Time-lapse Photography:

A Complete Introduction to Shooting, Processing, and Rendering Time-lapse Movies with a DSLR Camera
By Ryan Chylinski

First Edition: April 2012 (revised November 2012)
LearnTimelapse.com

Warning and disclaimer

The information in this book is distributed on an "As Is" basis, without warranty. While every precaution has been taken in the preparation of the book the author shall not have any liability to any person or entity with respect to any loss or damage caused or alleged to be caused directly or indirectly by the instructions contained in this book or by the computer software and hardware products described in it.

Trademarks

All Nikon products are trademarks or registered trademarks of Nikon and/or Nikon Corporation. All Canon products are trademarks or registered trademarks of Canon Inc.
Adobe, the Adobe logo, Photoshop and Adobe After Effects are registered trademarks of Adobe Systems Incorporated in the United States and/or in other countries.

Many of the designations used by manufacturers and sellers to distinguish their products are claimed as trademarks. Where those designations appear in this book, and the author was aware of a trademark claim, the designations appear as requested by the owner of the trademark. All other product names and services identified throughout this book are used in editorial fashion only and for the benefit of such companies with no intention of infringement of the trademark.

ISBN 13:   978-0985375713
ISBN 10:   098537571X

DEDICATION

To my family who always believes in me,

to my mentor Jim Rohn who taught me that the "book you don't read won't help",

and to the time-lapse community whose patience, helpfulness and creativity
inspires me to no end.

"Today is a big day. How would you like your eggs?"

CONTENTS

"THERE WAS NOWHERE TO GO BUT EVERYWHERE, SO JUST KEEP ON ROLLING UNDER THE STARS."

– JACK KEROUAC

IT'S 2:20 IN THE MORNING.

The alarm on my phone starts to beep and I fumble for it in the dark. 36+28=64, 84-13=31, 9x6=63, no wait 54!, The third correct answer finally deactivates the alarm and I'm now awake enough to remember what it is the heck I even set it for. I'm on Cape Cod for a family trip and I'm not going to let a night in a precious green zone go to waste. It's dark here, really dark and the excitement carries me the rest of the way out of bed.

I throw on thermal socks and pull my last battery from the wall charger grabbing my tripod and camera bag on the way out. It's only about a quarter mile walk to the small east facing pier I found on Google Earth. I make my way down the bank, set up the camera and carefully focus in at infinity. A few more test shots and I think I've got a good composition. The dock to the right provides a nice foreground, a moored boat should add some fun movement and of course the Milky Way, barely visible outside of my camera's preview window, but I know it should move slowly clockwise before the moon rises just off to the right.

I check everything over one last time: exposure time and the rule of 600, good; manual settings, check; interval, set. The test images look good. Let's begin.

It's cold tonight, but not too cold and as a blip of a shooting star diverts my attention to another part of the alive night sky, I can't help but think "I'm going to be here for a while... a very long while..."

"...and that's a beautiful thing."

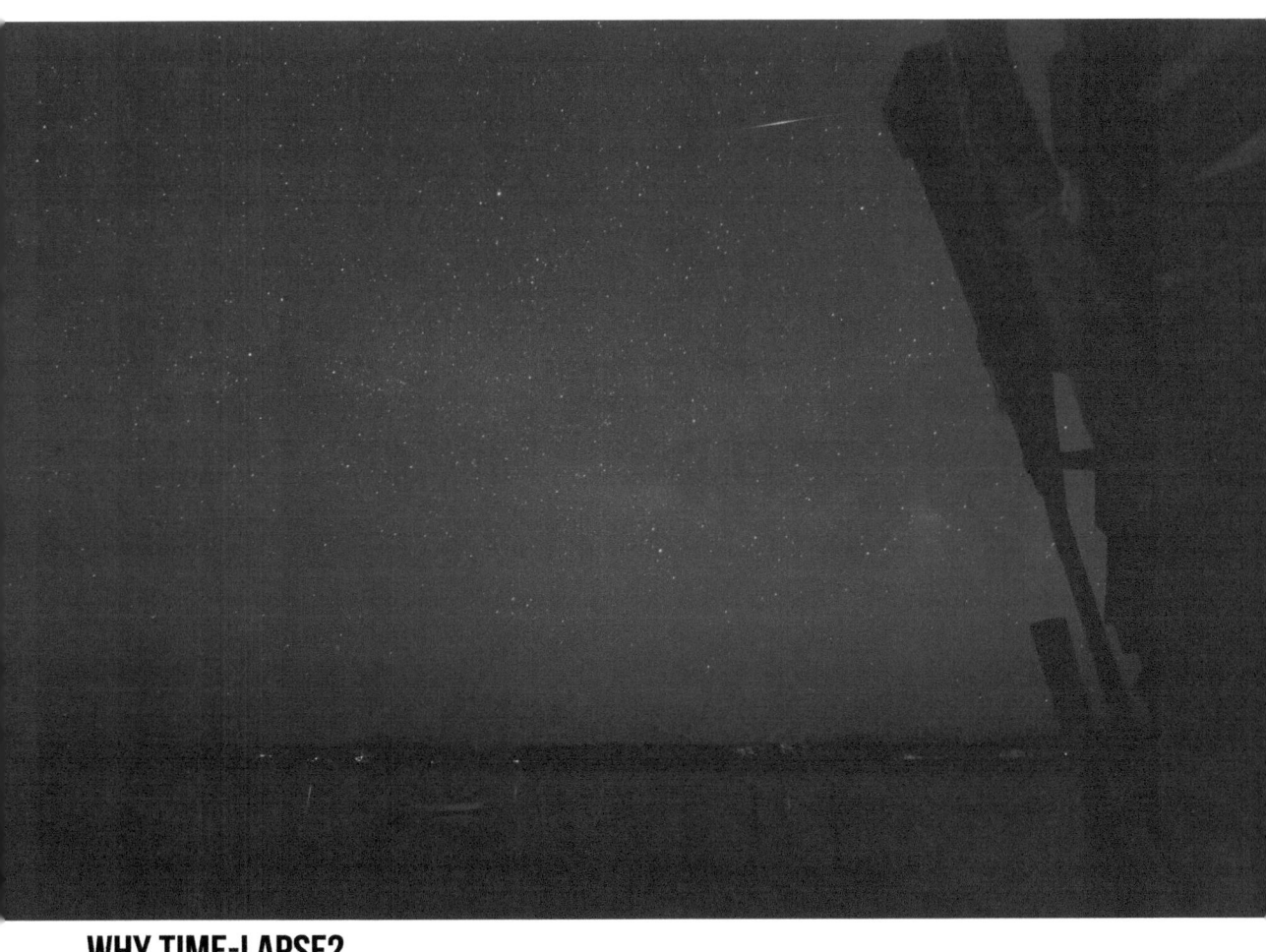

WHY TIME-LAPSE?

For me it's about freedom. Time-lapse is a strange thing: It frees you from the normal flow of your routine and all that busyness of life, yet at the same time it can connect you to your surroundings more than anything else. It is an awareness we seldom experience. As Lindsey Clark comments, time-lapse can be "a reminder that we are on a massive, moving orb and definitely not the most important thing even in our own lives."

I first saw it in the faces of family members: the fascination and the amazement when I shared a clip hot off the rendering queue. It's not just an image or a scene - it's how that place moved and worked; it was that place's story, at least for the brief time I was there. It starts to make people think and it gets them energized. It allows them, even if for a small moment, to armchair travel in the most incredible ways to what seems like impossible places.

Time-lapse has a way of slowing the world for the photographer while at the same time accelerating it for everyone else. I shoot time-lapse because it alters the way I think, it challenges my view of the world and teaches me things I can bring back and share with everybody else. It's also pretty amazing to watch.

The entrepreneurial aspect of the art is extremely exciting. So many photographers and filmmakers, having looked around and not found what they need to get the time altered shots they envision, have just gone ahead and built the tools themselves - often creating new companies or open source communities in the process.

The level of innovation, especially over the last few years, is incredible. Not only are we quickly fixing problems that have plagued photographers for years, but advancing camera controls and processing tools that used to be cost prohibitive are now becoming affordable for even the most basic hobbyist.

This is the change and energy that gets me fired up! This is why I'm so excited to share this with you. The more people that become involved with time-lapse the bigger the ideas, the better the innovations and the more amazing the stories we can tell.

It's a real honor and privilege to partner with you on this training journey. I hope this book is helpful and I would love to hear from you.

Best of luck,
Ryan Chylinski

Ryan@LearnTimelapse.com
@Timelapsejunkie

"I AM GOING TO MAKE A NAME FOR MYSELF. IF I FAIL, YOU WILL NEVER HEAR OF ME AGAIN."

- EADWEARD MUYBRIDGE

THE WAGER

The year is 1872. Leland Stanford, the Governor of California is steaming mad and red in the face. How long had he been arguing with his colleague one bar stool over? Two hours? Maybe three? *It had been at least twice that many rounds and this debate had gone nowhere.* "Unsupported transit" *was* real, he could see it in his mind. As a race-horse owner he was convinced that during the trot *all* four hooves left the ground. His companion would have none of it.

"How about a wager?" Stanford asked as he wiped the froth from his mustache. Maybe it was that *one* more drink, or maybe he stood up too fast from the stool, but as he drew back his arm from the handshake his stomach tightened into knots. Hands had met, the deal was sealed. $25,000 was not a problem... How to prove it scientifically was.

Stanford hired landscape and war photographer Eadweard Muybridge to settle the debate. Over the next few years Muybridge toiled and experimented at the race track. To capture the horse at the "magic" moment he designed and built a series of large glass plate cameras to be activated by thin threads which tripped as the horse passed (24 still cameras in all, 21 inches apart). Later designs would incorporate fast camera shutters controlled by clockwork timing devices.

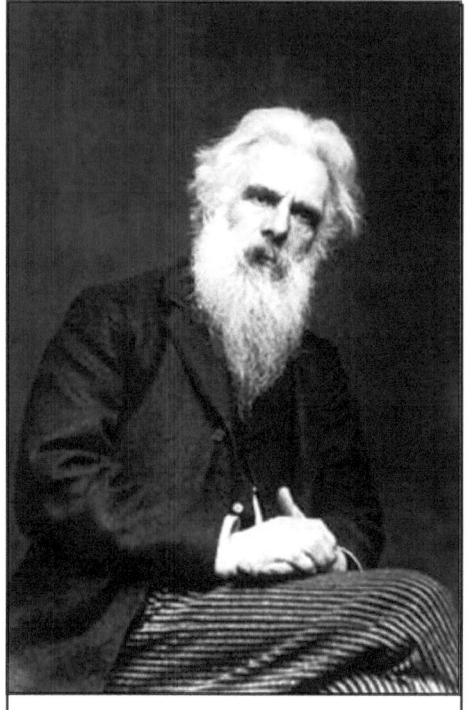

Eadweard Muybridge (1830-1904)

Cathy Curtis of the Los Angeles Times points out that Muybridge was famous for three things: 1) the strange spelling of his name, 2) his sensational acquittal for the murder of his wife's lover and 3) his indisputable photographic proof that horses gallop by lifting all four feet off the ground.

He would keep innovating until it worked.

Finally in 1877, a single photographic negative captured the precise moment clear enough to be unmistakable. Stanford's race-horse, *Occident,* was fully airborne at the trot.

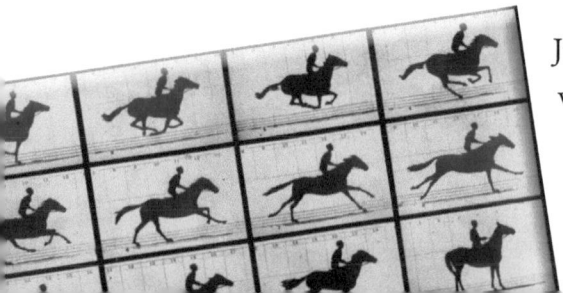

Jubilation would be short lived however. He had won the bet but there were *so many more* questions this technology could answer. Spurred on by the governor the work continued.

Decades of innovation

Earning the title 'the father of the motion picture', Muybridge's inventions and research into fast camera shutters and sensitive photographic processes allowed moving subjects to be captured and shared in unheard of and almost unimaginable ways.

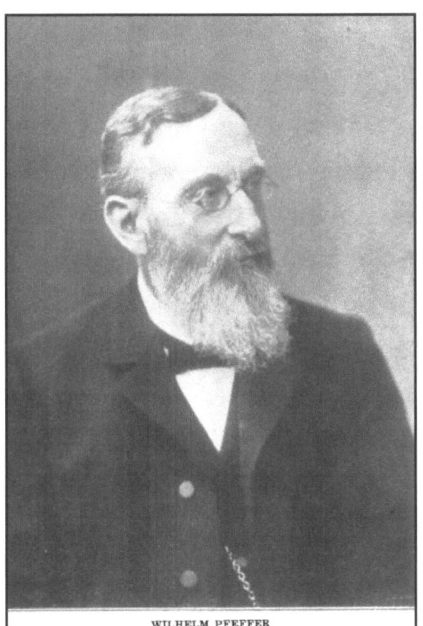

WILHELM PFEFFER
1845-1920

Wilhelm Pfeffer (1845-1920)
German botanist

His 1898 work as the director of the Leipzig Botanical Garden resulted in the world's first implementation of time-lapse photography.

Fascinated by Muybridge's work and inspired by the power of photography and the study of movement, a host of new visionaries would continue to innovate and expand the field, but it would take another decade before time-lapse photography would enter the minds of the leading practitioners.

THE FIRST TIME-LAPSE

Place yourself in 1898, only a few short years until the dawn of the 20th century. You're an intelligent person, interested in the new technology of the day and you're aware of some the latest advances. One day you are ushered into a university classroom to witness the truly incredible.

A short film is being shown. It's a film of a tulip plant, but not just any tulip plant, one that appears to be dancing back and forth growing taller and taller before your very eyes.

A bud forms at the center. It shoots up and you see the tulip flower blossom and spread its petals. The film is repeated and you are once again amazed at the images before you. You are seeing something you've *never* seen before.

Sure you knew plants grew, but not like this. Like peering through a microscope for the first time, you are seeing a whole new world and it's life changing. You knew things changed over time, but to actually see it happen was completely different.

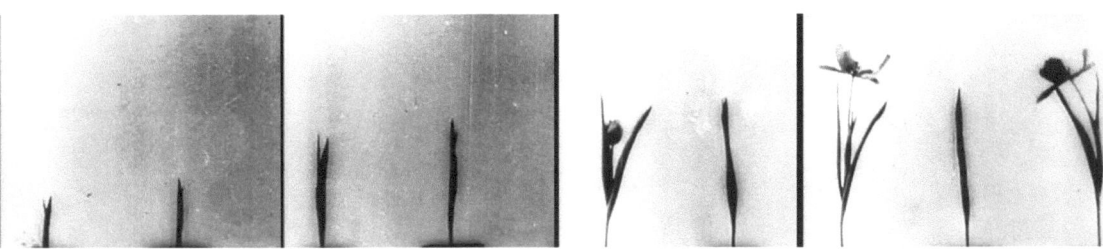

As you walk out into the courtyard you can't help but pause and think about all the things taking place around you, camouflaged and numbed by subtly and slowness. **No more.**

A blown mind

This technology and concept must have blown people's minds. Even today seeing the world from such a altered time perspective continues to amaze and astonish.

You've probably stumbled upon an incredible work of time-lapse and you just couldn't get the images and the feelings out of your head. Possibly you are fascinated by nature and the slow changes that occur over a period of time. A flower blooming, a sunset or a moonrise. Instead- maybe it was a construction project or a cityscape at night, full of activity and production. The capture of change in a way that we can't normally see is what makes time-lapse what it is. But what's really going on in the background?

WHAT IS TIME-LAPSE PHOTOGRAPHY?

Time-lapse photography is a cinematography technique whereby the frequency at which film frames are captured (aka the frame rate) is much lower than that which will be used to play the sequence back.

Put simply: We are manipulating time.

Objects and events that would normally take several minutes, days, or even months can be viewed to completion in seconds having been sped up by factors of tens to millions.

A century of real world science

The atmosphere, geology, astronomy, botany and microbiology. Rotting fruit, cell division, glaciers moving, cakes baking, construction and demolition. Thousands of subjects in hundreds of fields; dancing tulips were merely the start. More than a century of instructional and educational time-lapse aided research was about to begin.

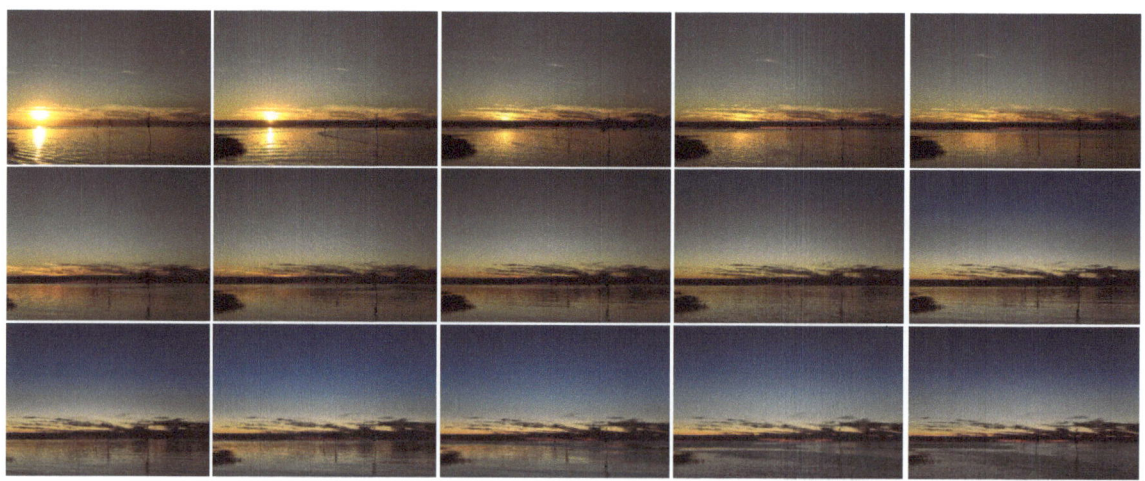

More than science, understanding

The best way to get a greater feel for the power of time-lapse outside of the educational realm is to watch a few. You have seen many before, (especially if you watch reality TV) but I am not really talking about those short clips between tribal counsel elimination decisions, it can go a little deeper *if we let it*. What I am talking about are the compilations that really grab your attention and make you think about the world around you - the ones that give you a better understanding about how nature changes and cities work; how stuff moves and how things flow.

AN UNFAIR EXAMPLE

OK, I know... It's certainly unfair to recommend any one time-lapse clip in particular as there are so many great works by amazing photographers, but there's one that just poked my brain and refuses to withdraw its finger. The clip is called "The City Limits" by Dominic Boudreault and I encourage you to watch it.

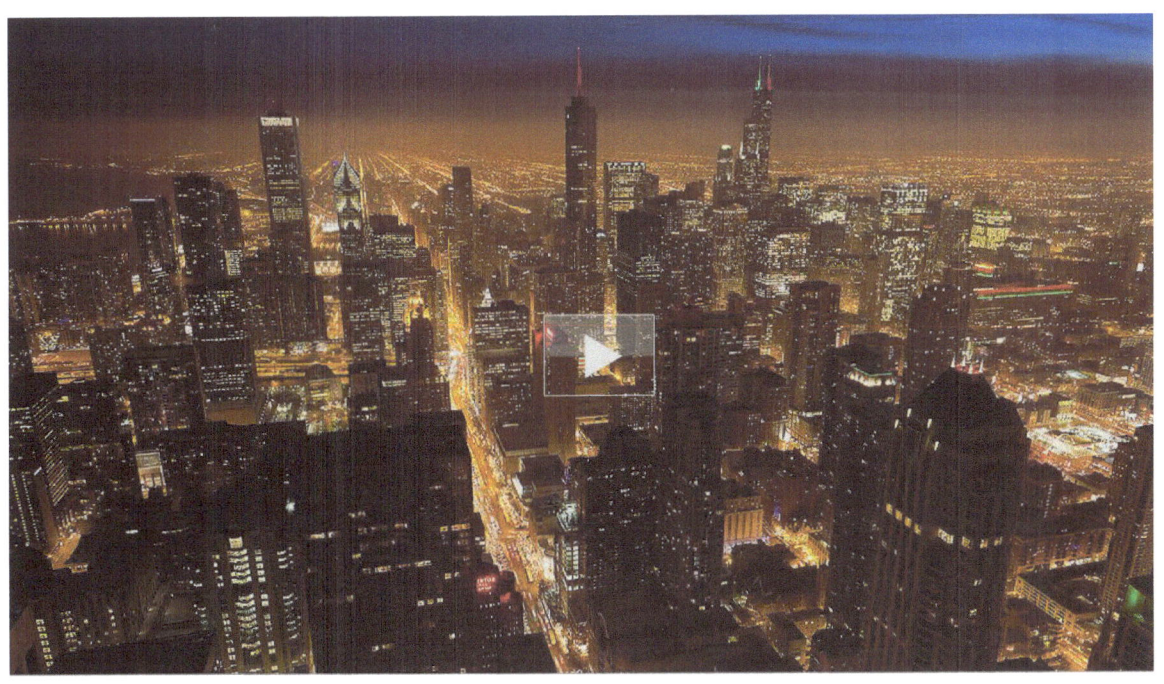

"The City Limits" by Dominic Boudreault. See more of his work: Dominicboudreault.com

His work was filmed in Canadian and American cities and shows the duality between these human built places and our natural world. It's this contrast, it's this story that he is using time-lapse to tell that does more than just amaze us with his image taking and editing skills, he shows us something that few artists can. He shows us time. This example is just one of many ways that time-lapse photography is so much more than a gee whiz editing effect.

It can be used to tell a story.

We've come a long way

A lot has changed since Occident's hooves' left the ground. From feature length collections of time-lapse compilations, IMAX films and medical imaging, to one-a-day photos of your face or your growing pregnancy on YouTube. It's both an art and science that fosters understanding and connection to the world around us.

Time-lapse requires patience, dedication, and some special tools and know-how in order to get the scenes we design in our minds to show up on screen, but it's certainly not hard. We'll walk through the process step by step, but it all starts with gear.

...and as a photographer is there any better place to start?

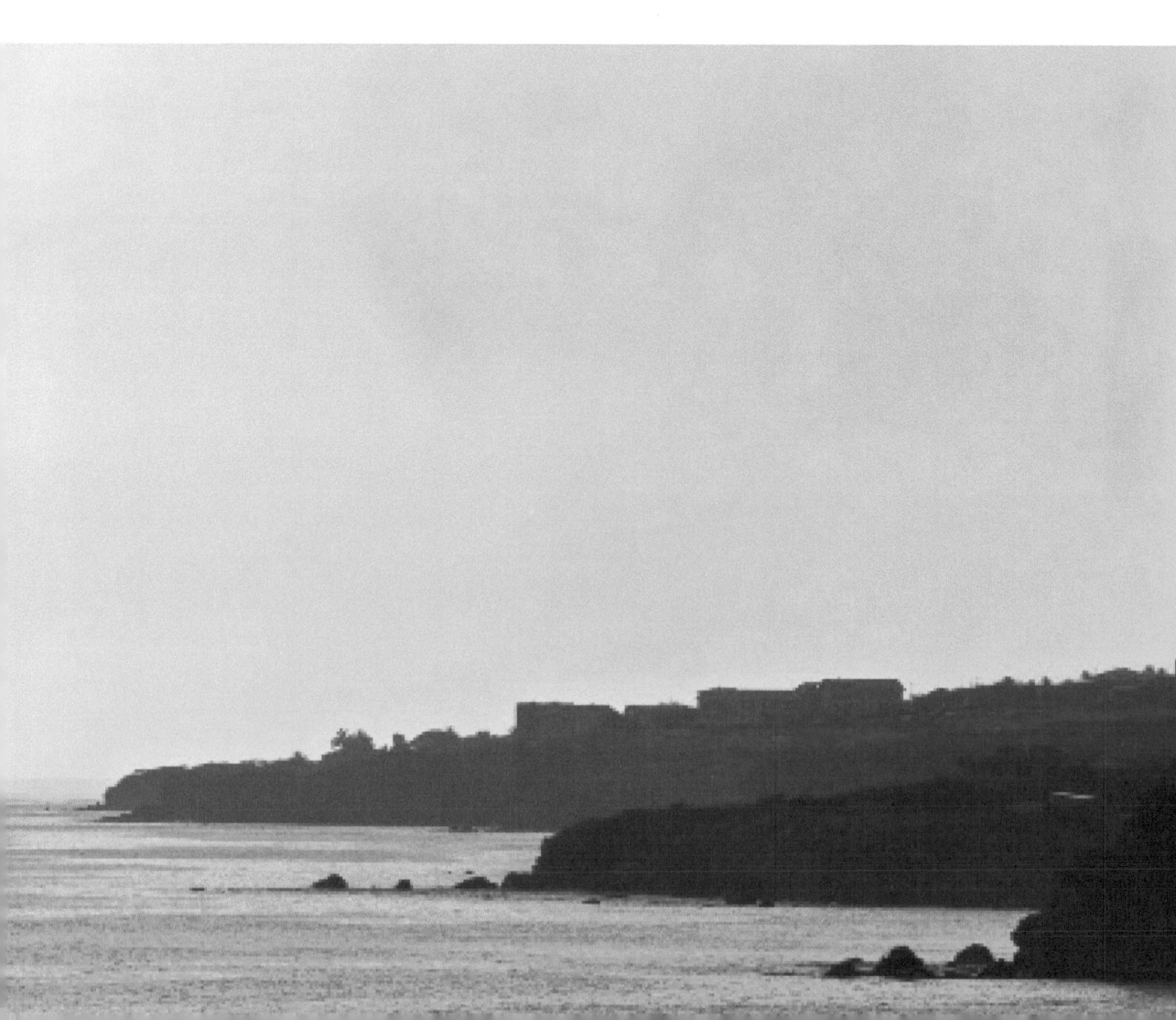

"NEVER FORGET THAT ALL THE GREAT PHOTOGRAPHS IN HISTORY WERE MADE WITH MORE PRIMITIVE CAMERA EQUIPMENT THAN YOU CURRENTLY OWN."

-BROOKS JENSEN

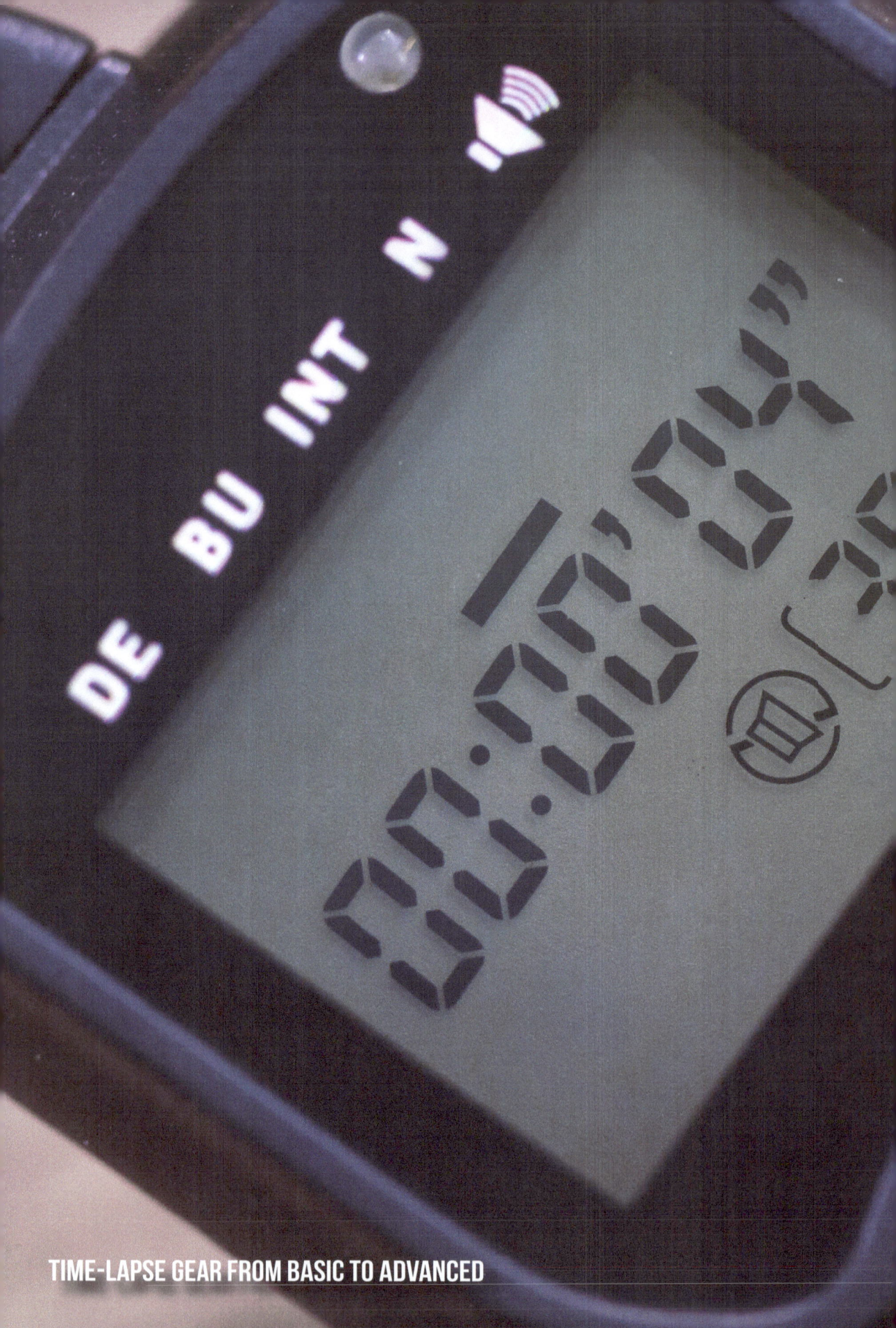

TIME-LAPSE GEAR FROM BASIC TO ADVANCED

1 TIME-LAPSE GEAR

• •

Chances are if you currently take photos with a DSLR camera you probably have just about everything you need.

No doubt that first time you said "*hey, wouldn't it be fun to dabble in DSLR photography? You know, just as a hobby.*" Our financial counselors, or our spouses for that matter, broke out in budget busting hives. There probably isn't a more gear obsessed group of enthusiasts out there, but don't worry, great time-lapse photography doesn't require much gear to begin.

And what about all that advanced stuff you ask? Well, as always the sky is the limit, but I can firmly say as a Dave Ramsey devotee that with some savings and a few Craigslisted garage items, creativity and drive will be your only limits.

Throughout this book I'll highlight what I currently use, free stuff and where to find it, as well as how to duck tape and hack your current gear into submission whenever possible.

This chapter begins with a minimum gear checklist to get you up and out the door as fast as possible. We'll then wet the appetite with a quick introduction to advanced gear (we cover this in more detail in the challenges section), then take a deeper look into the basic time-lapse necessities with some tips and thoughts for finding the right new or used gear that's best for you.

BASIC TIME-LAPSE GEAR

There are only four basics when it comes to time-lapse hardware:

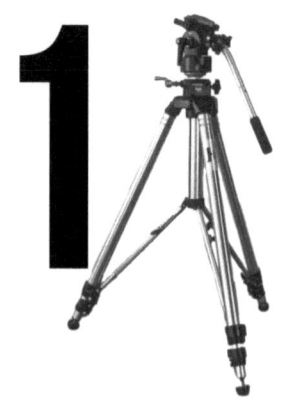

TRIPOD

A rock solid shooting platform that you are comfortable using is almost more important than the camera itself. The good news is that big, old, and heavy metal beasts usually make for great time-lapse tripods and in the world of photography *old* and *heavy* usually means *used* and *cheap*. The bad news is that sometimes your shot is more than a quick walk from the car and suddenly big and heavy doesn't sound so hot. We'll talk about what to look for in a good portable time-lapse tripod and a few things you can do to any tripod to make it as stable as possible.

INTERVALOMETER

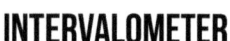

An intervalometer is an automated camera trigger, a programmable device that is used to snap hundreds of photos at precise intervals. In other words it's the heart of time-lapse photography. There are many different devices that we can use, some internal via camera firmware, some external like the one pictured at left, some cheap and some not so cheap. Having some kind of automated control is required and we'll talk about the different ways to achieve it.

CAMERA

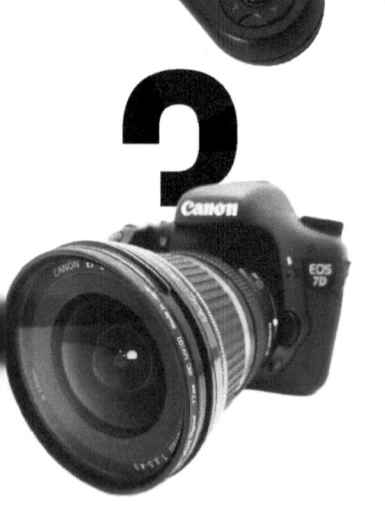

Is there such a thing as a good camera for time-lapse photography? Well, yes. I think it's a DSLR. While we'll touch on other ways to capture time-lapse images, this book is manly devoted to time-lapse photography using digital SLR (Single-Lens Reflex) cameras. Why? Results. I don't think you can find a more affordable package offering outstanding control, quality and ease of use. DSLR's get my vote.

ND FILTERS (sorta optional)

Like sunglasses for your camera, neutral density or ND filters reduce the intensity of light without altering its color. Less light intensity allows us to use slower shutter speeds in bright environments. Slow shutter speeds in turn allow us to capture motion blur on the moving objects in our time-lapse sequence. Wait a second? Blur!? Isn't that a bad thing? Well, no not really. Not in time-lapse photography. We'll talk all about it in later sections.

ADVANCED TIME-LAPSE GEAR

When it comes to advanced gear anything is possible right... Maybe not. I think you could argue that the art of time perception cinematography and the associated technology is evolving so quickly that much has yet to be thought up, let alone designed and offered in the marketplace. Unlike other fields, money might not be the only limiting factor to our time-lapse imagination.

Don't get me wrong there are certainly some incredible devices on the market and we don't have to go too far to find big price tags. Not only are these new designs eliminating mechanical and processing roadblocks, but they are allowing us to program camera movement and control in new and amazing ways adding many multiples of interest to our shots. We'll start with the two main areas of time-lapse innovation: motion and exposure control.

Motion control

We are all familiar with regular movie camera movement: panning (left and right), tilting (up and down), and dolly movements (smooth mounted movement along a track) but achieving those

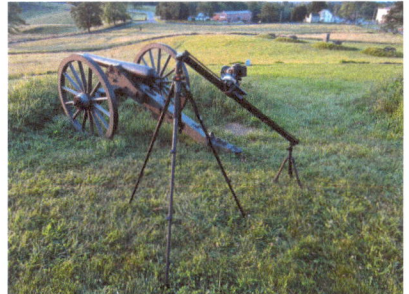 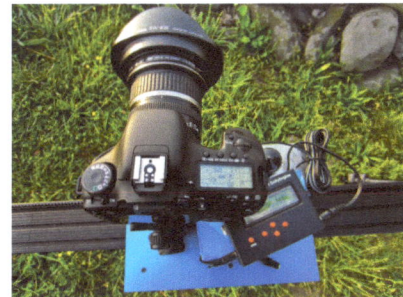

movements inside a time-lapse at precise programed intervals over potentially very long periods of time requires a whole new book of thought. I am fortunate to have one area of advanced time-lapse movement covered (dolly movement) with the purchase of a 6 foot Stage Zero Dolly by Dynamic Perception. We'll introduce more movement solutions later on in the challenges section.

Exposure control

Some of the best time-lapse sequences capture the extremes of light and dark in our envi-

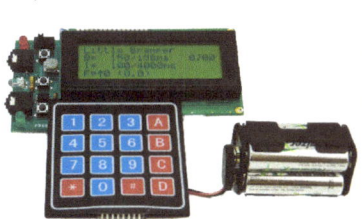

ronment, shots that are really dynamic in nature. Time-lapse images that begin in deep night using very long exposures and then continue into full day light requiring short exposures and often camera filters, need more than a simple timer to execute correctly. Advanced exposure control devices, both in camera hardware/firmware and post production software, help us plan and alter the cameras settings gradually as the conditions dramatically change in our scene. We'll talk more about these and the time-lapse Holy Grail in later chapters.

A FEW GOOD TRIPODS...

As the heavy feeling of disappointment sweeps over me, I realize all is lost. A windy shooting day led to a shaky time-lapse, which led to frustrated tinkering at home trying to correct it (failed), which led to 650 pretty photos of an awesome landscape but no usable time-lapse sequence. Bummer. While it's possible to correct bits of movement and maybe even save a few scenes with software, it's not fun (however with Adobe After Effects CS6 it is getting there).

Rock solid stability (or precise controlled movement) will be your most important and most essential component for good time-lapse photography. Unless you do a lot of hiking or travel (we'll talk about this on the next page) the bigger and heavier the tripod the better. Believe it or not, older models in the used marketplace are great for what we need. Do some digging and see what you can find.

A few things to look for:
- Seek big, heavy, and solid models
- Consider all materials not just the latest
- Consider both still and video tripods

A few places to look:
- KEH, B&H Photo, (both sites offer used)
- Local studios (they cycle gear frequently)
- Craigslist, eBay, Amazon (read reviews)

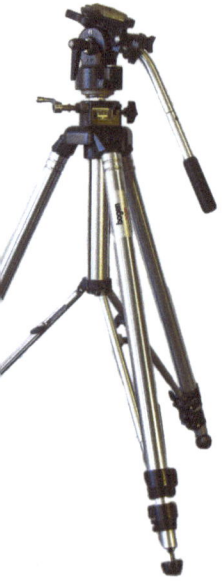

I was lucky to find this old Bogen 3036 tripod legs and three-way head on Craigslist for $70, which is a great deal. They don't sell this model new anymore but its clone/predecessor the Manfrotto 475B goes for $310 at B&H (and that's for the legs only!). It's heavy clocking in at 9.5 pounds for the legs and another 5 for the head. Perfect, for most situations that is...

Does it have to be heavy?
These big cosmodome like tripods work great but what if you do a lot of hiking to that secret epic overlook isn't exactly close to the trail head? We've included a few thoughts on what to look for in standard more portable tripods as well as a few things you can do to any tripod to make it more stable.

TIPS FOR PORTABILITY

Keep in mind a good tripod that meets your needs will outlast several cameras so consider budgeting a little more time and possibly cash to this category.
- Consider the materials used: weight and strength
- Check the load weight avoid sagging and flexing
- Height: eye level without using middle column
- The right head for your work: ball heads vs pan/tilt

HOW TO MAKE ANY TRIPOD MORE STABLE

Add more weight
Weight can be added to the top of the camera. Think bean bags, granule bags etc.(Stay away from dusty sand though)

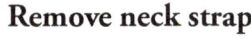

Remove neck strap
You don't want it to turn into a giant sail in the wind do you?

Turn off lens IS
Image Stabilization (and vibration reduction) lenses look for vibrations in your camera in order to reduce it – however if they don't find any (like when you are using a tripod) they actually can cause it. Unless your lens auto detects tripods turn it off.

Never extend center column.
You lose lots of stability. It's best to keep it down all the way and locked.

Batten down the hatches
Coil lose wires and attach extras like the remote timer to the tripod using Velcro straps or rubber bands. Blowing swinging things are very bad.

Tighten and lock
Make sure all clamps, knobs, and fasteners are clamped, knobbed (*wait that's not right*) and fastened.

Use center hook
Most tripods have a hook below the center column. Add weight by attaching heavy stuff to the center (backpack, water jug, a short uncle, etc.)

Biggest legs first
Avoid extending the smallest thinnest legs whenever possible. Keep the tripod as low to the ground as you can and raise with thicker legs first.

Spikes or rubber
On soft ground? Extend the metal spikes. On concrete or your dining room hardwood floor? Use the rubber feet.

What else do you like to shoot?

A lot of photographers own several head types and leg setups and swap them out based on where they are going and what they plan on shooting. If you do shoot a lot of video with your DSLR the ability to pan and tilt smoothly is sometimes very important. Some three-way heads are also specified as fluid heads and as the name implies, sealed liquid is used to create a mini hydraulic system which enables steady silky motion. If you find that you do a lot of wildlife photography the speed of a ball head might also be a good choice.

Not sure what to get? Consider renting

The best and truly only way to know if gear is right for you is to use it in the field. Renting camera equipment and accessories has become incredibly easy and very afford- able and this is one of many times you'll hear the suggestion. For a very small fraction of the retail price you can use top-of-the-line equipment on your next vacation, assign- ment, or to try out over a long weekend. There are many great companies out there but my favorites are Borrowlenses.com and Lensprotogo.com.

Starting point portable recommendations

A few good introductory models ($100-$200) might be the Manfrotto 190 Series, Benbo Classic or the Vanguard Alta series. I've used both and can say that they get the job done. I can't stress enough looking for used though, you can really find some great deals out there with a little patience. The next step up ($300-$400) might be the Manfrotto 055CX series which catapults us into the range of carbon fiber tubes. Beyond this the Gitzo Mountaineer series and other advanced models start to blur the boundary between practicality and an all out spend-fest.

Hey we can dream right?

INTERVALOMETERS

Intervalometers, remote triggers, remote timers, basically the physical devices or software applications that allow us to program a precise number of photo actuations at exact intervals. It's the heart of time-lapse photography. If you don't already have one, you need one and this section is for you.

DSLR Intervalometers come mainly in 3 forms:

1. A special shooting mode that comes built into some DSLRs (or tweaked with new firmware)
2. A dedicated external timer remote that plugs into your camera's side input port
3. A connection to an external computer/smartphone running time-lapse/automated image capture software

1 PREBUILT: DOES YOUR CAMERA ALREADY HAVE ONE?

Take a look through your camera's manual or do a search through the features section of your camera model's website. See an interval shooting mode that is part of your camera's functionality? If it's there you should be all set. Almost all digital cameras have the basic capability for interval shooting, just by knowing current and elapsed time, but in the end it's up the manufacturer to implement. The Nikon D2 series does have built-ins, older Nikons and most Canons for example need an external device.

MAGIC LANTERN

Have Canon, will Hack... enter Magic Lantern. I'll quote right from their Wiki: "Magic Lantern is an enhancement atop of Canon's firmware that frees your Canon DSLR, allowing you to use many useful features [including built-in intervalometer!!].... it now has functionality for both photo and video enthusiasts, including manual audio, zebras, focus assist tools, bracketing, motion detection and much more." see magiclantern.wikia.com [See also nikon-hacker.com, gh1-hack.info, or pentax-hack.info]

2 DEDICATED EXTERNAL DEVICES:

Don't worry if nary a timer function is found, my search came up blank too. I'll go out on a limb here and say that most DSLRs do not include one.

The external intervalometer world in 4 segments:

1. 3rd party manufacturers/aftermarket (some are perfectly good and cheap)
2. Name brands (good, but expensive)
3. Advanced (sometimes expensive but offer more features)
4. Home-built and DIY

We'll go through each of these four segments and point out some things you should consider before you buy.

3rd party and aftermarket manufacturers

Several 3rd party manufactures produce great DSLR compatible intervalometers (some even having the same form factor as the name brands) and sell at a fraction of the cost. This is very good news. Here are a few that I might recommend:

The most important thing is to make sure the product is compatible with your specific camera model.

- **Linkdelight ~$25 (linkdelight.com)**
  Linkdelight is a photographic and small electronics aftermarket company which sells an inexpensive and perfectly functional time-lapse timer remotes for most DSLR models. It does what we need it to do and is of good quality for most situations. Their brand now usually ships from US warehouses and has received good reviews and recommendations by other photographers. You just can't beat the price. Note: You *can* take unlimited shots with this model, just set the FRAMES mode to 0 (zero). Special disc batteries are a pain though.

- **Satechi ~$50 (Satechi.net or Amazon) Recommended**
  This is what I currently use and I am happy with the quality and functionality with no problems to report. It has the same features as the Linkdelight model plus the added ability to set shots between 1-399 and infinity (instead of 1-99 and infinity) and uses standard AAA batteries.

There are many others out there and I encourage you to look around. Take your time and again

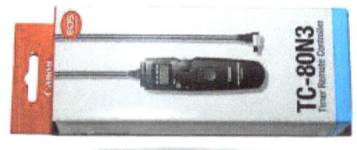
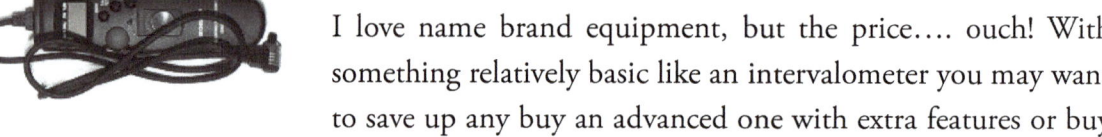

make sure the specific camera model is listed as compatible and look for some good reviews before you buy.

Name brand intervalometers

I love name brand equipment, but the price.... ouch! With something relatively basic like an intervalometer you may want to save up any buy an advanced one with extra features or buy 4 or 5 aftermarket models to have as backups: put one in the glove box, put one in your other camera bag and stick one in your back pocket. I jest, but my cat already chewed the wire and claimed my first Satechi (oops!). As far as build quality and long-term reliability is concerned, these models do score a little higher.

- **Canon Timer Remote TC-80N3**
  Cost: ~ $210 from Canon
  ~ $142 from Amazon

- **Nikon MC-36 Multi-Function Timer**
  Cost: ~ $180 from Nikon
  ~ $125 from Amazon

Don't forget to check eBay or Craigslist too. You may be able to find some deals on used gear especially name brand models as well as what we will discus next.

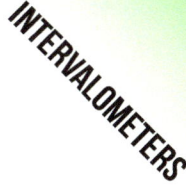

Advanced Intervalometers

Time-lapse photography is benefiting from a dramatic flow of innovation into the world of camera movement and shutter control. Some devices are made commercially available almost immediately while others are crowd-sourced strictly for sharing and experimentation. Here are just a few implementations you might want to learn more about:

- **Promote Control ~$300 (promotesystems.com)**

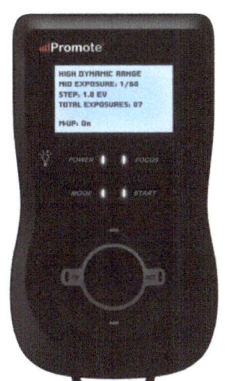

The Promote Control is marketed towards serious amateurs and pros (and for $300 that's probably about right). Offering advanced HDR (High Dynamic Range) photographic options and time-lapse functionality including Mirror-Up delay (an automatic wait for added photo sharpness) and HDR time-lapse multiple exposure support. We'll also see how this device and an added accessory can be used to vary our exposure settings gradually and become another way we can achieve those day to night continuous shots.

By subtly varying the exposure at a level much more precise than your camera alone can do, flicker free time-lapse footage of light varying scenes can be achieved. Largely a community driven development, these controllers, along with a few others, has allowed those who are worthy enough to seek the ultimate challenge: The Time-lapse Holy Grail.

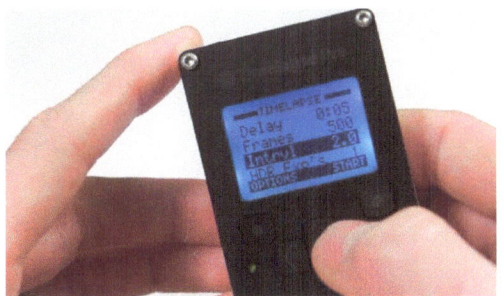

- **Time-lapse+ ~$99 (timelapseplus.com) [launched on kickstarter.com]**

Time-lapse+ is a universal intervalometer for Canon, Nikon, Olympus, Sony, Pentax and Minolta SLR cameras (basically as long as they have a connection for a cable release). Time-lapse+ is scheduled to include support for an unlimited number of photos, BULB ramping (shift exposure smoothly during the time-lapse), Auto BULB ramping based on the light meter, and more.

If you haven't checked out Kickstarter.com yet, please do. The site and community of creators and backers is incredible.

Homemade and DIY Intervalometers

Ever since the first time-lapse was filmed people have been hacking and programming their own destructions (I mean constructions) pushing the edge of what seems possible and sometimes practical. Feeling ambitious? Ready for a challenge? Tinker with a few of these designs or search for your own. Don't say I didn't warn you, it's addictive.

- Intervalometer using a 555 timer IC (search instructables.com)
- TI graphing calculator based time-lapse intervalometer (also @ instructables.com)
- Hacking a wireless remote for your camera (search for Luke Hill DIY time-lapse)
- Using a Nintendo DS, phenomenal idea (hdrlabs.com/occ)

And many, many more….

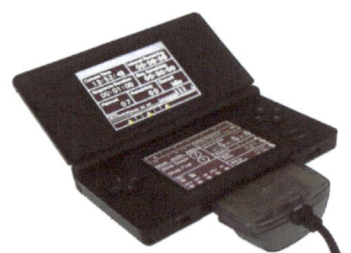

3 TETHERED COMPUTER/SMARTPHONE CONTROL

If you have a smartphone and don't mind dedicating its use for time-lapse every once and a while, or if you've got a laptop and don't mind schlepping it out into the field, tethered camera control might be a solution.

Computer Tether

One of the main benefits of tethered shooting with a laptop is the giant immediate feedback on your computer screen. Advanced time-lapse control applications also exist that really push the envelope of how you can control your camera's exposure over long sequences (I mean seriously amazing stuff). Most applications also allow you to save the images directly to your computer, usually solving any kind memory card limitations you might have. Here are a few computer tether applications to investigate:

Freeware
- DiyPhotoBits (diyphotobits.com)
- gPhoto2 (gphoto.org)
- Sofortbild (sofortbildapp.com)
- And more...

Commercial
- GBTimelapse (granitebaysoftware.com)
- DSLR remote pro (breezesys.com)
- DSLR Assistant (dslrassistant.com)
- Nikon Control Pro 2 (Nikonusa.com)
- And more..

Smart phone control

More and more smartphone DSLR camera control apps are hitting the marketplace. If you already have a smartphone why not download one and experiment? You'll probably need a special connection wire depending on which phone you have but many apps are coming out with advanced features only found on specialized dedicated devices or full fledged computers. I'm just beginning to experiment with these now and so far I'm having a lot of fun. It's worth it for the small cost to download and snag a wire.

Android OS (Android market)
- DSLR Controller
- DSLR Remote
- And more...

iOS (App store)
- DSLR.Bot
- Remote DSLR Camera Control
- And more..

A GOOD TIME-LAPSE CAMERA?

Unless you are shooting for the big screen I don't think you can beat DSLRs (and mirrorless cameras) for a affordable package offering outstanding control, quality, and ease of use.

In the market for a new camera? Time-lapse is obviously on your list, but it's probably not the only thing you want to record. Try to plan ahead and think about your photographic interests, aspirations, and what you want to shoot, or film for that matter. While I can't say which camera is right for you, I can help you ask the right questions.

Here are few things to consider:
- What do you want to do with your camera? Try to think long term.
- Where do you want to take yourself with photography?
- What is your budget?
- Are there particular features that are important to you?

Where do you want to take yourself?

Weekend warrior, full-time professional, enthusiast, hobbyist or fill_in_the_blank? One is not necessarily better or worse than the other, but having a clear idea of what you want to become is most helpful in setting your camera and photography budget. Are you planning on producing income with your photography?

What is your budget?

The dreaded "B" word.

We talked about this before so I'll just add:

1. Answer honestly
2. Stick to your plan

Budget vs. Passion

Since a camera is probably the most expensive piece of time-lapse gear you'll buy I'll highlight a line that I am sure you've heard before: *"The single most important component of a camera is the twelve inches behind it." -Ansel Adams*

Give Ansel Adams a coffee can, some electrical tape, a pin, and some film and he could make a great photo. At the same time give him quality equipment and he could blow us away with amazement. Quality gear matters but not as much as what you do with it. Balance the two and all will be right with the world.

My camera is a Canon 7D

I use a Canon 7D (~$1,200) for my photography, time-lapse, and HD video work. I am by no means immune to the twinges of more advanced models, but I've found a great mix of features, customization and image quality at a mid-range price point that was right for me.

A thought on time-lapse shutter wear: Your camera's shutter mechanism *does* have a lifespan (the 7D advertises ~150k actuations) and while some people easily exceed that mark you *will* wear things out faster by taking lots of time-lapse photos. Personally I think its more than worth it but it's something you might want to factor into your decision making process.

FEATURES AND RESEARCH

Here are a few considerations that might be helpful as you evaluate your options:

Is a built in intervalometer important?

No, not really. All DSLRs have the capability to record time-lapse compilations but some have interval shooting functionality built right into their menu system. Look in the camera's feature listing for something called *interval timer shooting mode*. If it's listed then you've got it. If it 's not, like in the case of the 7D, you will need to either tweak its firmware (Advanced: not possible for all cameras) or connect an external device (intervalometer or smartphone etc).

So you want to photograph star trails or star lapses?

If you think astrophotography and star trails or star-lapses might be in your future (and it's still in the budget), you may want to consider a full frame DSLR. Full frame cameras have a larger image sensor (roughly 24mm x 36mm) which is bigger than their smaller *crop sensor* cousins. Bigger sensors allow for better low light shooting options. I get pretty good night sky shots with my 7D (crop senor, 1.6x magnification) but it lacks that extra bang for wide angle shooting and true astrophotography. I encourage you to do more research and see if a crop or a full frame DSLR is right for you?

Use OPR (Other People's Reviews)

I've learned a lot about what gear works, doesn't work, and is completely irrelevant to me and not worth the extra cost. I've also learned how other photographers use certain features in ways the manufacturer probably never intended. The next page highlights a few good resources, blogs and forums to check out if you are looking to buy a DSLR:

Rent and test first

I talked about renting before but I really can't stress enough how cool it is to take a new model into the field and try it out for a few days before buying. Amazing.

- Borrow Lenses (borrowlenses.com)
- Lens Pro To Go (lensprotogo.com)

General camera tests, reviews and forums

- Digital Photography Review (dpreview.com)
- Imaging Resource (imaging-resource.com)
- Camera Labs (cameralabs.com)
- Planet 5D (blog.planet5d.com)

Reviews and new/used stores

- KEH used gear (keh.com)
- B&H Photo (bhphotovideo.com)
- Adorama (adorama.com)
- Amazon (amazon.com)

I spent a lot of time learning about features, reviewing different camera models, studying image tests etc, found a few I liked, tried them out. I shopped around. I pulled the trigger and haven't looked back. Okay... maybe just a little.

<u>YOU Don't look back</u> *(at least not for a while)*.

It is a big purchase, but you did your homework so stop reading reviews and shoot more photos!

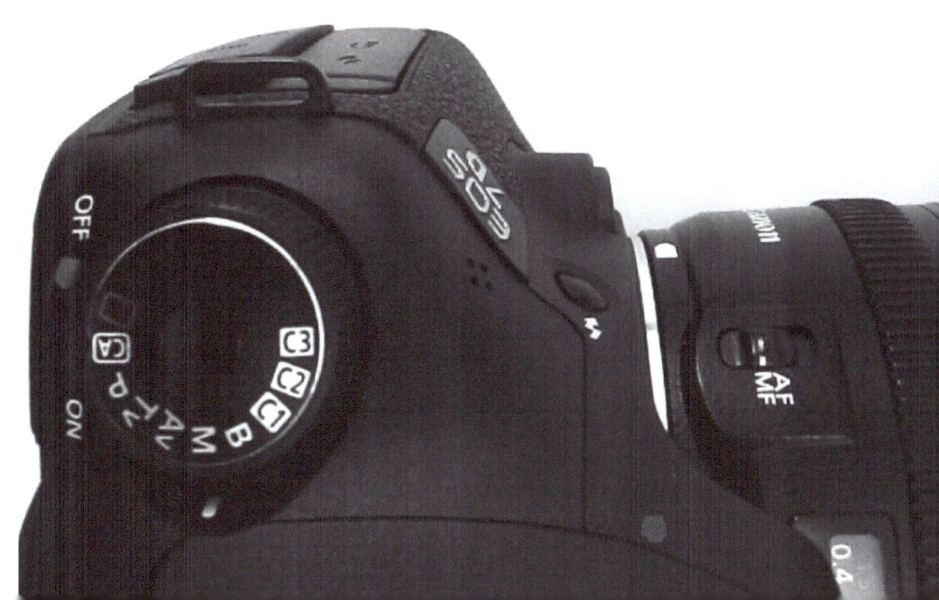

ALL ABOUT ND FILTERS

Like sunglasses for your camera, neutral density or ND filters reduce the intensity of all colors of light passing through your lens equally leaving you with less light without changing the hue or color rendition. It's really all about choices, and ND filters give us more.

Think about it this way: to achieve a "correct" exposure there are many different shutter speeds and aperture combinations that we could use to get a good result (called reciprocity). If we attach an ND filter, the exposure value is reduced because there is less light entering the lens. With less light we now have the flexibility to lower our shutter speed while keeping the same aperture and still get the exposure we want. Same image brightness, lower shutter speed. Nice!

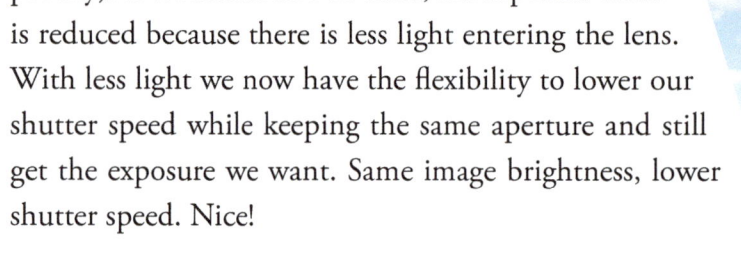

ND Filters help by:
1. Allowing for wider apertures, assuming a fixed shutter speed
    For example: a shallower depth of field in bright conditions
2. Allow for slower shutter speeds, assuming a fixed aperture
    For example: motion blur in bright conditions

Dragging your shutter

This is why we really love ND filters. In still photography a fast shutter speed and minimal (or no) image blur is usually the goal. In time-lapse photography, because we string so many still frames together to create a moving sequence, we actually want a little motion blur in each image to create the illusion of smoother moving objects. This intentional blurring is called "dragging your shutter".

We'll talk more about motion blur when we set up our first shot in the next section but for now just think of the blur as "extra information" about how the scene is changing. This extra motion, when strung together other slight motion blurred images, adds fluidity to the scene and makes it feel more realistic.

DE-MYSTIFYING FILTER SELECTION

ND filters are sold based on "gradings" depending on how much light they reduce. A higher grading signifies a filter that blocks more light.

Two different types of notations are commonly used to tell them apart:
1. Filter factor (listed as: ND2 or ND4 etc.)
2. Filter density (listed as: 0.3 ND or 0.6, etc.)

The *filter factor* simply tells us how much additional light will be required with the filter mounted in place. For example a factor of 4 (ND4) means we need 4 times as much light to equal the same exposure. Since each one "stop" of light reduction corresponds to a halving of light the ND4 filter results in 2 f-stops of reduction. We can now shoot at f/4 instead of f/8 and get a more selective depth of field, or we could shoot at 1/15th of a second instead of 1/60th to get some nice motion blur.

Filter density is also another common notation used. For each *filter density* change of 0.3, the camera's f-stop is reduced by 1, and the darker the filter will appear. The chart below helps us put this in perspective.

ND filters can be stacked... but it's better to use fewer

F-stop reduction using ND filters can be increased by stacking 2 or 3 filters end to end for an additive effect. Just be careful, too many and you might begin to see a barrel effect or narrowing around the lens edges. Reflections might also be a problem so keep your filters to a minimum.

If possible, stick to the name brands

There are a lot of cheap off-brand alternatives out there, especially on eBay, and while some may be okay, time and time again I hear of complaints. Hoya, B+W, Lee and Tiffen are good names to stick to. My B+W ND8 and ND16 work well.

Amount of Light Reduction		Common Manufacturers	
f-stops	Fraction	Hoya, B+W	Lee, Tiffen
1	1/2	ND2, ND2X	0.3 ND
2	1/4	ND4, ND4X	0.6 ND
3	1/8	ND8, ND8X	0.9 ND
4	1/16	ND16, ND16X	1.2 ND
5	1/32	ND32, ND32X	1.5 ND
6	1/64	ND64, ND64X	1.8 ND

I recommend at least a 3 stop reduction filter or higher.

Anything lower and you just wouldn't have the reduction effect you need for most daylight shooting situations.

You may want a GND filter

A Graduated Neutral Density (GND) filter restricts light across an image in a smooth pattern. Especially helpful for landscape scenes, ones where there's often a horizon line separating lighter and darker areas, the built in transition helps to properly expose for such drastic contrast.

TIME-LAPSE LENSES

What makes a good time-lapse lens? We'll, it depends on what you are going to shoot, but for time-lapse we usually want to capture as much dramatic change as we can in our scenes and that means a wide field of view. Let's discuss a few ideas on lens selection.

Lens field of view

Basically all that "stuff" you can see when you look in a particular direction. A lens' field of view is determined by its focal length which is the measure in millimeters from the center of the lens to the principle point of focus for the lens. Don't worry too much about the definition we really just care about what happens when we change it.

A normal lens is said to have about the same field of view as the human eye. A telephoto lens has a longer focal length and it's field of view gets narrower as its magnification increases. A wide angle lens on the other hand has a shorter than normal focal length which results in a wider field of view.

A wide-angle lens is a time-lapes' best friend

In most cases time-lapse photographers are trying to capture as much as they can and that usually means big scenes and wide fields of view. My Canon EF-S Wide-angle 10-22 mm F/3.5-4.5 lens was a great moderately priced choice for most of the scenes I record. What kinds of scenes will you most likely shoot?

Consider your cameras sensor size

The same focal length lens will deliver a different field of view depending on the size of your image sensor. For example my Canon 7D in considered a crop sensor, that means it's APS-C format sensor size results in 1.6x crop factor to my field of view. Great when I want telephoto reach, not so great if I want to get really wide. Luckily camera manufacturers produce special lenses designed to help compensate for some DSLRs sensor crop factors. An EF-S lens ("S" stands for "short back focus") sits closer to the image sensor, which allows for wider angles, a larger aperture, and overall less cost. Look into specialized lenses if you have a crop camera.

How does the lens aperture (f-number) affect my choice?

Lenses list the maximum and usually minimum available apertures as part of their printed specifications. The larger the range the greater the artistic flexibly. Lenses with larger maximum apertures (smaller f-numbers) are significantly better for night and low light photography. These "fast lenses" capture more light in much shorter times but usually cost significantly more. If you are really serious about astrophotography and star-lapses get the largest max aperture you can afford.

HELPFUL TIME-LAPSE EXTRAS

Here are a few extras that might be extremely helpful for next time-lapse project:

Battery Grip

Most DSLR's have an accessory available that allows you to extend the size of the camera's battery compartment and house two batteries instead of one. I'll be honest and say that most time-lapse sequences (with the exception of astrolapses) can get by on one fully charged battery, but the piece of mind knowing I can shoot a sequence, pick up the camera shoot stills, shoot some video, then setup for a second sequence is well worth the extra $75. I highly recommend a battery grip.

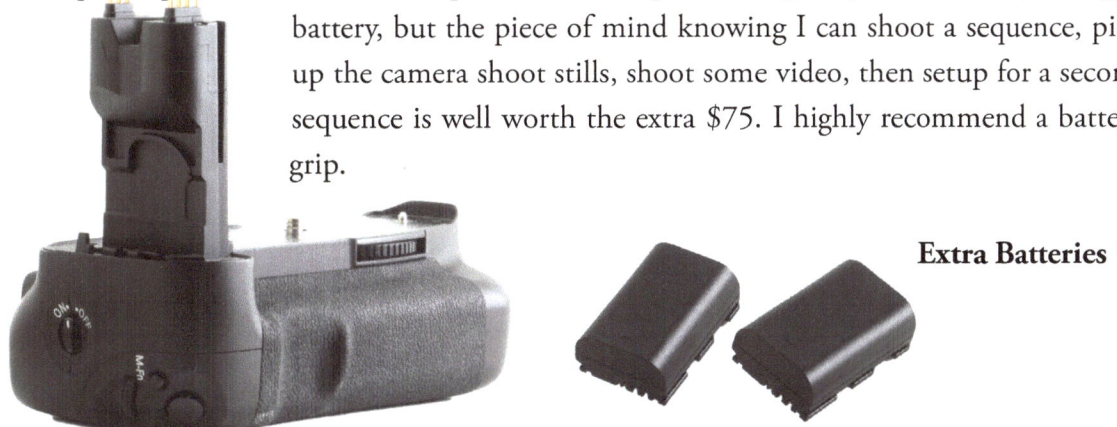

Extra Batteries

Change batteries mid sequence with the battery grip trick

A Google search and Melanderci at the timescapes forum came up with a great little trick to extend your shots as long as you have enough fresh spare batteries. Here's how to change them mid time-lapse: Open the door of the battery grip, find the little button that gets pressed when the door is closed (upper left), now wedge something there to keep it down (pen cap, some toothpicks taped together) then turn the camera on.

You are now able to swap out the battery one at a time without disrupting the time-lapse, just be as careful as you can not to move the camera (maybe try to time moves between shots or pause the time-lapse briefly). It's also suggested to write "DO NOT CLOSE DOOR" or else old habits are sure to jump up on you.

Card reader and extra memory cards

If you don't already have one I highly recommend it. Since we'll be transferring large numbers of photos there no sense in using camera battery power while we wait for images to transfer. You might want to spend just a few more dollars and invest in a name brand unit. Memory cards are very expensive protect them.

Save some serious juice while shooting by turning image review off. Once you are confident in your exposure and composition there is no need for the screen to fire up and show you each time-lapse image.

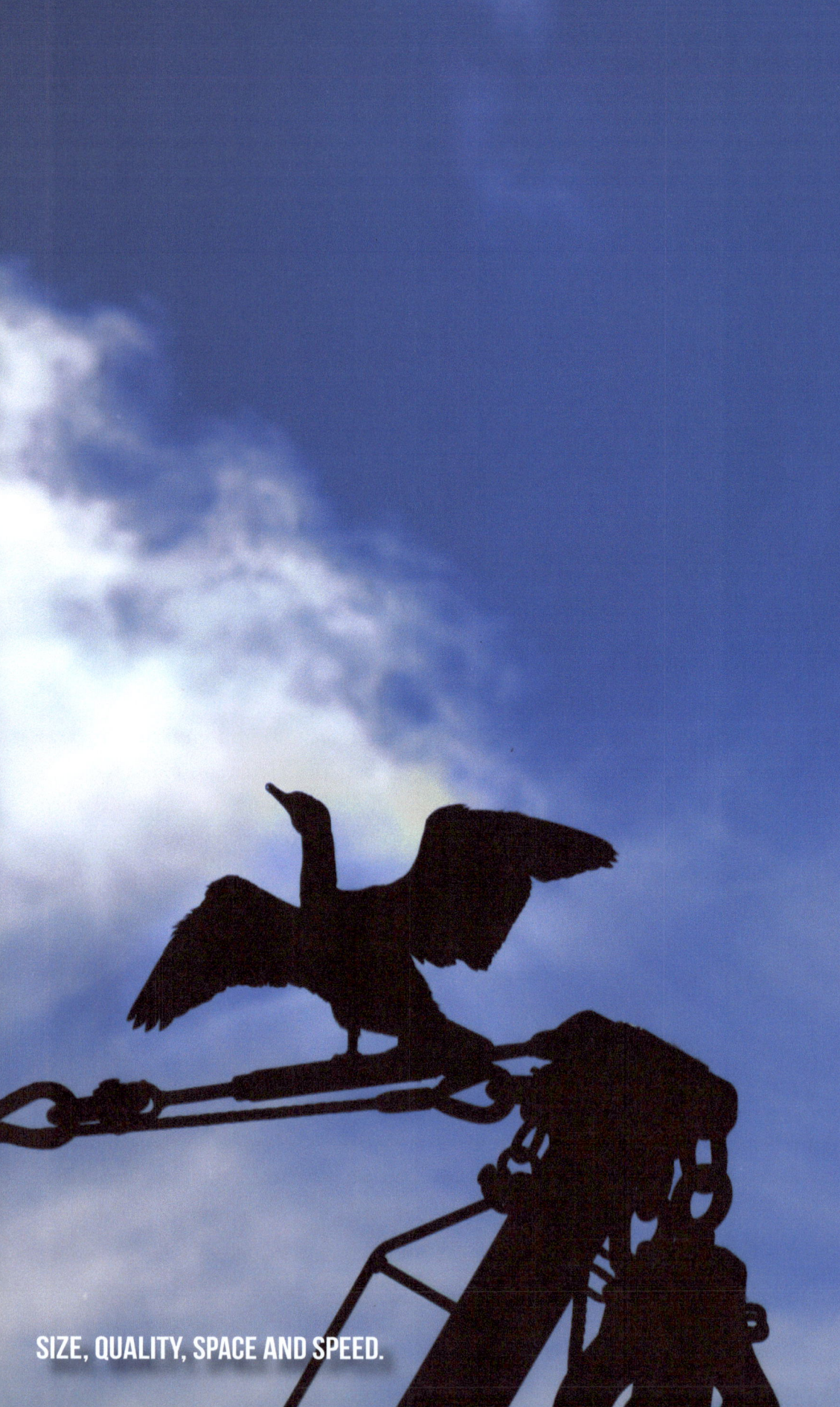

SIZE, QUALITY, SPACE AND SPEED.

2 BALANCING TIME-LAPSE IMAGE SETTINGS

Size, quality, space and speed; It's nothing new if you've worked with digital images before but with time-lapse sequences poor planning can quickly cut a scene too short or leave you with a blinking "Card Full" message just as the sun peaks out over the mountains.

OK, I'll admit it. For the first few months after purchasing my DSLR I only shot in the highest resolution RAW format possible. Bigger file sizes must produce better quality images right? Here I was with an 18.0 Megapixel digital camera, why wouldn't I want to shoot at it's fullest potential?

Potential, yes. Practical, not always. I almost had it right back then but my understanding of what makes a good image was a little hazy. I failed to think about the end destination.

Now I still do most of my shooting in full RAW, but only when I know I have the memory capacity to allow for it, and more importantly, have a need for the added flexibility it provides. In other words I plan for it.

This chapter is about 3 things: Image resolution, photo file types and how to fit it all on your memory card.

IMAGE CHOICES

Knowing what resolution and file format you need and can afford to use before you begin shooting will prevent headaches and save time-lapse shots. It will also ensure you capture the highest quality images your project requires. Let's start with a debate that's, well, no longer a debate (for some that is):

RAW VS JPEG

While some photographers would say that the argument is over, RAW has won, knowledgeable pros shoot in the format best suited to their particular situation. Shooting in RAW does have many benefits but also comes at a cost of large file sizes. With cheap memory this almost isn't an issue anymore but for time-lapse sequences we aren't just talking about a few dozen images, usually not even a few hundred images, sometimes we're dealing with thousands of images and we'll need to weigh the costs and benefits carefully. Here's what I mean:

Take an 18 Megapixel camera for example. At full resolution:

- **1 JPEG image weighs in at around 6.6 MB**
- **1 RAW image tips the scale at around 25.1 MB**

Keep in mind that's for the same resolution 18 MP image. As you can see there's a big difference in file size, but that's not the only difference. Here are a few thoughts on the pros and cons of the JPEG versus RAW format.

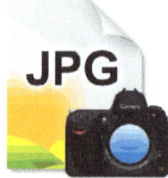
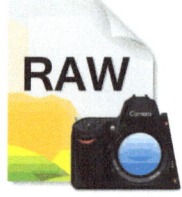

JPEG Pros
- JPEGs take up less space
- JPEG is a file format that has been adopted as a standard and can be displayed quickly almost anywhere

JPEG Cons
- JPEG is considered a lossy format, each time a file is saved data is compressed and information is lost
- JPEG is a one time interpretation of camera data (white balance, exposure settings, etc.) and cannot be re-outputted/changed like RAW

RAW Pros
- RAW is like a digital negative holding all pixel data captured by your camera
- RAW editors allow the easy adjustment of all exposure settings and then allow syncing those settings across the entire sequence without quality loss

RAW Cons
- Raw files are big, really big compared to JPEG
- RAW formats are proprietary to each camera manufacturer and require some degree of processing to display

It's all about pixel data...

When you snap an image in JPEG the camera's firmware quickly goes to work taking all the pixel information from the image sensor, applies your white balance, exposure settings, etc then following complex algorithms compresses the image before saving it to memory. This takes place very fast and no additional processing or special software is required, but all the original pixel data used to create that file is thrown away.

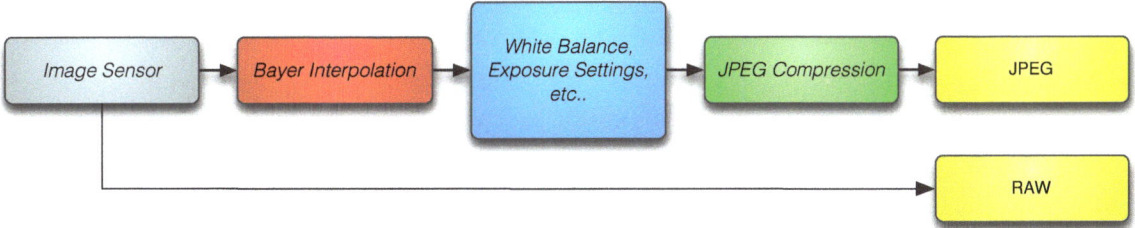

RAW format on the other hand isn't necessarily an image file per se, rather it's an unprocessed collection of all possible pixel data from the sensor. Instead of the camera processing and compressing the file into an image, RAW relies on you and your computer to apply a set of instructions on how those pixels should be displayed. Feel the images can be improved by adjusting the exposure or changing the white balance? Simple. Using your RAW processor just tweak the instructions the computer uses to interpret those pixels and easily sync those adjustments across all images in a large sequence.

START LEARNING IN JPEG

JPEGs are easier to work with, take up less space, and will allow the faster processing of more time-lapses to learn the basics.

Choose RAW for time-lapse (with one caveat: card capacity)

Consider starting out in JPEG format

RAW images are great but they can also be a big (in more ways than one) pain in the arse the first few times you use them. If you are brand new to time-lapse (or RAW for that matter) consider learning the basics on JPEGs then when you are more comfortable shooting and manipulating large collections of images, switch over to RAW.

THEN USE RAW FLEXIBILITY

If you have the space RAW format flexibility will pay off

Then switch over to RAW

Shooting a time-lapse sequence is a pretty big investment and a collection of RAW images will help ensure that more of your investments pay off. Not only will you have much more nondestructive creative control over your images after they are captured, but syncing those changes across an entire sequence during processing is simple.

"You should always shoot in the RAW, but not in the buff, because you might get arrested."
- Confucious

Extra pixel data is great, but only if you have the space to store it.

There's one more choice we need to make before we start tallying space requirements, and that's image resolution.

IMAGE RESOLUTION

Resolution is defined as the actual dimension of the image being captured measured in pixels. For example an 18MP camera can capture a maximum of 5184 pixels across by 3456 down.

Quality		Pixels (megapixels)	Printing Size	File Size (MB)
JPEG	◢L	Approx. 17.9 (17.9M)	A2 or larger	6.6
	◢L			3.3
	◢M	Approx. 8.0 (8M)	Around A3	3.5
	◢M			1.8
	◢S	Approx. 4.5 (4.5M)	Around A4	2.2
	◢S			1.1
RAW	RAW	Approx. 17.9 (17.9M)	A2 or larger	25.1
	M RAW	Approx. 10.1 (10M)	Around A3	17.1
	S RAW	Approx. 4.5 (4.5M)	Around A4	11.4

That's a lot of pixels, but we don't necessarily have to capture that many if we don't want to. We have options.

Selecting "M" if we are shooting in JPEG or "M-RAW" in RAW will produce slightly smaller resolution images, followed by even smaller "S-RAW" or "S".

Letters and the different pixel counts they represent can be a little tough to compare so it makes more sense to show the different resolutions in relation to one another:

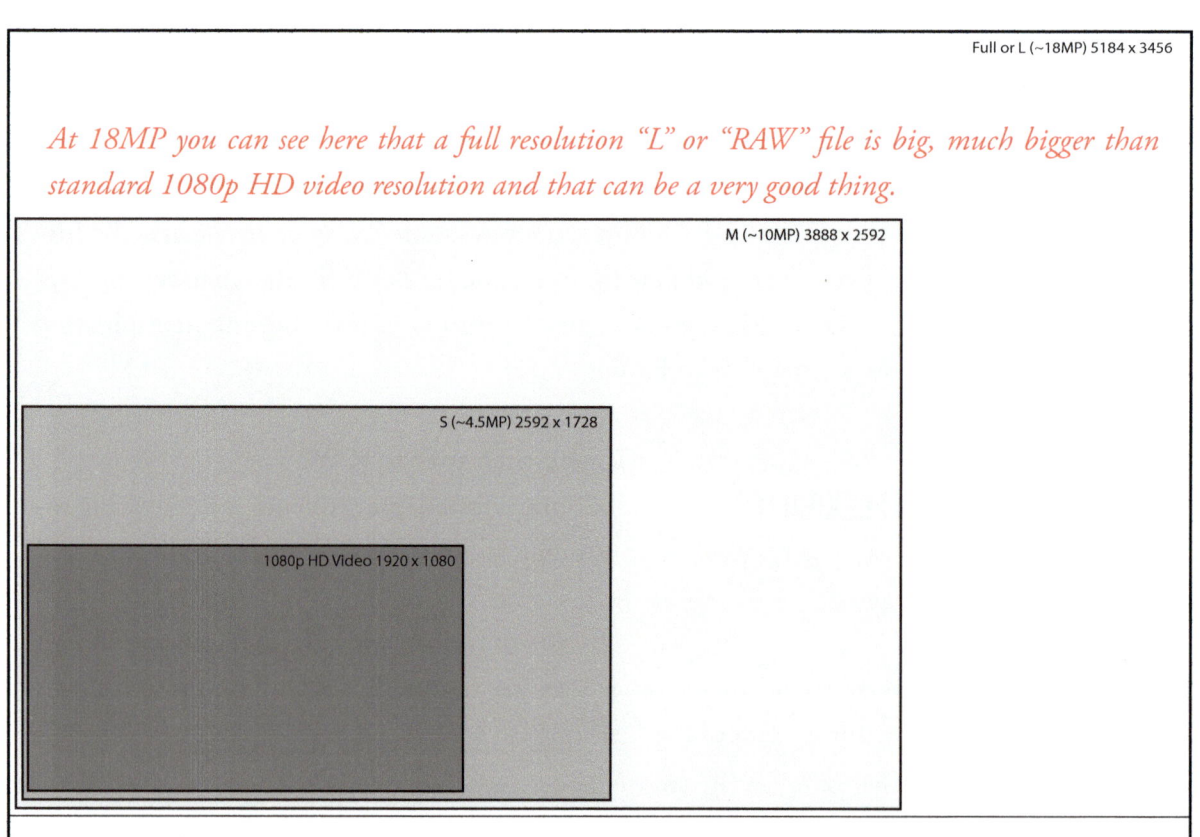

Full or L (~18MP) 5184 x 3456

At 18MP you can see here that a full resolution "L" or "RAW" file is big, much bigger than standard 1080p HD video resolution and that can be a very good thing.

M (~10MP) 3888 x 2592

S (~4.5MP) 2592 x 1728

1080p HD Video 1920 x 1080

ADVANTAGES OF HIGH RESOLUTION TIME-LAPSE IMAGES

It's all about flexibility. Shooting at the highest resolution your camera allows give you the largest individual time-lapse sequence frames to crop,

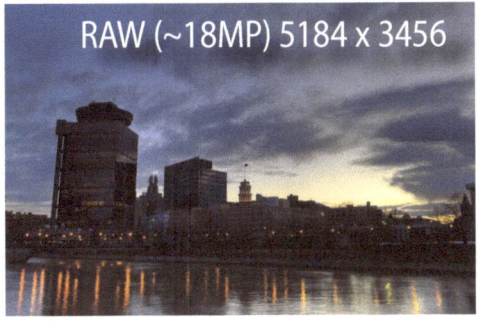

pan, tilt, zoom, basically manipulate in different ways without risking image quality loss in post production.

SHOOT AT HIGH RESOLUTION

Large images provide export and editing flexibility in post production

The image at left was taken at a maximum 18MP resolution which produces an image 5184 x 3456 pixels large. Because my original master image is so much larger than what I am planning to export to (HD quality or 1920 x 1080 pixels.), I can do one or several different things:

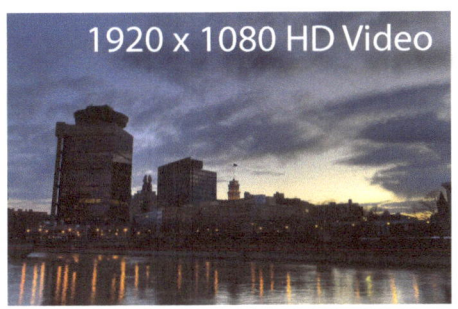

Shrink

You may want to keep your full composition just how it is, unchanged and stationary. You can simply shrink your images to match your desired final destination, in this case full HD video, however keep in mind the aspect ratio difference from the camera's 3:2 and HD video's 16:9, you will be forced to slightly crop the top and/or bottom.

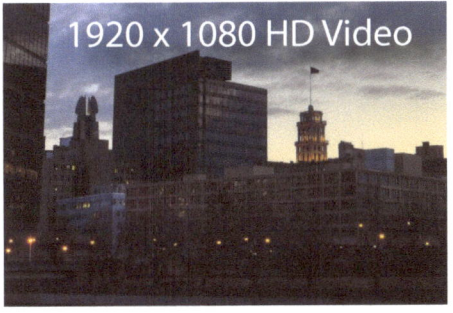

Crop

Cut out parts of the shot you don't want to feature then zoom to full HD resolution. All those extra pixels allowed me to crop out a large portion of the shot and expand the buildings and flagpole to become full screen. Cropping allows you to easily shift the viewers attention to something different than the full composition.

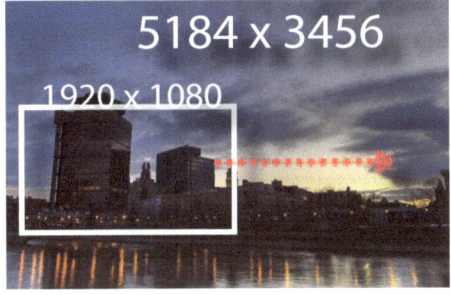

Pan, Tilt, Zoom

Using a few extra steps either when rendering the time-lapse sequence itself or afterwards inside an editing application, high resolution images allow room for programed movement. ***An easy and very awesome way to add interest to the time-lapse scene.*** We discuss adding movement in each rendering workflow found in chapter 5.

HD VIDEO ASPECT RATIO

When shooting to export to HD video don't forget to consider your final framing and the differences between your camera's 3:2 aspect ratio and the HD aspect ratio of 16:9.

Any photos you take and want to shrink to HD will experience about a 15% (200 pixel) crop.

It's up to you during post processing which end (or a combination) gets cropped. You could also add a tilting effect to your video and move from one portion to the other over time but keep this potential image loss in mind when composing your shots.

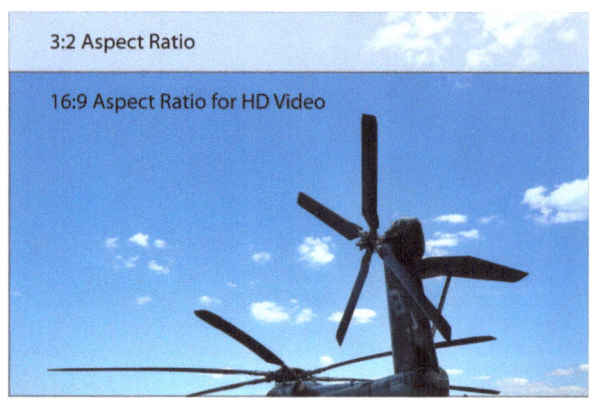

FITTING IT ALL IN

Moore's Law is working it's magic on memory; it's getting bigger (or should I say smaller?) and cheaper all the time, but it certainly isn't free, not yet anyway. As time-lapse photographers we'll always worry about memory capacity in the field and planning what we want to capture and how many images we are capable of storing *before* we start shooting is paramount.

The number of time-lapse images you can safely save depends on three things: your camera manufacturer, the size of your memory card (or cards) and your choices for file type and resolution.

The chart below is based on an 18MP DSLR that produces around a 20MB full RAW image file. See that a simple resolution change from full RAW to mRAW boosts your image counts by about 18%. Choosing sRAW instead of RAW almost doubles your image counts adding about 80% more. Choosing JPEG versus RAW almost triples the number of photos you can store.

Estimated Number of Time-lapse Images				
Card Capacity (GB)	RAW	mRAW	sRAW	JPEG
2	93	109	169	266
4	186	219	338	531
8	372	438	676	1,063
16	744	875	1,353	2,126
32	1,488	1,751	2,705	4,251
64	2,976	3,501	5,411	8,503

We'll double check this capacity number before we shoot, but it will be only one of many things we need to set up properly before we start recording. That's what the next chapter is all about.

"TEACHERS DON'T WORK IN THE SUMMER, AND PHOTOGRAPHERS DON'T SHOOT IN THE MIDDLE OF THE DAY."

- JOHN LOENGARD

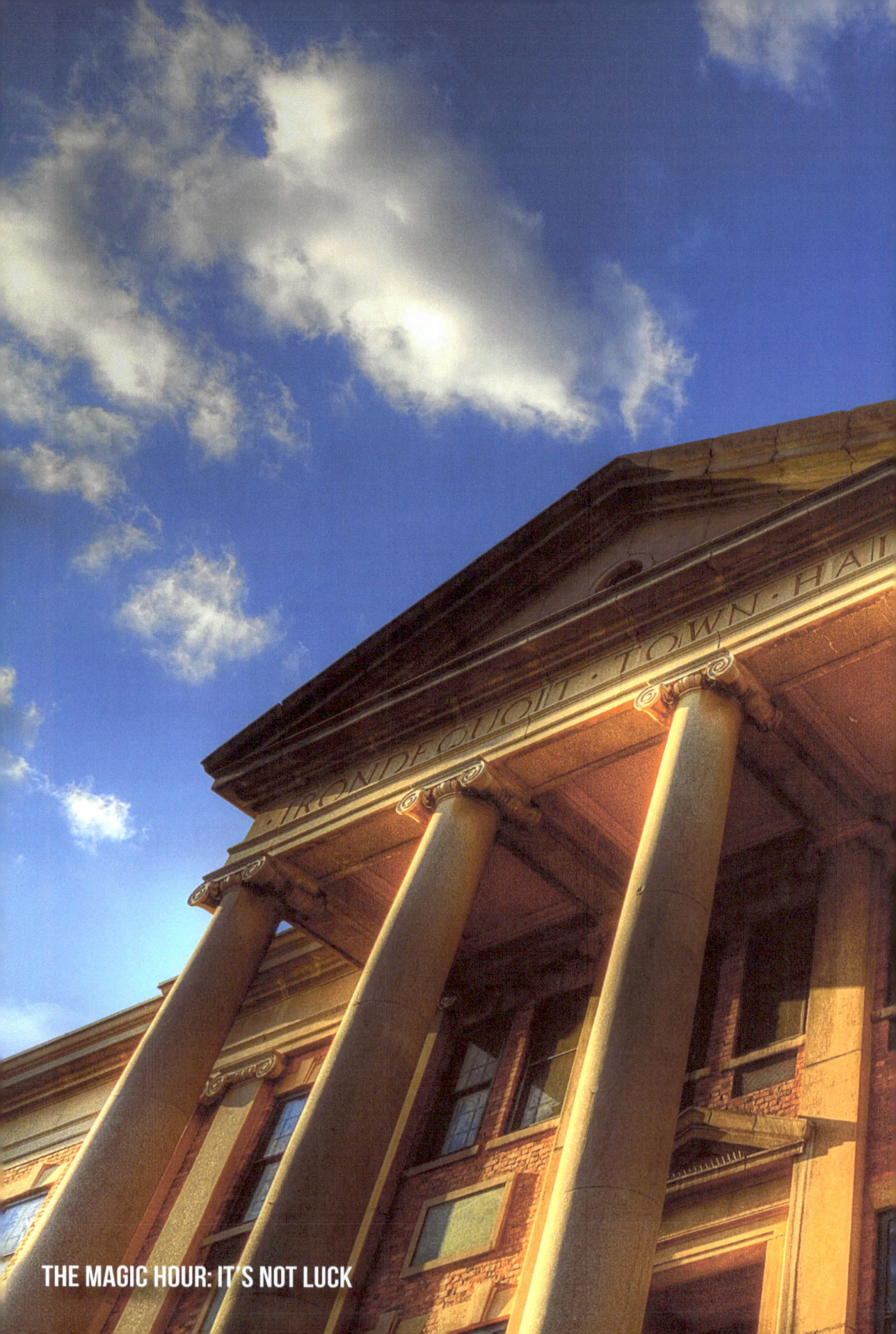

THE MAGIC HOUR: IT'S NOT LUCK

3 SHOOTING TIME-LAPSE

This section walks you through the fundamentals of shooting DSLR time-lapse then sets you loose to develop and tweak your own workflow and style.

These first few tests should focus more on experimenting and a little less about creating a technically perfect rendered sequence (there's plenty of time for that later). Get a few fun tests under your belt and the time-lapse bug is sure to carry you through.

In later chapters, after you've had a chance to survey the basics, we'll walk through some specific scenarios and advanced topics.

It seems counter-intuitive but if you to leave this section with more questions brewing in your mind than when you began I'll say you're right on track.

You'll see as we walk through your first time-lapse that the more you begin to understand about the topic the more you realize you don't know and need to experiment, and it's the experimentation that really propels you forward.

Can I shoot a time-lapse of a scene as it changes from day to night without flicker? Can I really capture the Milky Way as it moves across the sky?

SHOOTING TIME-LAPSE BASICS

Recording a series of time-lapse images is not difficult. In just a few simple steps you'll have the images you need to render your movie. As a matter of fact if the entire process could be broken down into 4 colored boxes and a blue start button, here's what it would look like:

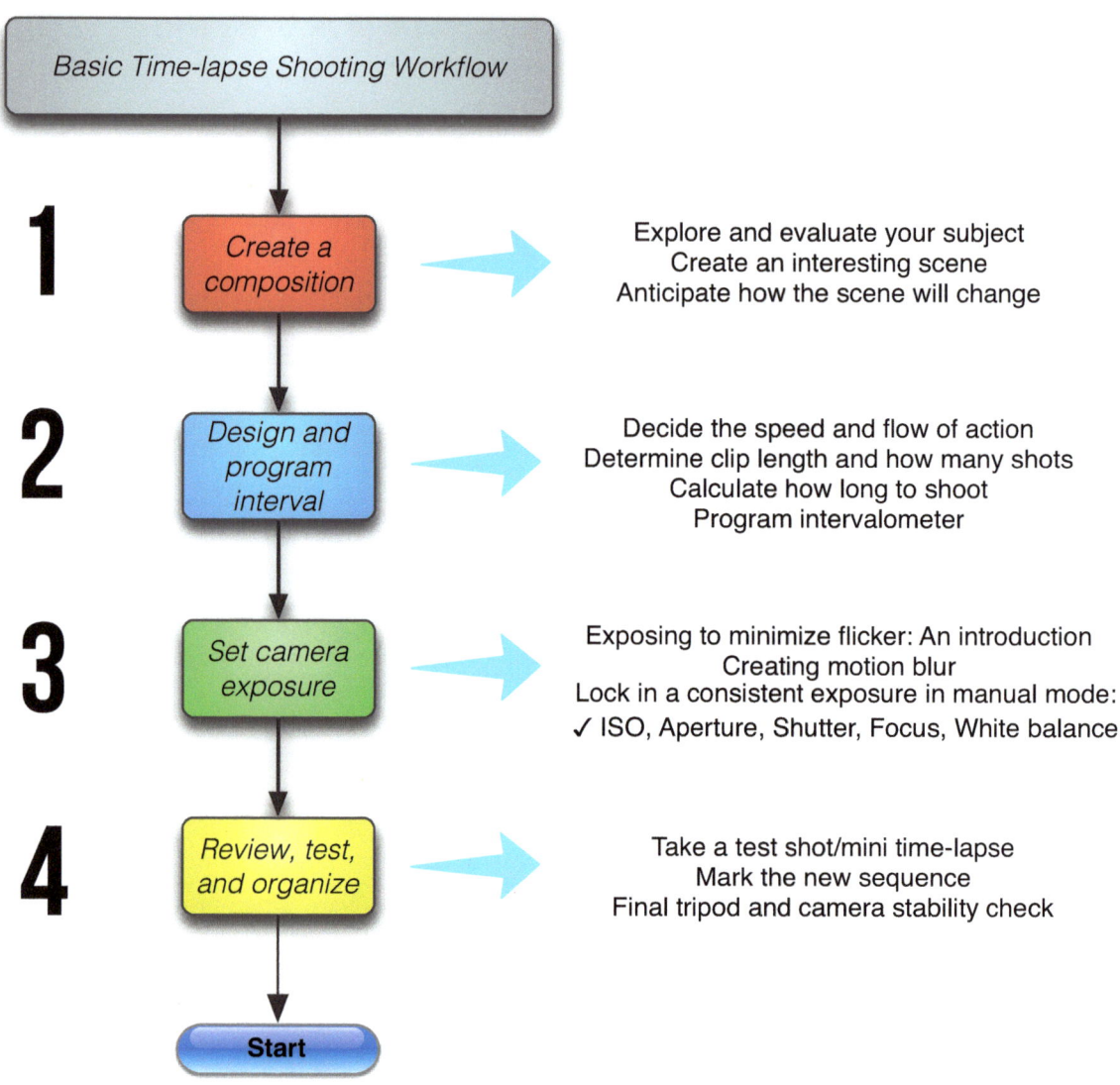

WHAT MAKES A GOOD TIME-LAPSE?

Well...you kind of just know it when you see it, right? It's tough to put into words but I'll give it a shot. I think some of the most interesting and the most memorable time-lapse compositions are ones that have a really good mix of dynamic and static elements, lots of contrast between changing or moving things and those that are stationary. The best scenes are both captivating now and intensely interesting later. They are of the places you want to see at the times you would want to see them. Here's what I mean:

Say you wanted to film the Milky Way moving across the sky. An awesome time-lapse by itself, but how might you really add interest to the scene?

What if you positioned the camera nice and low to the ground and brought in some foreground elements? In this case a silhouette of a treeline which will really show the contrast between the moving night sky and the (appearing to be) stationary Earth.

What if we got lucky and also added something to the scene like this lighthouse? What if we got even luckier because the spinning lighthouse beacon (although bright and a overblown) will show a cool spinning effect when sped up?

Say you wanted to film the bright sunrise over the mountains. What could you add to the scene to really make it interesting?

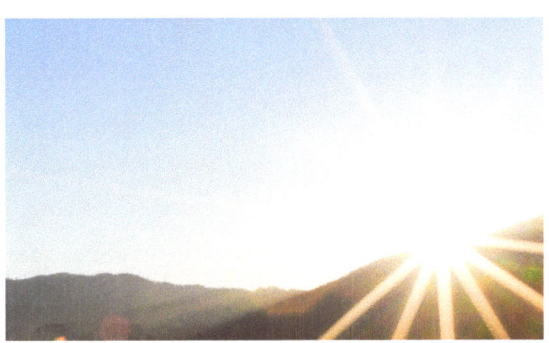

What if again we found something in the foreground to highlight, in this case the beach and this big rock which will show the changing shadow from the sun as it rises? We can also get some interesting motion from the small waves hitting the shore.

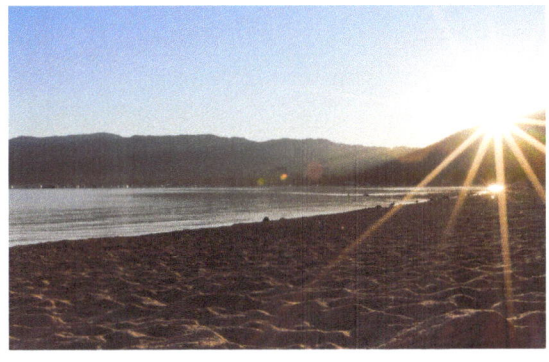

Wow, talk about making you feel small and insignificant. Although a bit more challenging the night sky is one of my favorite things to photograph.

Don't worry too much for your first time-lapse.

Find a place close to home where something is happening: maybe your backyard on a partly cloudy day, maybe your local park or playground with dads pushing swinging kids, or if the sun is streaming in your windows, just stay inside and observe your apartment in the daylight. *Look for a no-pressure spot where you can take your time and experiment, take notes, relax, then quickly download and see what you captured.* Then again, just because I am going to stay close to home on this first walkthrough doesn't mean you have to.

1 [Create a composition] SELECTING YOUR COMPOSITION
THE ART OF WALKING AROUND

I used to be normal, and I got normal shots. Whatever you do don't approach a scene, set down your tripod and begin shooting because guess what? *You'll end up with a shot (actually hundreds and hundreds of shots) just like everyone else's.*

Unless you are rushing to capture some rare elk migration or a total eclipse, start by taking a few extra moments to walk around your scene. Observe your environment in real time, don't zero in on anything just yet, roam around, take in the big picture and then begin to focus on individual elements. Remember that the best time-lapse might be of a scene directly behind you, from an angle at ground level, or at some other time during the day. *In other words slow down and think about your options.*

Once you find a good spot peer through your lens and ask yourself a few questions:
How will the edges of my composition look?
Am I considering my foreground?
Do I want to limit focus?
What is interesting about this scene?
What time-lapse motion will occur? (more than 1?)
Will my audience enjoy watching it change for 10 seconds?

NOW, CREATE YOUR SCENE
Seek out and balance interest
Remember sometimes it's all about balance. We're really only brushing the surface of artistic photo composition in this book, but there are a few important rules that can quickly lead to better scenes:

The Rule of Thirds:

Images just seem more interesting if the elements within them are balanced and the main subject is not directly in the center. Divide your scene into thirds, horizontally and vertically, and place your main subject on one of these coordinates, but don't be afraid to break the rules for dramatic effect.

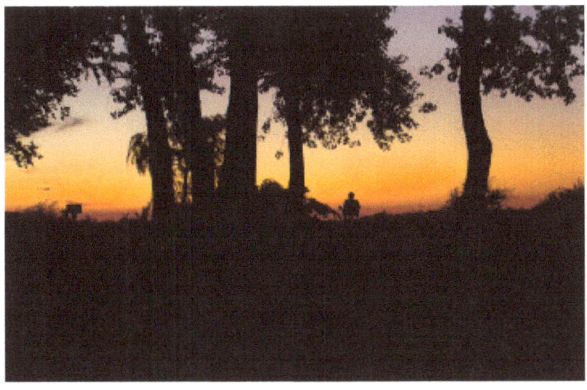

The magic hour:

There are two times a day when outdoor things just look better. Light at the beginning and ending of each day is softer, warmer and the shadows are longer. Time-lapse done well can make most scenes more interesting but shooting during the first and last few hours of the day can really be amazing.

Plan ahead and be patient. I've missed lots of great shots stuck in the car driving to my location as the sky turns amazing colors of orange and red. Realize that it might take you a while to find the right composition and setup your shot.

Anticipate what will be exciting and interesting in your compiled scene, combine it with the best light possible and then compose your shot in such a way that the viewer can understand why you did it.

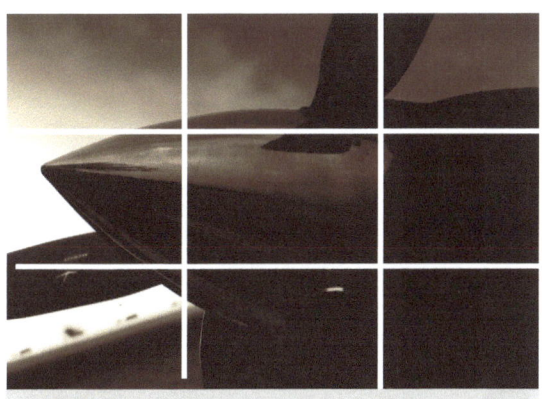

The rule of thirds is all about moving your subject off to one side or another; in this case the tip of the cone and the changing cloud reflections are a little to the left of center.

NOW, ANTICIPATE THE CHANGE

Time to polish the crystal ball

As time-lapse photographers we have an incredibly creative tool that few other photographers have, and that's **change**. Try to anticipate how your scene will change over time and what composition best captures this change.

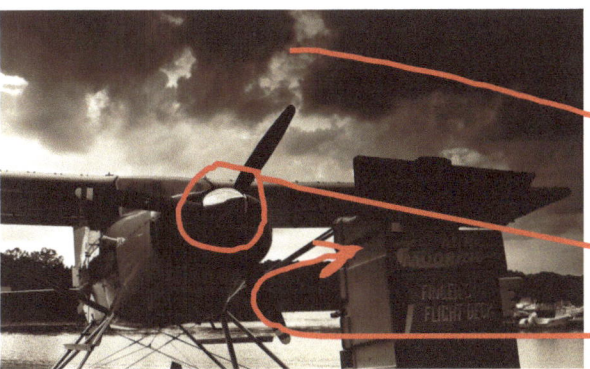

Fast clouds moving from west to east

Moving sky reflection in airplane nose cone

Boats moving out of the channel

Is something moving from one side of the frame to another? Do I capture enough of it on both sides (or one side)? What about the time of day? How is the light going to change over the next few minutes or in the next hour? How fast are the clouds moving? Are boats moving in and out of the channel? What about reflections?

In addition to making sure the composition is set up to capture the action we anticipate, begin to think about how fast that action will be taking place and what the best interval might be to create the effect we want.

Time-lapse subject ideas
The number of potential time-lapse subjects is massive. Interesting change is all around you.

- Transportation - cars, trains, boats
- Drivelapses from inside cars
- Crowds - stadiums filling, concerts
- Busy human places - malls, airports, parks, city streets, etc.
- Cooking - baking, mixing, making
- Food - rotting, bugs eating
- Construction projects
- Clouds - anywhere and everywhere

- Tides and natures changes
- Sunrises, Sunsets, Shadows
- Fast growing plants - vines/flowers
- Human change - pregnancy, weight loss, aging
- Stars, the night sky, the Milky Way, the Moon
- People getting stuff done
- And so much more...

2 Design and program interval

SELECTING THE INTERVAL
SPEED, LENGTH AND PROGRAMMING THE SHOTS

With one number you have control over two things:
1. How fast the time-lapse change appears to be taking place
2. How smooth that action appears on screen

DECIDE HOW TO BALANCE SPEED AND FLOW
Since the time-lapse interval is the amount of time that we program the camera to wait between each exposure, different scenes containing slow or fast movement will require different intervals. For example if we are filming fast clouds on a windy day we will need to keep our interval relatively short. If we program too long of an interval (maybe anything over 2 seconds) we risk the scene appearing jumpy or jerky when we play back the final compilation.

The stuttery and jumpy scene is due to the fact that we didn't collect images fast enough; too much information was lost between each frame. Now, sometimes we want things to be a little jumpy and pop from one location to another (like in tilt-shift effect time-lapses), but in most cases we are aiming for smooth motion.

No two scenes are exactly alike. These common interval durations should give you a head start:

COMMON BASELINE INTERVALS

1 SECOND

- Moving traffic
- Fast moving clouds
- Drivelapses

1 – 3 SECONDS

- Sunsets
- Sunrises
- Slower moving clouds
- Crowds
- Moon and sun near horizon
- Things photographed with a telephoto

15 – 30 SECONDS OR LONGER

- Moving shadows
- Sun across sky (no clouds) (wide)
- Stars (15 – 60 seconds)
- Fast growing plants (90–120 seconds)
- Construction projects (5–15 min.)

If you arrive at a scene and aren't really sure what interval to use, it's usually best to use one that is faster than you need rather than slower. You can always speed up too many frames at home in post by throwing away images or changing your frame rate, but you can't easily fill in those missing intervals to correct big jumps.

Matching intervals to slow or fast scenes may seem a little difficult at first but as you continue to gain experience seeing the rendered results of the decisions you make this will begin to become second nature.

Now that we've matched up the interval to the scene we're photographing we need to figure out how many photos we need to take, and consequently how long we need to let the camera snap away. But before we can do that we need to decide how long we would like the final video to be.

DECIDE THE LENGTH OF YOUR VIDEO

It's a general rule of thumb to shoot for at least 8 to 12 seconds of time-lapse video length. Anything shorter and we just start to realize how incredible the scene is and then *blackness*, the video clip is over. Unless we have a specific use in mind, it might be a good idea to err on the longer side of 10 seconds for a few reasons.

First, it gives us the option to trim a portion of the front or back of the clip or add fading or cross dissolving when we play with the footage in a video editor. Second, sometimes we're combining several scenes and paring them with music. Having a little bit of flexibility with a long enough clip to break and fade to match the beat or change in the music comes in handy.

AIM FOR ~10 SECONDS OF FOOTAGE
Don't cut your time-lapse shots too short in the field, you can always trim in post

A review of frame rate:
Before we calculate how many photos we'll need to take to get the desired clip length we want we need to determine how fast they will be played back. That's where frame rate comes in.

Frame rate refers to the number of individual images we fit into one second of video. More frames per second (FSP) means we are playing back images faster and more will need to be captured to produce the same length of video. The faster we play back the frames the faster the action appears to take place in our movie. We'll talk more about frame rate later when we export our series of images into a video, but for now understand that it plays a pretty important role in how many photos we need to capture in the field.

UNDERSTAND HOW MANY SHOTS YOU NEED AND HOW LONG TO SHOOT

Here's an example of how to calculate how many shots you will need?
Scenario: It's an awesome sky and fast moving clouds are being painted a warm orange from the evening sun. We've decided that we would like to create a 10 second cloud time-lapse movie with an extra 2 seconds to fade in and out.

First, calculate the number of frames required:
We want 12 seconds of compiled cloud footage to be shown at 30 frames per second. This will require [12 x 30] 360 frames to be captured.

Shot length calculation (in seconds)	☒
video length * frame rate * interval = total shooting time	

Then, determine the interval:

We can see that the clouds are moving moderately fast and we want a nice smooth video. We decide to shoot at a 2 second interval.

Now, calculate the shooting time:

At a 2 second interval and with the goal of 360 frames, we need to snap images for [2 x 360] 720 seconds or [720 / 60] 12 minutes. *Keep in mind this does not include the actual exposure time but that really only comes into play for long night time exposures.*

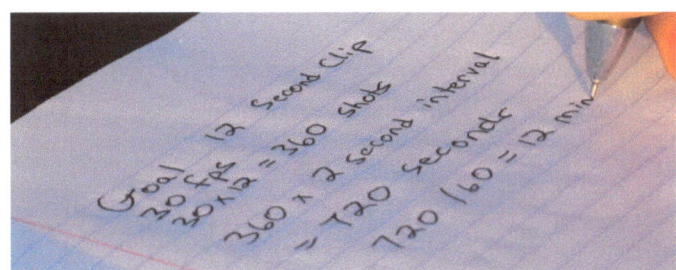

That's it. We've determined our two main time-lapse variables, a proper interval and the number of shots we need. We've also figured out about how long we need to allow the shooting to take place to capture all those images. Now it's time to program them in.

PROGRAMMING YOUR INTERVALOMETER

Intervalometers are really simple devices. Most models are really only four variables complex, and since most of the time you'll only be concerned with two of them, learning will be quick.

Chances are if you have a basic external intervalometer it will look a lot like the one below but even if it doesn't, just about all timer controllers function in the same way and a quick translation should match up your input variables.

DELAY (DE) : Just like a regular self timer. Program this delay time if you want to start your time-lapse recording at a later time. For example, if you have the courage to leave your camera unattended this works great for an early morning Milk Way shot.

BULB (BU) : Controls your camera's bulb mode exposure time with the time you program here. We'll walk through an example on how to use this in our astro-lapse challenge.

INTERVAL (INT) : The amount of time that we program the camera to wait between each exposure. Your intervalometer will continue until your camera fills its memory or you reach a programmed maximum number of exposures.

NUMBER OF SHOTS (N) : How many exposures do we want. Most devices can be programmed from 1 to 399 or to infinity. For infinite exposures select " - - - " as the number of shots.

I usually select infinite shots relying instead on my watch to know when to stop the sequence, this way if something changes or the scene starts to look even better I can just let it roll on for a while longer and trim the clip as needed later. Be careful though as you can quickly fill up your card and leave no room for the next scene on your trip.

Most timers also allow you to select an interval "beep" to sound for each exposure and more importantly they allow you to deselect this feature for silent shooting.

Tip: Don't forget you can also use your timer remote as a standard off-camera shutter release for long exposures (batteries or not).

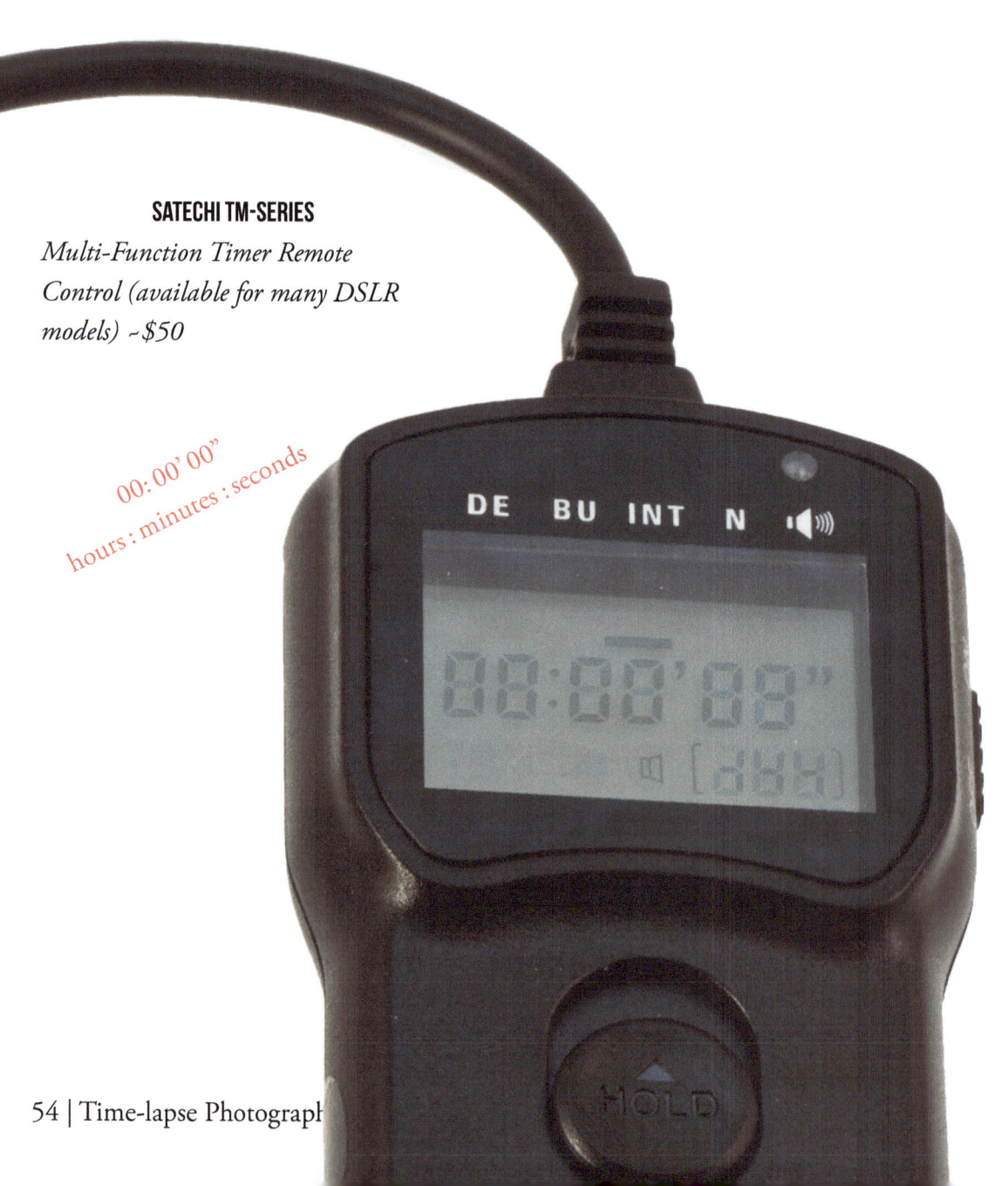

SATECHI TM-SERIES

Multi-Function Timer Remote Control (available for many DSLR models) ~$50

00: 00' 00"
hours : minutes : seconds

Exposure is all about controlling the amount of light that hits our camera's image sensor. Too little light and our images look dark, tone and colors are dull, shadows lose detail and become black. Too much light and our images are overexposed, colors become washed out, bright areas lose detail and become blown out in white.

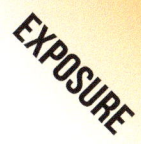

3 *Set camera exposure*

EXPOSURE SETTINGS
MANUAL CONTROLS, MINIMIZING FLICKER AND CREATING MOTION BLUR

Millions upon millions of dollars and decades of research has gone into creating cameras that can predict what you want to photograph, sense current lighting conditions, and then automatically adjust the mechanical and electrical parameters to create a good exposure, and as time-lapse photographers we don't use any of it, *(cue hysterical madmen laughter)*. Well... most of the time.

Automatic aperture, shutter speed, ISO, white balance, focus etc, it automatically works and it automatically works well, it's just usually not the best for shooting time-lapse. Here's why:

TIME-LAPSE FLICKER: AN INTRODUCTION

Take a look at these three time-lapse frames:

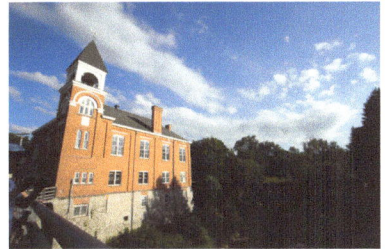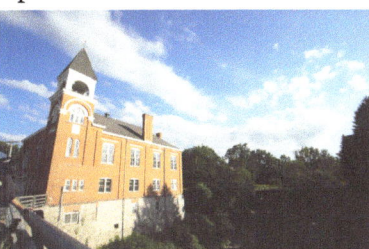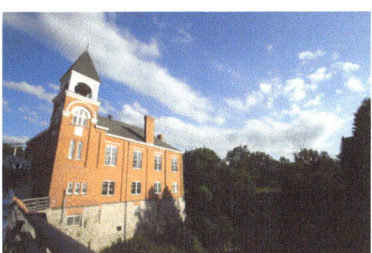

1/100th sec. at f/8   1/80th sec. at f/8   1/100th sec. at f/8

Notice how the middle photo is slightly brighter? Now we could argue which appears to be a better exposure, but in time-lapse photography not only do we have to care about how each *individual* image looks, we also have to care very much about how each image looks in relation to the ones before and just after it.

If we were to view these images in rapid succession what starts to look like a good time-lapse video is suddenly spattered with some images that look brighter or dimmer making the film appear to "flicker" or "strobe". It's the bane of many a time-lapse photographer, and it's called time-lapse flicker. *"Some of these photos are not like the others?!"*

- Big Bird upon rendering his first time-lapse shot in full automatic mode

WHY DOES TIME-LAPSE FLICKER OCCUR?

Essentially instead of the camera's exposure settings and mechanical configurations remaining perfectly constant or purposefully changing in very slight and gradual ways, large unintended exposure jumps occur in some sequence frames which create images that look out of place when compiled together.

How can we minimize/correct time-lapse flicker?

- Eliminate or reduce the camera's automatic exposure controls
- Use manual lenses or trick our camera into thinking our automatic lens is manual
- Correct it after it occurs by using de-flickering software in post production

We'll talk a lot more about flicker in the next chapter but for now understand that the most common and simplest way to minimize it is to prevent the camera from making *any* exposure decisions as it snaps our series of time-lapse photos.

If the camera exposes each time-lapse image in the exact same way we should experience fewer sudden light or dark jumps, and that's the goal. Here's how to do it:

CONFIGURE MANUAL CAMERA CONTROLS

Manual mode (M on your camera dial) is usually the best shooting mode for most time-lapse scenes with relatively constant light. It allows us full control over all elements of the exposure.

Now it's OK if you are a little rusty on full manual control. Read through the basics on the next page or two, then cement in the fundamentals with a few of the suggested resources in the resources section. You may also want to rummage around and find your camera's manual (or bring up the PDF online). It will be helpful in locating the menus and options if your aren't familiar with them as we review some time-lapse exposure considerations.

Let's walk through a quick overview of your camera's manual exposure controls and how these settings affect not only the individual images, but how it affects the entire time-lapse compilation when we combine and view our images in rapid sequence.

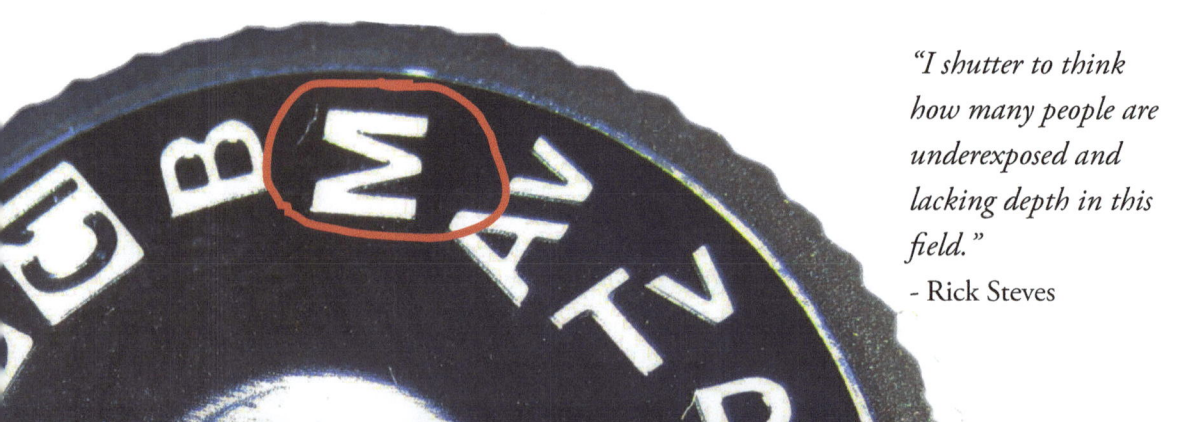

"I shutter to think how many people are underexposed and lacking depth in this field."
- Rick Steves

TIME-LAPSE EXPOSURE TRIANGLE:

You've probably seen a similar exposure triangle before. It highlights the fact that different camera settings can be combined in different ways to achieve the same exposure result. In other words aperture, shutter speed, and ISO settings work closely together. We'll quickly deconstruct this triangle as we discuss why manually configuring each one is the easiest route to a flicker free time-lapse.

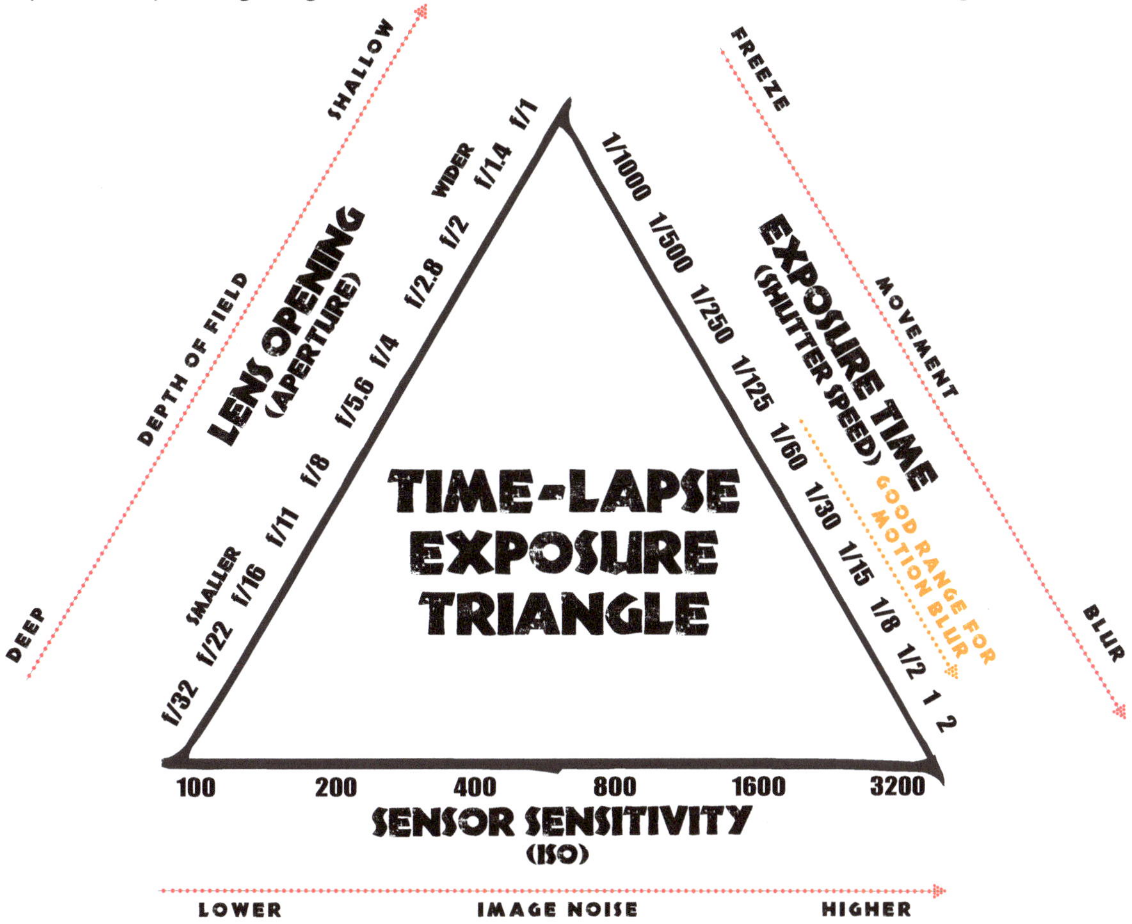

SHALLOW

FREEZE

DEPTH OF FIELD

LENS OPENING (APERTURE)

WIDER f/1.4 f/1

f/2.8 f/2

f/5.6 f/4

f/8

SMALLER f/11

f/16

f/22

f/32

EXPOSURE TIME (SHUTTER SPEED)

1/1000

1/500

1/250

1/125

1/60

1/30

1/15

1/8

1/2 1 2

MOVEMENT

GOOD RANGE FOR MOTION BLUR

DEEP

BLUR

TIME-LAPSE EXPOSURE TRIANGLE

SENSOR SENSITIVITY (ISO)

| 100 | 200 | 400 | 800 | 1600 | 3200 |

LOWER   IMAGE NOISE   HIGHER

MANUAL ISO

ISO is a measure of the sensitivity of your image sensor. Think amplification. Since the data read off the sensor needs to be amplified before it can be analyzed, an increased ISO setting provides increased amplification.

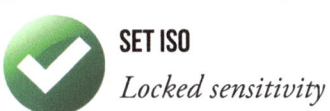

SET ISO
Locked sensitivity

Those once weak light levels are now more significant which allows for smaller apertures and shorter exposure times. Electrical noise however is also amplified with a high ISO so it's sometimes best to only use higher ISOs (>200) when it's absolutely necessary (handheld shooting, indoors/low light, etc).

By deselecting automatic ISO determination and locking in a set number we prevent the camera from creating brighter or darker images due to changes in sensor sensitivity.

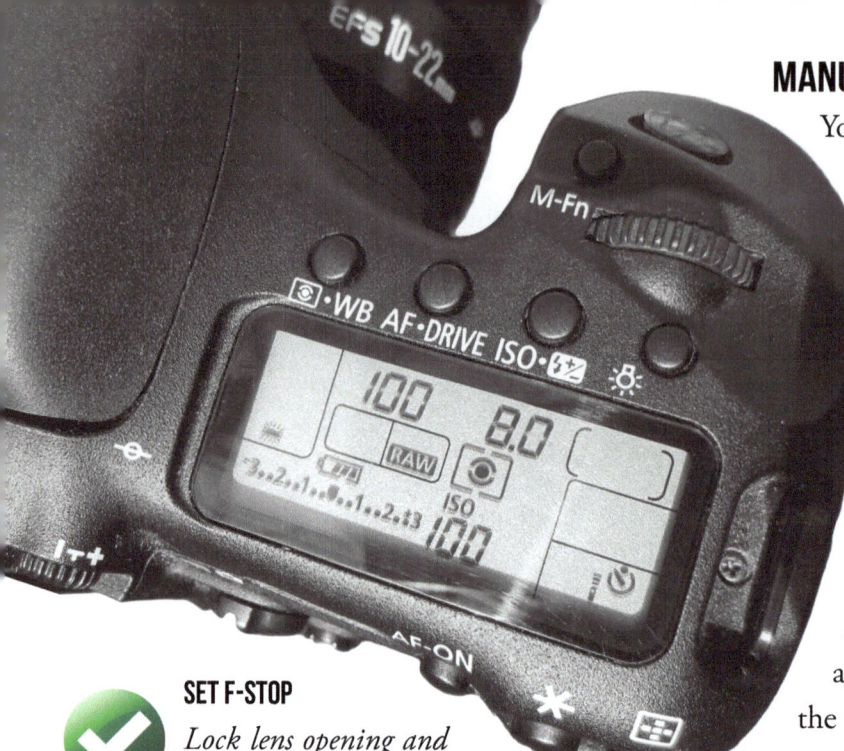

MANUAL APERTURE

Your camera's lens aperture is an iris composed of interlocking metal blades that open letting in more light, and close letting in less.

This mechanical movement back and forth becomes very important when we introduce aperture flicker on the next page but for now concentrate on how the aperture allows us to control the time-lapse viewer's eye.

SET F-STOP
Lock lens opening and depth of field

Even after setting a specific aperture in manual mode small frame-to-frame inconsistencies sometimes occur. Aperture flicker is discussed in detail in Chapter 4.

The size of the opening is specified using a measure called f-stop. A bigger f-stop number means a smaller aperture, strange I know, but it makes more sense if you think of the iris as light stoppage device; the bigger the f-number the more the stoppage. More stoppage means a smaller hole for light to travel through.

Don't just *stop* at light though, the aperture size also determines the depth of field or how much of a scene can be in focus. Shorter depth of fields blur out the background of an object. A deeper depth of field allows everything in the image to be in focus. Use depth of field as another tool to control the viewer's eye when designing your composition.

By shooting in full manual mode and setting a specific aperture we minimize bright and dark time-lapse flicker by preventing the camera from jumping from one f-stop to another. We also prevent changes in depth of field from by keeping a constant range of focus.

Deep　　　　　　Depth of Field　　　　　shallow

Lens Opening
(aperture)

Smaller　　　　　　　　　　　　　　　　Wider

f/32　f/22　f/16　f/11　f/8　f/5.6　f/4　f/2.8　f/2　f/1.4　f/1

MANUAL SHUTTER SPEED

Your camera shutter is a mechanical device that controls how long the image sensor is exposed to light when you take a photograph. A longer shutter allows more light to hit your sensor and thus creates a brighter image.

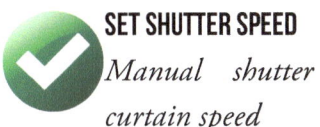

SET SHUTTER SPEED
Manual shutter curtain speed

By shooting in full manual mode and setting a specific shutter speed we minimize bright and dark time-lapse flicker by preventing the camera from jumping from one exposure time to another.

Freeze   Movement   Blur

Exposure Time
(Shutter Speed)

Good range for motion blur

1/1000 1/500 1/250 1/125 1/60 1/30 1/15 1/8 1/2 1 2

MOTION BLUR/DRAGGING YOUR SHUTTER

The longer your shutter stays open the greater the chance that things moving in your scene may blur. Motion blur or a little captured movement in a single image is actually a good thing for time-lapse. Think of that little bit of blur like extra information about what's happening to some of the parts of the image during that very brief period the shutter is open.

Since our time-lapse images are played back-to-back very rapidly, the slight blurring in each individual photo blends together creating an added smoothness to the entire sequence.

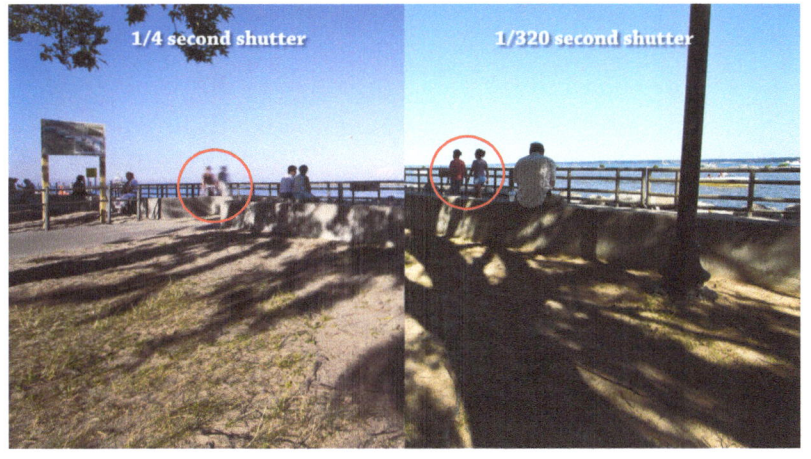

1/4 second shutter   1/320 second shutter

DRAG SHUTTER
Keep shutter <1/100th of a second to smooth motion.

HOW TO DRAG YOUR SHUTTER:

Simple: Keep your shutter speed relatively low. As a rule of thumb, try to keep your shutter speed under ~1/100th of a second.

Depending on your subject you may be able to achieve good smoothing results at faster speeds but it is usually a good idea to stay within this range.

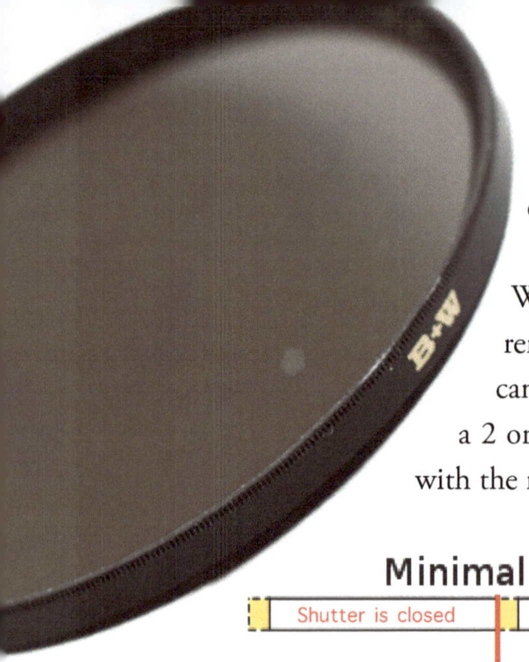

You may need a neutral density filter

If you are photographing a time-lapse of a bright scene you may need to use an ND filter to allow a properly exposed shot while still using a slower "dragged" shutter.

We talked about ND filters in the gear chapter but remember these reduce the amount of light entering the camera without altering colors. You may want to start with a 2 or 3-stop reduction ND4 or ND8 filter and experiment with the results.

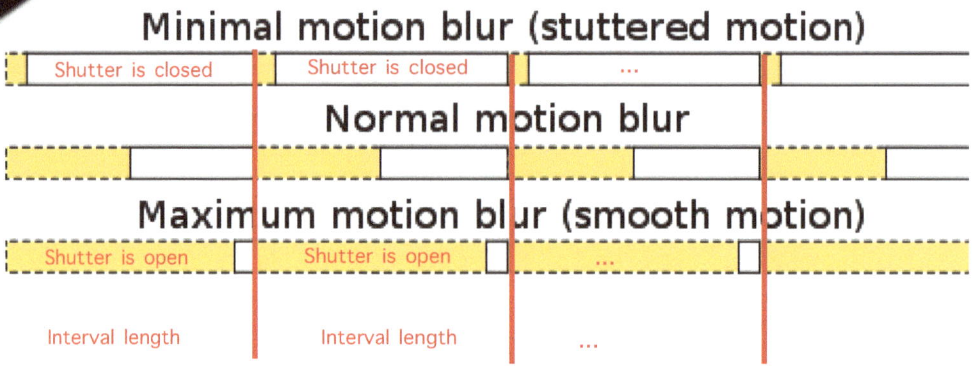

Minimal motion blur (stuttered motion)

| Shutter is closed | Shutter is closed | ... |

Normal motion blur

Maximum motion blur (smooth motion)

| Shutter is open | Shutter is open | ... |

Interval length   Interval length   ...

AVOID DROPPED FRAMES

Frame interval > Exposure time

Think of your camera's buffer like a pipe connecting the camera's image sensor to the memory card. It takes a little bit of time (depending on your image resolution and card read/write speed) for the information to be processed and flow from one place to the other. If we try to send images too quickly some may get lost (our camera will skip a frame), bad news for time-lapse.

Faster memory cards will help but as a good rule of thumb keep your exposure at about 60% – 80% of your interval to give your camera enough time to clear the image buffer before the next frame is taken.

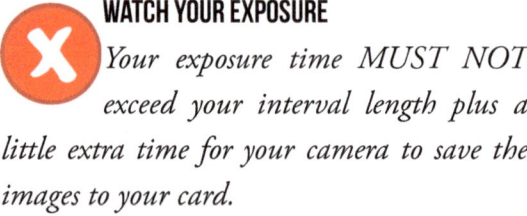

WATCH YOUR EXPOSURE

Your exposure time MUST NOT exceed your interval length plus a little extra time for your camera to save the images to your card.

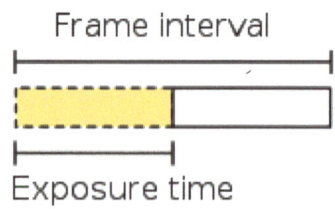

Frame interval

Exposure time

MANUAL LENS FOCUS

Switch your lens to manual focus and either adjust the focus yourself or allow your camera to automatically focus (by pressing the shutter button half way) and then make the switch from automatic to manual focus.

Selecting manual focus prevents the camera from focus hunting as each photo is taken and from seeking a different focus range throughout the compilation.

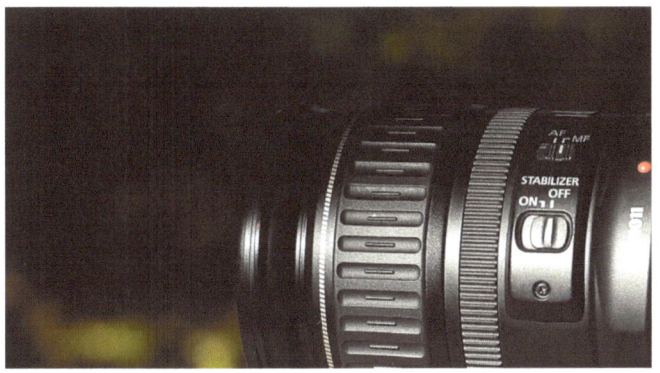

SELECT MANUAL FOCUS
Prevents focus changes between time-lapse frames

Tip: Using your depth of field button (usually found below the lens), as well as live view mode, helps to makes sure the right subject is in focus.

WHITE BALANCE

Different types of light have different color characteristics and your camera's white balance selection adjusts accordingly to produce colors as accurate as possible.

For example in early morning hours natural light is cooler and your photographed scene may take on a slight blue hue. As the day wanes on light becomes warmer and you might notice more red or orange. White balancing counteracts these changes reducing or eliminating color tints in your photos.

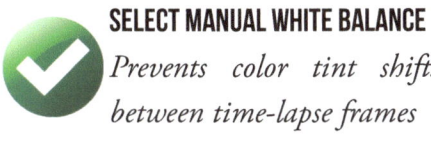
SELECT MANUAL WHITE BALANCE
Prevents color tint shifts between time-lapse frames

Selecting manual white balance prevents the camera from analyzing and adjusting each photo independently and avoids flickering color changes in the final time-lapse compilation.

FILE FORMAT

How much room do you have on your memory card? How many memory cards do you have? Is this the only time-lapse you will be shooting before you can download your photos? These are just a few last minute image size and quality questions to think about before you begin.

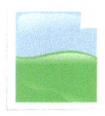
CONSIDER RAW FORMAT
If you have enough space, RAW affords more options in post production

I usually shoot in the largest RAW format possible. Shooting in full RAW creates large image files (~17-22 MB per image) and requires a big memory card but like we talked about in the last chapter it allows the most flexibility to crop, pan, and zoom when we stitch our images together in an editor.

Sometimes we don't always know exactly how a final compilation will be used. Remember we can always downsize and throw away data if we need to but we can never collect more unless we head back out into the field and re-shoot.

4 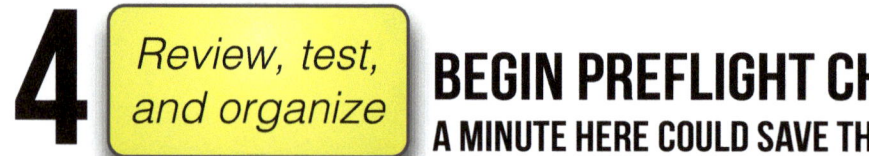 BEGIN PREFLIGHT CHECK
A MINUTE HERE COULD SAVE THE ENTIRE DAY

Make sure your tripod is set and locked, all loose wires are wrapped and secured from becoming giant sails in the wind (Velcro straps and rubber bands come in handy), and give a final look at your composition and picture the action that will be changing over time. How does it look?

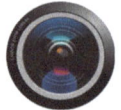

TAKE ONE PHOTO
Preview your shot, zoom in and check your exposure and composition

PREVIEW A TEST SHOT
If you aren't in a hurry to catch some epic action that's starting right now you may want to snap a few shots and preview them.

Consider zooming into the preview screen and double checking your focus and depth of field. Double check the sides of your composition and take a look at your foreground.

CONSIDER A 10 FRAME MINI TIME-LAPSE TEST

That's right, record a mini one. I've caught lots of mistakes by recording a quick time-lapse for a minute or two, stopping and then using the scroll wheel to preview the images in quick succession. I don't do it all the time but it's one more simple check that allows you to see how changing action, shadows or lights affect your composition without being surprised at home.

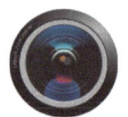

RECORD A QUICK SEQUENCE
A one or two minute test may save an entire afternoon

BEFORE YOU START: ISOLATE YOUR SEQUENCE

Sometimes when you get home and import all of your images, one time-lapse sequence can bleed into another making it tough to distinguish between where one ends and another begins, especially if the only change is the interval or a slight composition change.

Either navigate in your camera menu and create a new file folder before starting the sequence or do what I like to do...

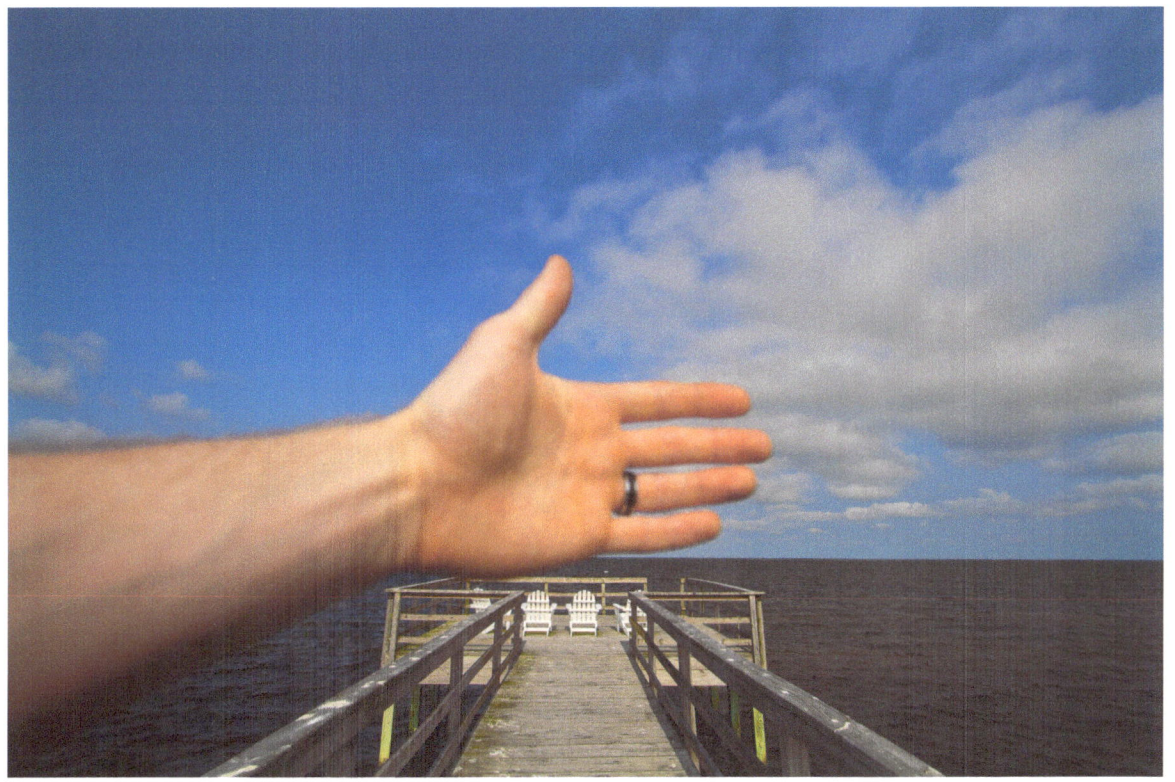

"The best helping hand that you will ever receive is the one at the end of your own arm."
- Fred Dehner

TIME-LAPSE EXPOSURE SETTINGS:

Here's a final review of the important exposure considerations for time-lapse photography:

SHOOT IN FULL MANUAL MODE:

Photographing in full manual mode prevents the camera from making independent exposure decision before each image is captured. Any exposure changes in the middle of a time-lapse series might create a kind of flicker and should be prevented.

CONFIGURE THE FOLLOWING EXPOSURE SETTINGS:

- **ISO:** By deselecting automatic ISO determination and locking in a set number, we prevent the camera from creating brighter or darker images due to changes in sensor sensitivity.

- **Aperture:** By setting a specific aperture we minimize time-lapse flicker by preventing the camera from jumping from one f-stop to another. We also prevent changes in depth of field throughout the sequence by keeping a constant range of focus.

- **Shutter Speed:** By setting a specific shutter speed we minimize time-lapse flicker by preventing the camera from jumping from one exposure time to another.

- **Focus:** By selecting manual focus we prevent the camera from focus hunting as each photo is taken and from seeking a different focus ranges throughout the compilation.

- **White Balance:** Selecting manual white balance prevents the camera from analyzing and adjusting each photo independently and avoids tint shifts in the final time-lapse compilation.

CREATE A LITTLE MOTION BLUR:

Since our time-lapse images are played back-to-back very rapidly, slight blurring in each individual photo helps to blend them together creating an added smoothness to the entire sequence. As a rule of thumb, try to keep your shutter speed under ~1/100th of a second. In order to get such a low shutter speed in daylight conditions we will probably need to use an ND filter.

WATCH YOUR TOTAL EXPOSURE LENGTH:

Your exposure time MUST NOT exceed your interval length plus a little extra time for your camera to save the images to your card.

CHECK YOUR FILE FORMAT:

Make sure you have enough room on your card all your required time-lapse images at the image size that you selected. Do you need to save space on your memory card for other shots today?

CONSIDER A TEST PHOTO AND A QUICK MINI-LAPSE:

Previewing an individual exposure and possibly scrolling through a few images in a test time-lapse might save a whole afternoon's worth of shooting. It's worth the extra time, trust me.

"LET ME TELL YOU SOMETHING MY FRIEND. HOPE IS A DANGER-OUS THING. HOPE CAN DRIVE A MAN INSANE."

- STEPHEN KING
(THE SHAWSHANK REDEMPTION)

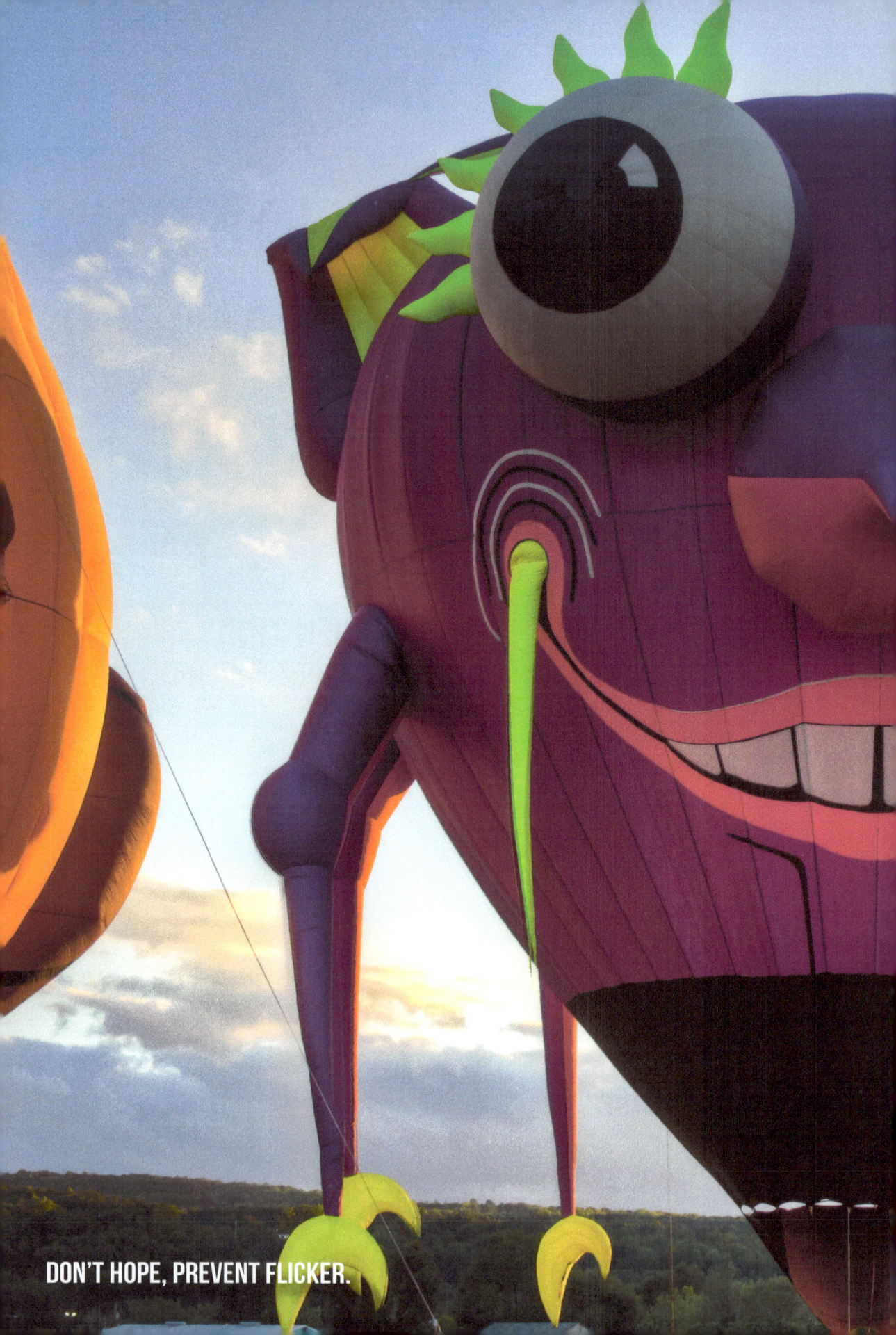

DON'T HOPE, PREVENT FLICKER.

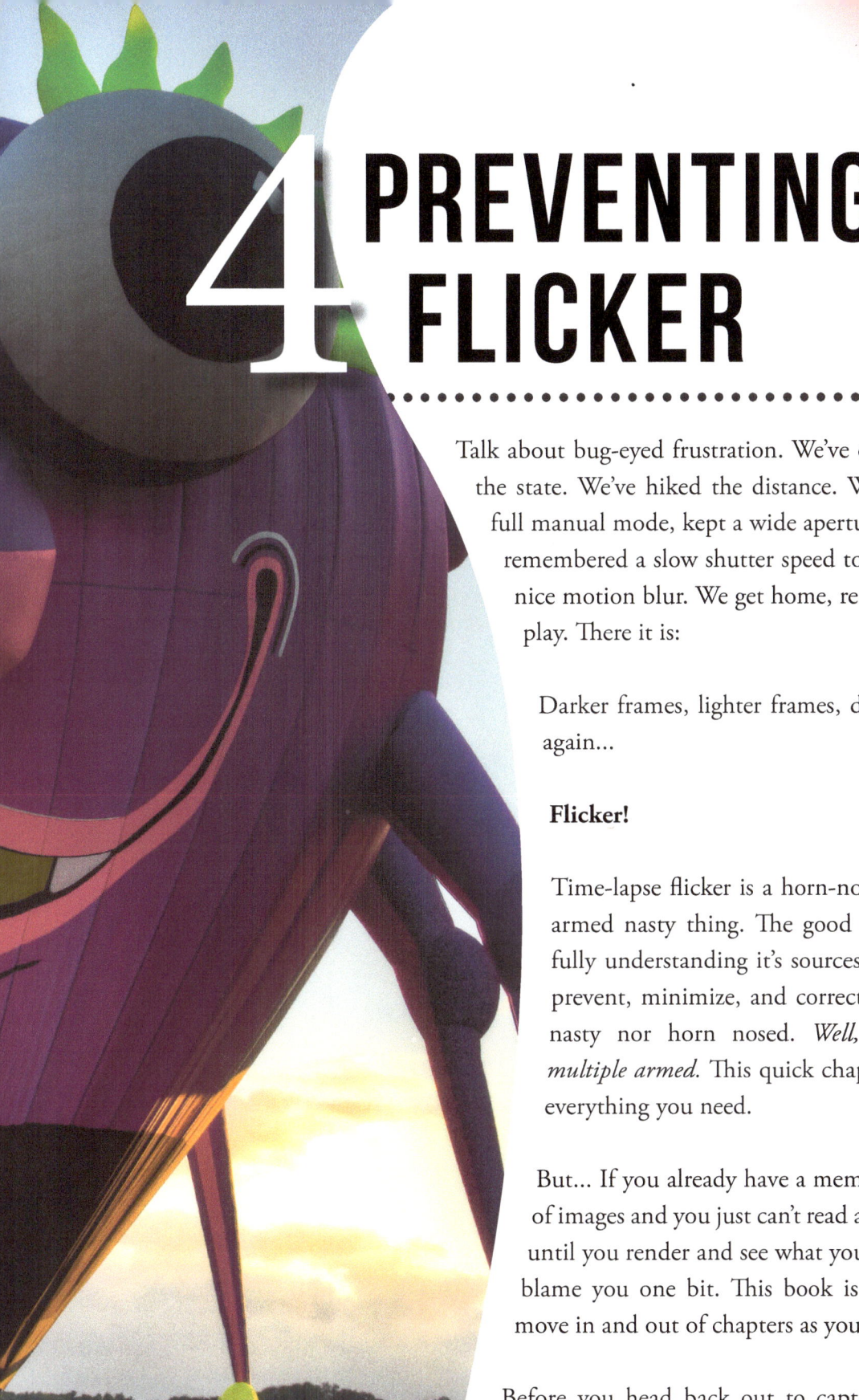

4 PREVENTING FLICKER

Talk about bug-eyed frustration. We've driven across the state. We've hiked the distance. We've shot in full manual mode, kept a wide aperture, and even remembered a slow shutter speed to create some nice motion blur. We get home, render, and hit play. There it is:

Darker frames, lighter frames, darker frames again...

Flicker!

Time-lapse flicker is a horn-nosed multiple armed nasty thing. The good news is that fully understanding it's sources and how to prevent, minimize, and correct it is *neither* nasty nor horn nosed. *Well, maybe just multiple armed.* This quick chapter provides everything you need.

But... If you already have a memory card full of images and you just can't read another word until you render and see what you got, I won't blame you one bit. This book is designed to move in and out of chapters as you need.

Before you head back out to capture the next scene make sure you have a firm grasp of flicker and all it's sources. That's where we'll begin.

PREVENTING FLICKER

We know that large unintended exposure jumps are the enemy, but a perfectly constant exposure or perfectly gradual exposure adjustments aren't exactly as easy to achieve as they might seem.

Preventing flicker usually requires an attack on three fronts:

- The right in-camera settings to eliminate automatic frame to frame luminance changes
- Understanding the camera's mechanical exposure inconsistencies
- If all else fails deflickering in post-production

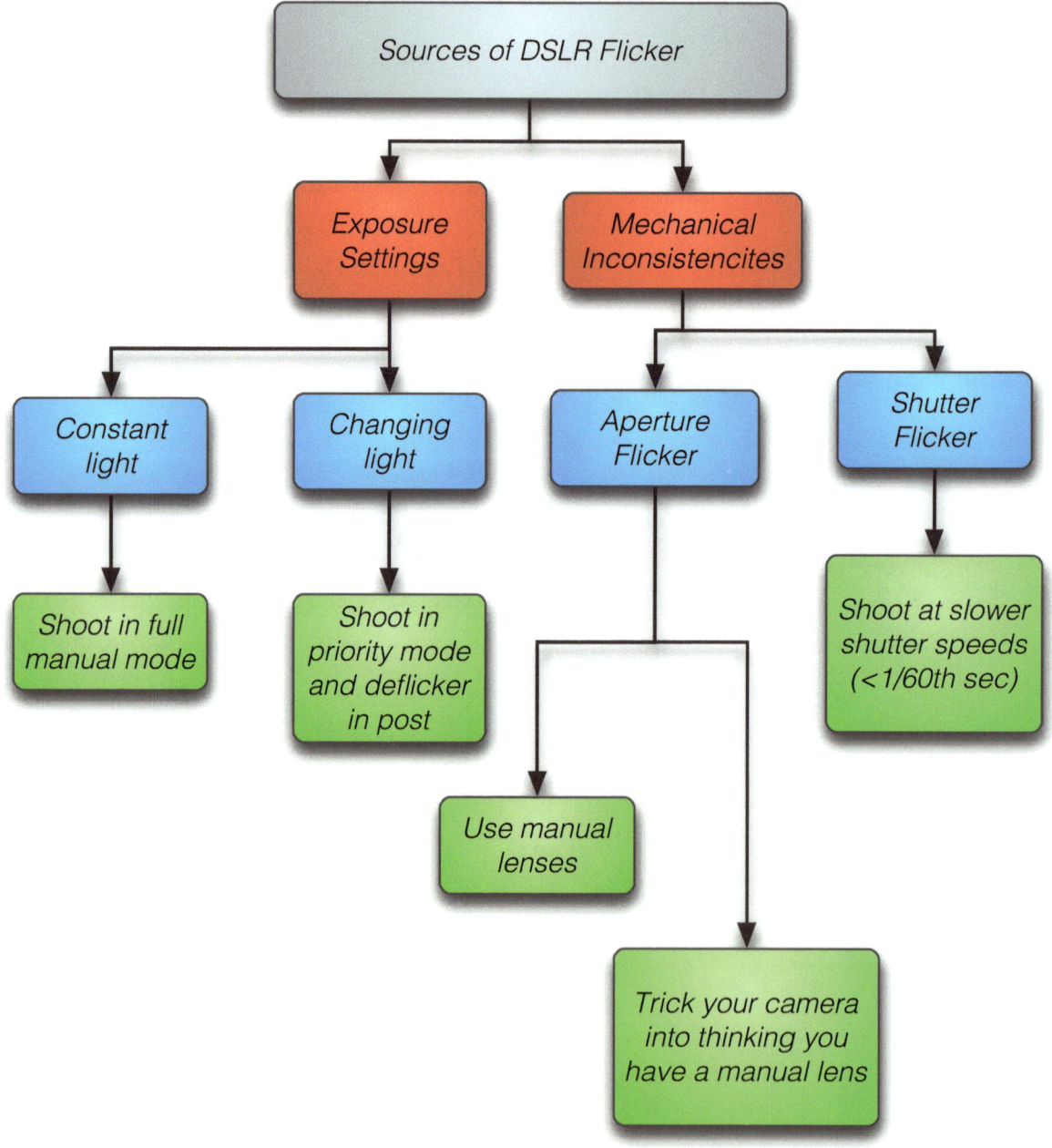

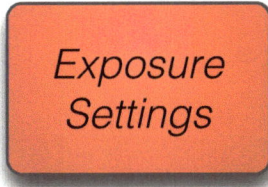

EXPOSURE SETTINGS

How we allow the camera to take each time-lapse exposure greatly influences the amount of flicker we encounter when we combine our images into a rapidly playing sequence.

MANUAL MODE

We learned in Chapter 3 that the best and simplest way to minimize flicker is to switch off your camera's ability to make exposure adjustments for each image we snap.

Constant light   **Shoot in full manual mode**    **SELECT FULL MANUAL MODE**
Prevent the camera from changing exposure variables during the time-lapse sequence

Manual mode works well for most scenes, but what if we want to continue to properly expose some action even when the light changes over time?

PRIORITY MODES

Say you are shooting a time-lapse sequence of a sunrise. Locking in a set manual exposure at the beginning would quickly over expose your images as the scene changes. What was once a properly exposed pre- sunrise low light photo quickly becomes overexposed and fades to white as the sun peaks up over the ridge.

Changing light   **Shoot in priority mode and deflicker in post**   **WITH CHANGING LIGHT SELECT PRIORITY MODE**
Adjusts exposure variables over time to maintain a constant exposure

By shooting in camera priority mode, specifically in aperture priority mode (Av mode on your camera dial), the camera will adjust the shutter speed automatically throughout the sequence and maintain a good shot. All those adjustments are

 **SOME FLICKER WILL OCCUR**
Our trade off for automatic adjustments to capture changing light is some flicker in our final compilation

nice but we'll have to offer a little time-lapse flicker as payment, here's why:

WHY FLICKER OCCURS IN PRIORITY MODES

Simply put DSLR's have *steep* steps between exposure values which can cause noticeable dark or light jumps from one time-lapse frame to the next.

Exposure Value or EV is a number used to represent all the different shutter speeds and f-stop combinations that combine to produce the same exposure. EV is also used as an interval value on the photographic exposure scale, with 1 EV corresponding to 1 stop (the doubling or halving of light).

Think of a step ladder, if your goal was to get to the top as smoothly as possible, many small

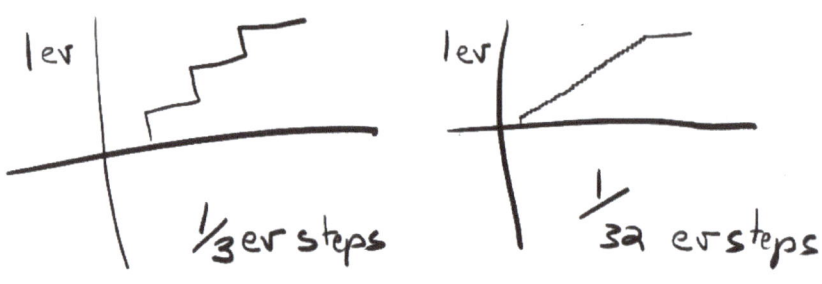

steps would allow a less noticeable ascent than say one or two big steps. It's the same way with your camera's exposure values. When we only have steep choices we get abrupt dark and light exposure jumps. To make things even worse imagine you were on the edge of a decision wether to continue up the ladder or head back down.

Down one step, up two steps, down another step, your direction might change a few times before you commit to one direction; big steps could create a pretty severe wobble (and headache). The smaller the EV steps the smoother the transition between exposures, the bigger the steps the more abrupt the changes.

Without special modification to the camera's firmware or advanced external input devices, DSLR's are only currently capable of 1/3 or 1/8 EV steps. Future DSLRs are likely to allow smaller EV steps from both the firmware and lens stepper motor right out-of-the-box, but today's DSLRs require a few special considerations to minimize these steep jumps:

METERING

How we configure the camera to evaluate the light in a frame is a good place to start. By selecting evaluative metering the whole frame is averaged instead of just one particular spot (like in partial or spot metering) and exposure jumps are less likely to occur.

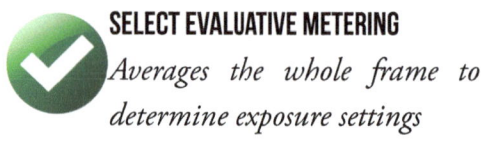

SELECT EVALUATIVE METERING
Averages the whole frame to determine exposure settings

Selecting Evaluative Metering (Canon), or Evaluative/Matrix Metering (Nikon) forces the camera to utilize the entire scene within the camera's viewfinder to select an appropriate exposure value.

COVER YOUR EYEPIECE

Use your eyepiece cover or black tape to block stray light from entering the viewfinder

Stray light entering through your camera's eyepiece can sometimes affect the camera's automatic metering and increase the likelihood of exposure value jumps and wobbles.

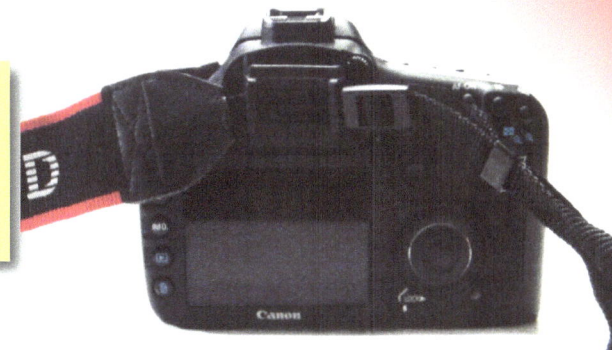

Stick to aperture priority mode

Although both aperture and shutter priority (Tv on your camera dial) can be used, having the shutter speed change and not the f-stop does have a few advantages. Not only will our depth of field remain constant throughout the shot but in some cases cameras can utilize smaller EV steps.

Mechanical Inconsistencites

MECHANICAL INCONSISTENCIES

The second most common, but usually less severe cause doesn't have anything to do with your camera's exposure decisions at all but rather lies in the mechanical components in the camera itself.

Errors, inconsistencies, deviations, call it what you'd like but even though automatic DSLR camera apertures and shutter curtains are highly engineered devices, they cannot produce the exact (and I mean perfectly exact) mechanical formations each and every time a photograph is taken, even if the settings between shots are not changed one bit.

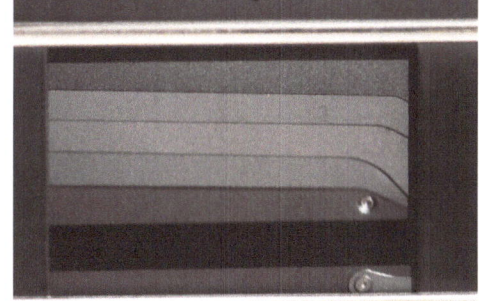

Vertical-travel focal-place shutter firing at 1/500 of a second.

MINIMIZING SHUTTER FLICKER

DSLR cameras have mechanical curtain shutters that control the amount of time the camera's image sensor is exposed to light. Think of two opaque curtains, somewhat accordion like, that can expand and collapse in front of the sensor.

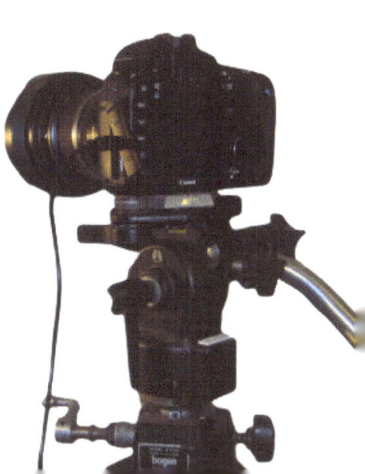

During slow shutter speeds the first curtain is released from an expanded position and folds downward revealing the image sensor. After the required exposure time the second curtain, which was in a folded state, is now released and expands to block the sensor.

As you can imagine for very fast shutter speeds much more precision is required. At these faster speeds both curtains need to be active at the same time. In order to get very quick exposures the second curtain is triggered before the first is fully opened. The result is a horizontal slit or gap that travels vertically across the image sensor.

The faster the shutter speed the narrower the slit and the shorter the exposure.

> **Shutter Flicker**

> *Shoot at slower shutter speeds (<1/60th sec)*

Very small curtain timing inconsistencies from one frame to the next produce slightly brighter or slighter darker frames when we watch them together in quick succession.

The good news is that shutter flicker is usually much less pronounced and even easier to fully eliminate. By simply keeping our exposures below 1/60th of a second we should be able to effectively prevent this form of flicker.

CONSIDER SLOWER SHUTTER SPEEDS
Minimize the chance for small shutter curtain frame-to-frame differences by shooting at speeds slower than about 1/60th of a second.

> **Aperture Flicker**

MINIMIZING APERTURE FLICKER

The same frame-to-frame inconsistencies that sometimes affect a high speed camera shutter also affect the lens aperture and it's the last form of flicker we need to worry about.

The camera's aperture functions much like the iris of your eye - it controls the diameter of the lens opening and subsequently how much light passes through to the image sensor. Now normally when shooting in full manual mode we would think that the aperture setting or f-stop would remain perfectly constant between shots. A shutter curtain moves but a lens opening is stationary right? Not exactly and that's the problem.

Instead of remaining perfectly constant each time a photo is taken the lens diaphragm opens fully (See photo 1 at right) before dialing down to the selected aperture (photo 2) just before the shutter fires. Each time it moves from wide open to the desired f-stop those small inconsistencies can again show up in our photos.

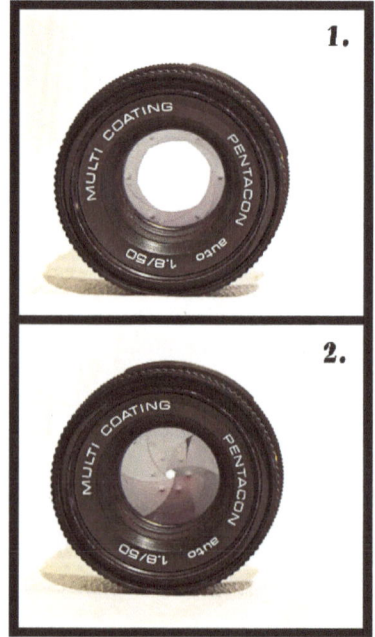

By selecting a larger lens opening we reduce the amount of movement and thus the chances of experiencing deviations.

Wide aperture shooting isn't always going to be possible however, especially if we are shooting in daylight and want to drag our shutter. Good thing there are a few easy ways around this...

USING MANUAL LENSES

Use manual lenses

The easiest way to fully solve the problem is to use a lens with a manual aperture ring. No automatic movement, no flicker. These lenses were simply designed to use manual external f-stop controls and lack the electronic controls and the forced automatic dialing down.

CONSIDER A MANUAL LENS

If you've got one, manual lenses avoid the forced diaphragm movement that can causes aperture flicker.

Easily solved but not so easily found, or fit for that matter as most will require some sort of lens adapter.

Now don't feel like you have to run out and buy anything special just yet, there's a quick way to trick your camera into think its automatic lens is manual.

USE THE LENS TWIST TRICK

Trick your camera into thinking you have a manual lens

The lens twist trick disconnects your lens electronically while keeping it in place, fooling your camera into thinking it's a manual lens. If we set the aperture before we disconnect electronic control then it will remain perfectly constant throughout our sequence of time-lapse shots.

Here's how to do it:

1. Set your desired aperture setting in manual mode
2. Press and hold the Depth of Field preview button to set the diaphragm (usually a small black button below your lens)
3. Press the lens unlock button and slightly rotate the lens clockwise

The lens is now still connected firmly (well, sort of firmly) connected to the camera body and it is set and locked at the desired aperture.

Don't forget to fully reattach the lens before disconnecting from your tripod or packing it away.

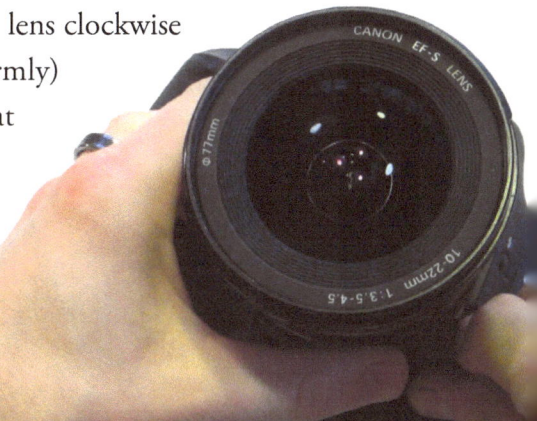

FLICKER PREVENTION OVERVIEW

Here's a final review of the important considerations for time-lapse flicker prevention:

WHAT IS FLICKER?

Instead of the camera's exposure settings and mechanical configurations remaining perfectly constant or purposefully changing in very slight and gradual ways, large unintended exposure jumps occur in some frames which create images that look out of place when compiled together.

FLICKER IS CAUSED BY: 1) Exposure settings and 2) mechanical inconsistencies

EXPOSURE SETTINGS TO MINIMIZE FLICKER: **For scenes with constant light shoot in full manual mode.**

Photographing in full manual mode prevents the camera from making independent exposure decision before each image is captured.

Configure the following manual exposure settings:

- **ISO:** By deselecting automatic ISO determination and locking in a set number, we prevent the camera from creating brighter or darker images due to changes in sensor sensitivity.
- **Aperture:** By setting a specific aperture we minimize time-lapse flicker by preventing the camera from jumping from one f-stop to another.
- **Shutter Speed:** By setting a specific shutter speed we prevent the camera from creating brighter and darker images due to exposure length.
- **White Balance:** Selecting manual white balance prevents the camera from analyzing and adjusting each photo independently and avoids tint shifts in the final time-lapse compilation.

For scenes with drastic changes in lighting we can take advantage of priority modes:

Automatic exposure control will allow more flexibility but we will experience much more flicker. We can usually correct this using de-flickering software in post production. Don't forget to cover your eyepiece.

MINIMIZE THE CHANCES FOR MECHANICAL INCONSISTENCIES: Inconsistencies in mechanical formations can occur between shots resulting in a slightly different exposures even though camera settings remain identical. There are two forms of mechanical flicker:

Aperture flicker: Minimize the chances for small frame-to-frame lens diaphragm inconsistencies by preventing movement:

- Use a manual lens
- Use the lens twist trick to fool your camera into thinking an automatic lens is manual

Shutter flicker: Minimize the chance for small shutter curtain frame-to-frame inconsistencies by shooting at speeds slower than about 1/60th of a second.

"I MAKE MY BEST GUESS AFTER STUDYING THE ENVIRONMENT AND THEN I CAST MY LINE.

ONLY POSTPROCESSING WILL REVEAL "THE CATCH," WHETHER MUNDANE OR SPECTACULAR."

- TODD SALI

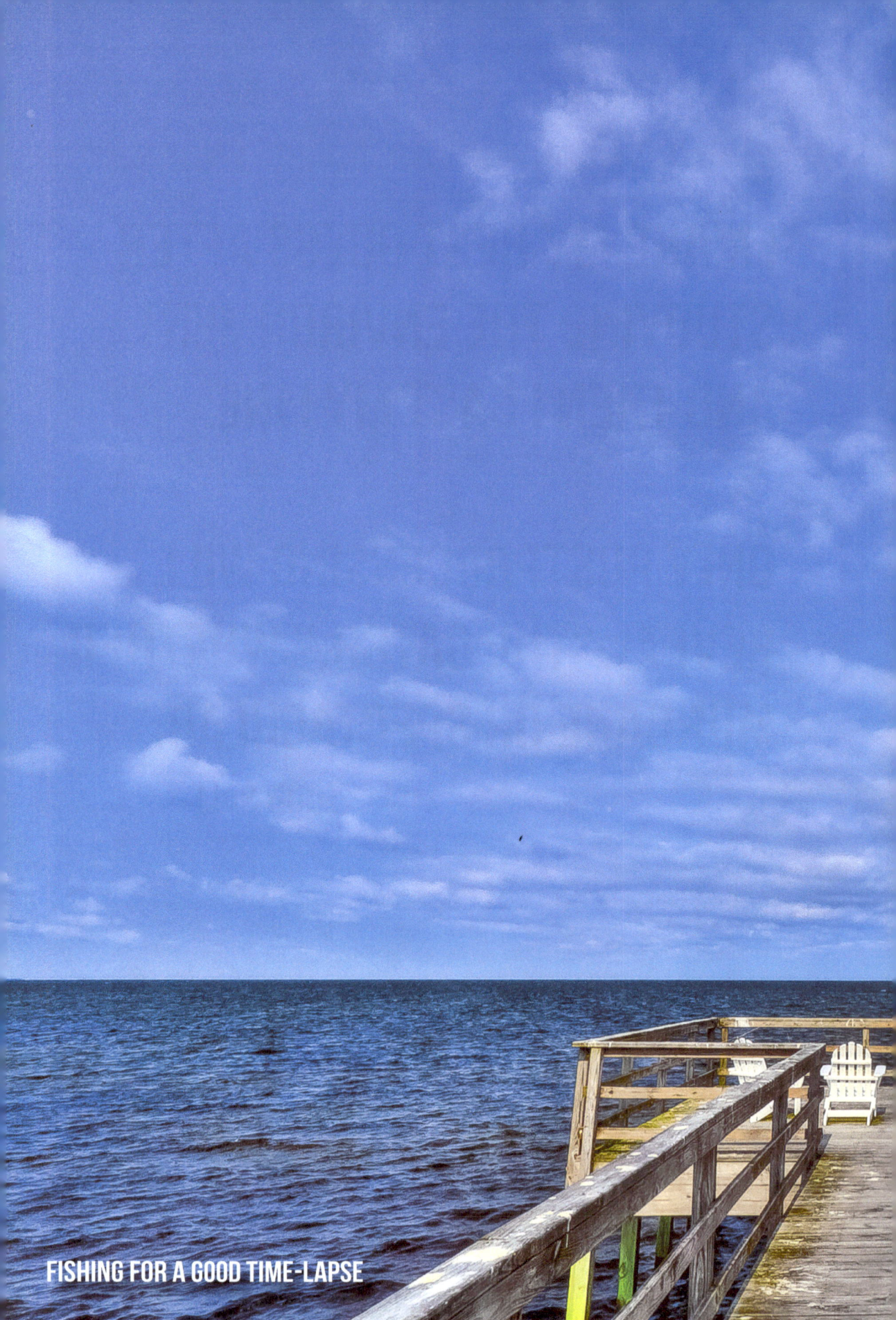

FISHING FOR A GOOD TIME-LAPSE

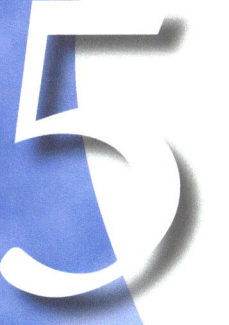

5 CREATING TIME-LAPSE

Compiling the images is where it all pays off.

Creating your time-lapse movie from hundreds of still images is not very complicated, however approaching the rendering process without a set workflow can make things seem more complex than they actually are.

I assure you once it's built and you've run through it a few times you'll be able to cruise through the time-lapse process.

We'll start with the camera to time-lapse workflow in it most basic and abstract form.

- Importing your images
- Editing, a few different ways to attack
- Deflickering, if necessary
- Rendering the images together
- Post production, music, + clips, etc

We'll then continue with an overview of these steps then compare and contrast three basic time-lapse rendering software workflows each with their own set of applications that cover a wide spectrum of cost, learning curves, and interfaces. We'll then finish with a dive into all three and create three different time-lapse compilations step-by-step.

Let's start developing your own custom creative workflow.

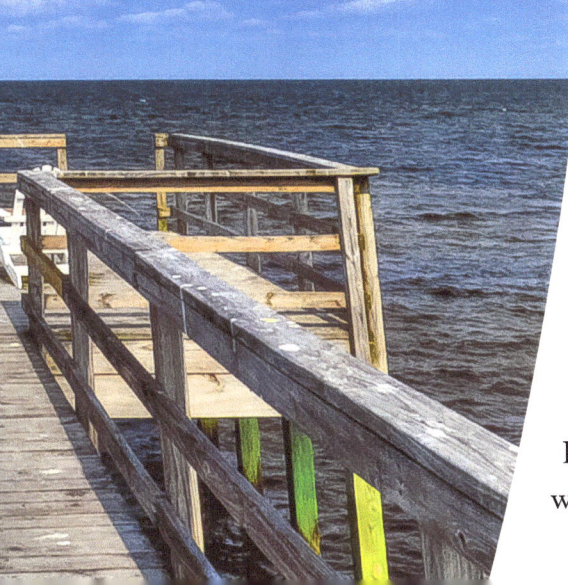

BASIC TIME-LAPSE WORKFLOW

Here's the basic time-lapse movie creation process from camera memory card to final rendering. We'll quickly review each process then jump right into specific software workflows.

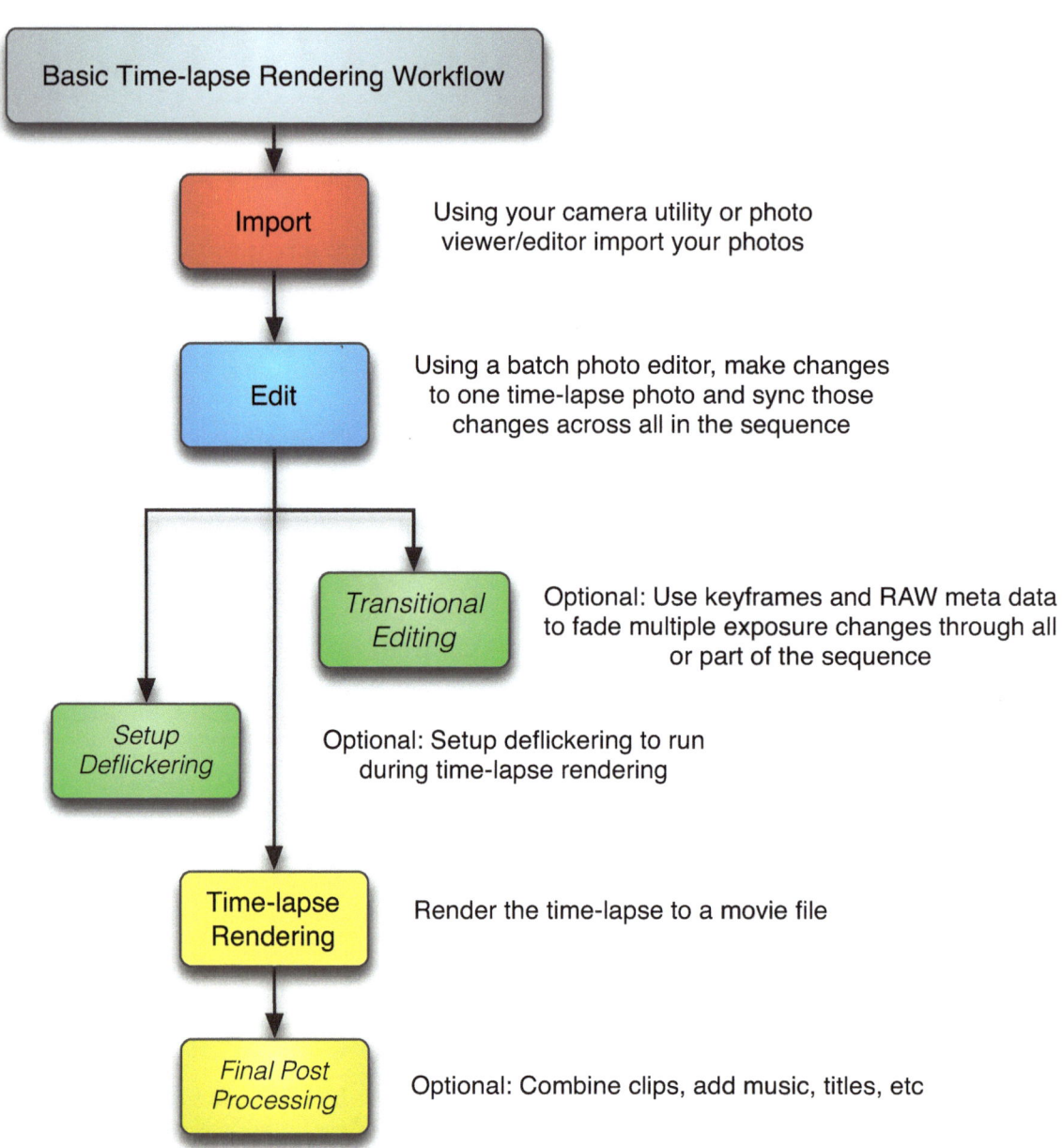

TIPS FOR IMPORTING A SEQUENCE

Keeping your time-lapse images organized is important. Not only are we dealing with collections of hundreds of photos which need to stay in a precise sequence, but the collection as a whole is often tens of gigabytes large. Moving that much data more than we have to isn't fun.

1. GET THE IMAGES OFF THE MEMORY CARD

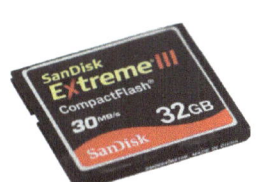

Maybe I read too many horror stories of fried cards (*or just drink too much coffee*), but sometimes after I record a particularly compelling scene, I mean when I know I really nailed one, I can't get them off my memory card and on to a backed-up computer fast enough.

Importing too quickly though, into a disorganized and impossible-to-find-later hard drive isn't that much better, and there are just a few things that we need to do during the initial import step to keep our images organized and efficient.

Location and subfolder: Pick a large hard drive, or better yet use a second (or third) dedicated drive and keep your time-lapses separate. Store all your time-lapse sequences in a main time-lapse folder, each sequence descriptively labeled with its own subfolder.

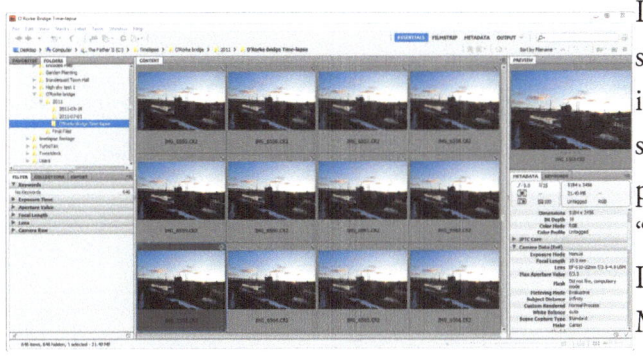

I used to store the sequences in the same place as all my other photos. Sure it was still in a separate subfolder but sometimes when scrolling through a photo browser application looking for "Cape Cod - Grampa's Birthday Photos", I'd accidentally click on "Cape Cod - Milky Way Time-lapse February 2012" and be forced to wait a few seconds as my computer churns a little to display 600 image previews. Not a big deal but keeping sequences in their own area helps keep me organized and fast.

Don't rename during import: Most applications, including Bridge and Lightroom, can rename all the images during the import to a custom name followed by a sequence number. This is what we want in the end and it's sometimes okay if we're sure this card has one and only one time-lapse sequence with no test shots or extras, but often this is not the case. It's better to rename manually when we view all the image thumbnails together, that way those test shots, multiple sequences, etc., don't get auto-named to a single sequence.

2. SEPARATE AND RENAME THEM

Now that the images are on the computer flip through and separate other time-lapse sequences, single photos, and videos into different subfolders. If you happen to be using Adobe Bridge consider a nice feature called *batch rename*. It quickly moves images to a new titled folder and renames them at the same time. Pretty helpful.

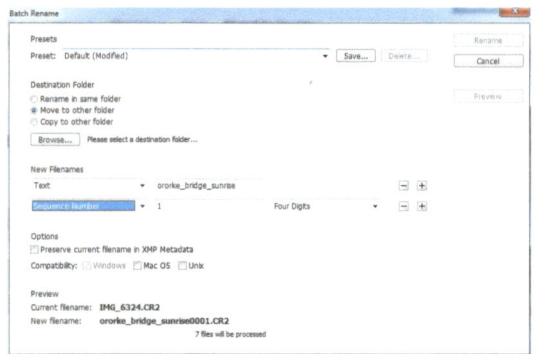

Time-lapse photographers really care about file names. Screw up the name and order of a thousand photos and we've got a little problem.

Our goal in the end is to have all images in a specific sequence labeled with a helpful file name followed by a three or four digit sequence number.

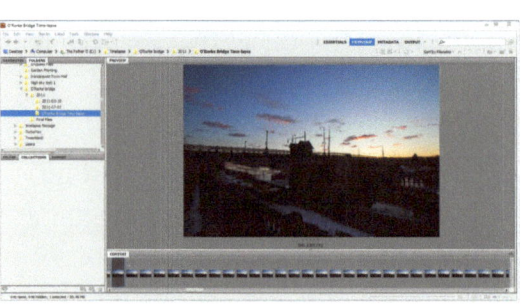

For example:

ORorke_Bridge_Sunrise_001.CR2
ORorke_Bridge_Sunrise_002.CR2
ORorke_Bridge_Sunrise_003.CR2

After all the files are imported, scroll through the series and get a sense for how the time-lapse will look. Selecting the "Filmstrip" view and then holding the right arrow key is a good way to preview the time-lapse in action.

3. THINK ABOUT RAW PROCESSING

We are beginning to get a sense of our initial exposure and how lighting conditions or other variables in the scene may have changed over time and affected the shot.

Continue the high level preview by zooming in, usually a 4x4 thumbnail grid is good, and

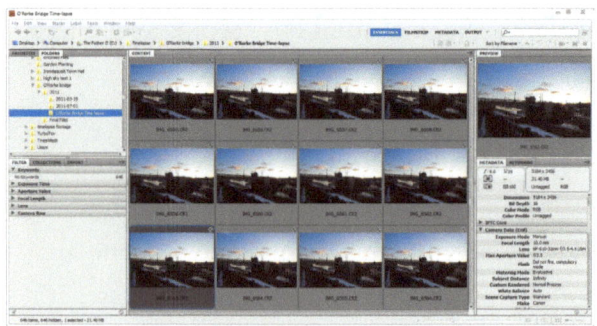

scroll through the images again, this time a little slower and look for unwanted things that may have entered the frame, birds for example or sensor dust or an unwanted person or distraction.

We'll touch on image correction little later but for now simply get a feel for what needs fixed.

TIPS FOR BATCH EDITING A SEQUENCE

We talked about the many advantages to shooting time-lapse images in the RAW format and this section is where all that additional exposure information comes into play. If your time-lapse is in JPEG format, no worries, just keep any changes to a minimum as they will impact photo quality.

HOW DOES BATCH EDITING WORK?

Using an editor capable of batch processing, we'll pick out a single image from our sequence, make some processing corrections and adjustments to that one image and then if it makes sense to do so, apply them across the entire time-lapse. Trust me it's not nearly as hard as it sounds.

Your DSLR camera likely shipped with a pretty good RAW image editing workspace or at least a trial version of one. Canon's Digital Photo Professional or Nikon's Capture NX2 are common out of the box editors. Some of the most popular and most powerful RAW editing applications can be purchased separately such as Adobe Lightroom, Apple's Aperture or Adobe Camera RAW (ACR) which comes installed with versions of Photoshop. The examples on the next few pages show the ACR screen layout which is a pretty standard configuration you'll find elsewhere. Terminology and functionality should be very similar no matter what application you use.

WAIT! DON'T FORGET YOUR SCENE IS CHANGING:

An added challenge to correcting and adjusting time-lapse images is that our scene's exposure changes over the life of the shot, sometimes very dramatically, as in a sunrise. What might look like a good change for the first few exposures, might break the images at the end of the sequence.

 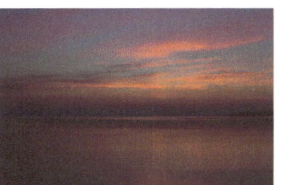 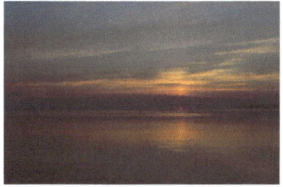 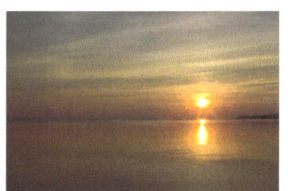

There are two ways to avoid problems:

1. Do a Test. Apply changes to one image then synchronize (letting the software automatically apply those same settings) throughout the sequence covering both lighter and darker images that changed over time (typically the first few and the last few shots). If your changes still look good at all extremes then chances are it's OK to copy across all images.

2. Use a specialized application like LRTimelapse to apply changes gradually across the entire sequence or using keyframes apply different gradual changes to different parts of the time-lapse, for example increasing exposure substantially until the sun rises, then decreasing the exposure as the scene gets brighter and so on.

Let's run through a few time-lapse corrections and enhancements using a standard image editor.

START WITH THE HISTOGRAM:

Sometimes it's hard to tell if an image is over or underexposed and the histogram is a good place to start. Usually a well exposed photo is one with tones that are distributed throughout the histogram and not concentrated on one side or the other. Notice two triangles on the upper corners of the graph, click these to engage clipping indicators (aka "the blinkies") to see where your photo may be losing image data due to overexposure (red blinkies) or underexposure (blue blinkies). Keeping in mind this scene changes substantially over time, these adjustment panel descriptions may give you a head start editing your sequence:

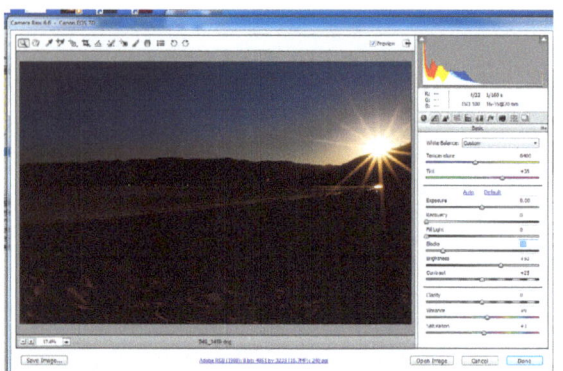 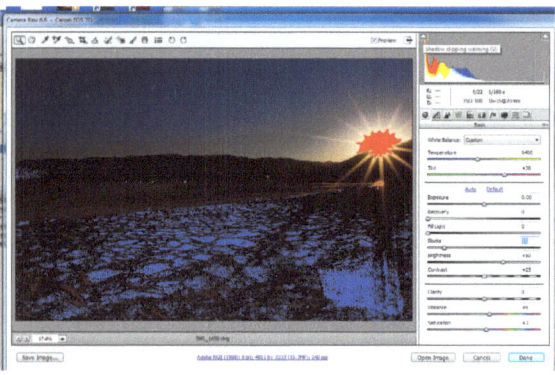

CORRECTING COLOR:

You can either accept the white balance as it was configured by your camera, you can choose a different WB preset or you can create a custom modification using temperature and tint sliders.

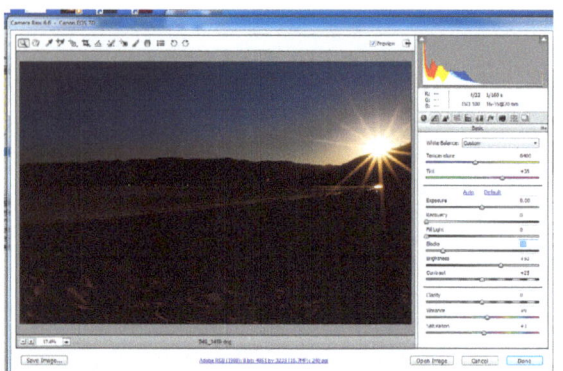

ADJUSTING LIGHTS AND DARKS:

Auto is sometimes a good place to start, but keep in mind it's all about how you want the viewer to see the scene, not a scene that's properly developed.

Exposure - Big changes and reach to brighten and darken

Recovery - Primarily targets brighter tones, top 5 or 10%

Fill Light - Focuses on darker (lower 3/4) tones, brings up

Blacks - Increase density of deepest tones (with fill light)

Brightness - Focuses on 1/4 tones and midtones

Contrast - Whites whiter and darks darker (tonal range)

Clarity - Midtone snap, small changes in contrast

Vibrance - Analyzes and modifies weaker colors (nonlinear)

USING A GRADUATED FILTER:

Sometimes an exposure is correct in one area but not really in another, like in this bridge sunrise below. The foreground is a little underexposed and the background is already beginning to be overexposed, even before the sun peaks over the bridge.

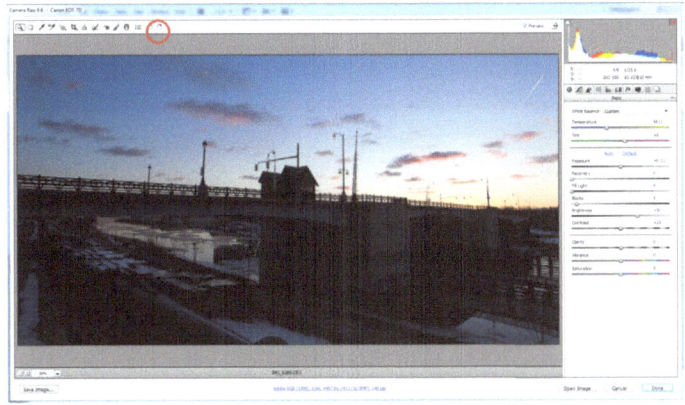

We can use a tool called a graduated filter to apply the changes in exposure to the areas we want much like how an actual graduated neutral density filter would have helped in this situation.

Click on the graduated filter button.

You'll notice that we have a new set of controls.

Go ahead and make an exposure change, maybe decrease exposure, then click and drag on the area of the image you would like to apply this to. Two dots connected by a line should appear. The first dot and line signifying the adjustment is at its full intensity and the second dot is where its faded to a complete transition.

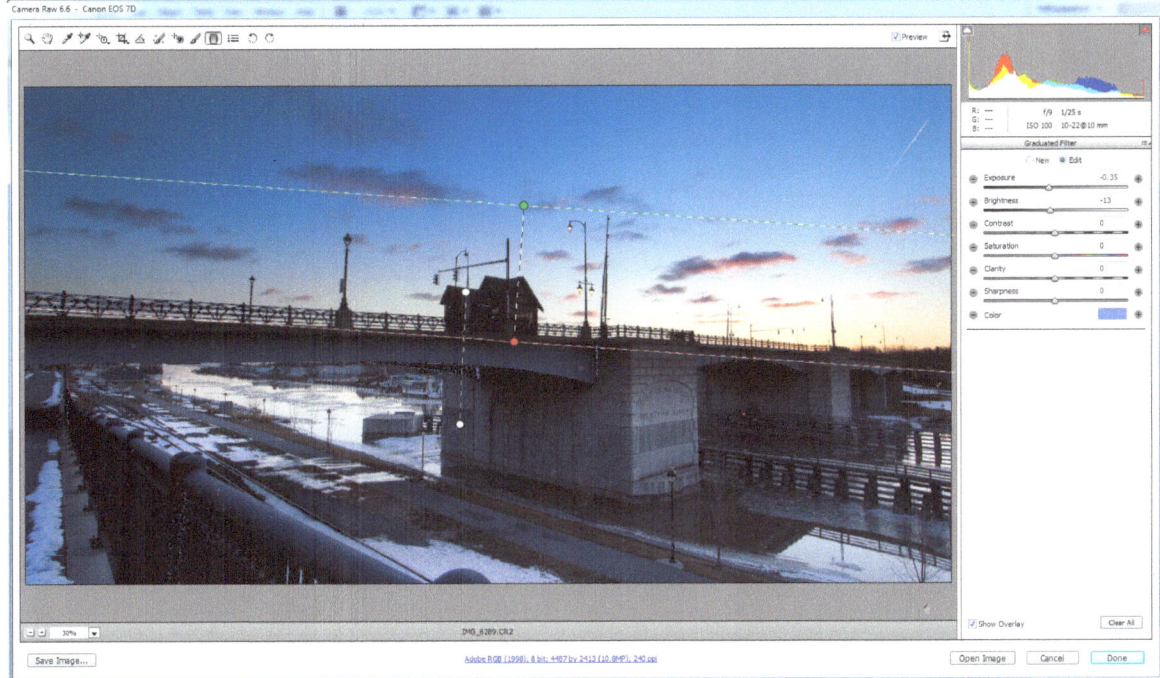

TRANSITIONAL EDITING

(This is an optional step using LRTimelapse and Adobe Lightroom)

Instead of applying one set of changes across all images, LRTimelapse and Adobe Lightroom allow control over where and how changes are applied throughout our time-lapse. Say we filmed a sunrise and wanted to tweak the look or correct for an error, with regular batch editing any changes we make would have to be applied equally across the entire sequence.

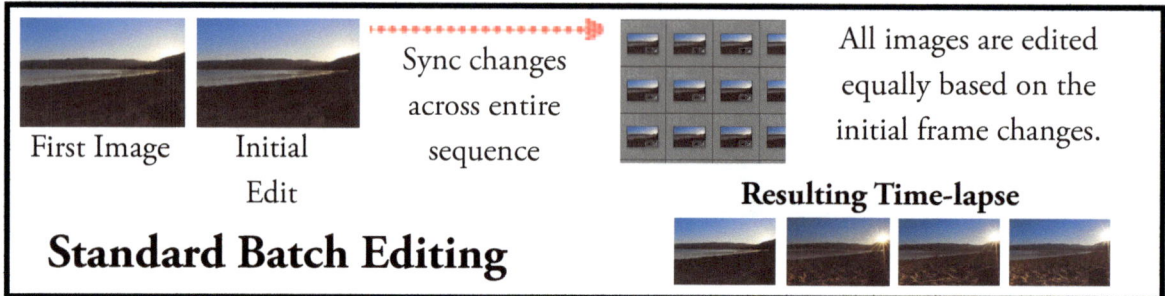

Standard batch editing can correct most time-lapse image problems, but what if our issue didn't need correcting until the end of the sequence? What if we wanted different changes to be applied to different parts of the time-lapse? Transitional editing with LRTimelapse allows us (using image metadata) to make changes to keyframes, or selected images scattered throughout the sequence. We can quickly make changes to these select few images and allow the software to spread those changes out amongst all the frames inbetween them. We can essentially apply whatever changes we want gradually wherever we want. Awesome.

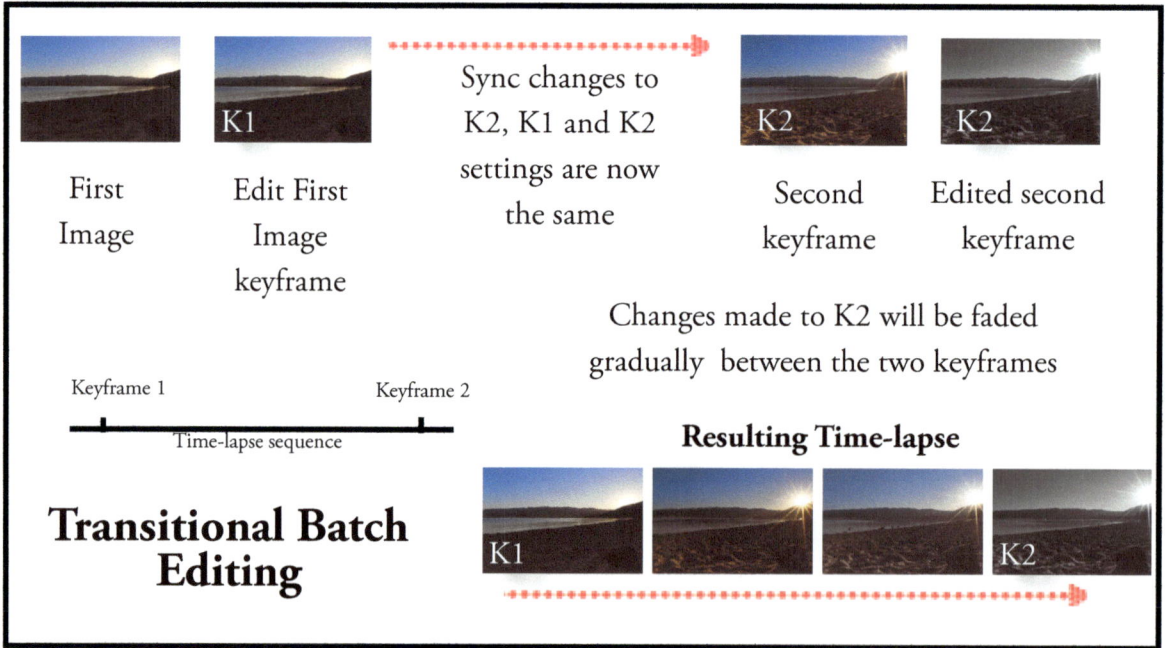

We'll cover this process in detail in the LRTimelapse software workflow.

DEFLICKERING
(This can be an optional step based on need)

Much like transitional editing, deflickering takes those abrupt changes in brightness and spreads them out slowly over nearby frames for a smooth transition and less noticeable (or eliminated) brightness or darkness pops. There are three applications that are commonly used to deflicker time-lapse and all three are included in the software workflows:

MSUDeflicker or GraftDeflicker

These two free de-flickering filters are available for the open source VirtualDub capture and

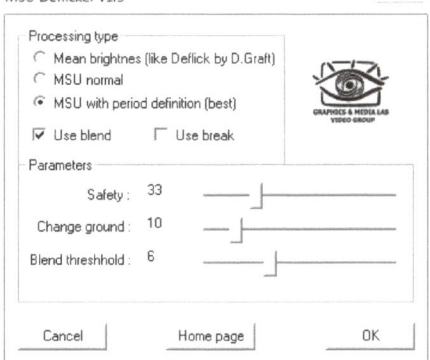

processing utility. We'll use MSUDeflicker in our free/donationware time-lapse rendering workflow. It's simple, free and gets the job done.

LRTimelapse

You've already heard a little about this application but in addition to allowing transitional time-lapse editing it handles deflickering with a single click.

GBDeflicker

Available as a plugin for Abobe After Effects and Adobe Premiere as well as a standalone windows application, GBDeflicker by Granite Bay Software is often touted as the standard for time-lapse deflickering.

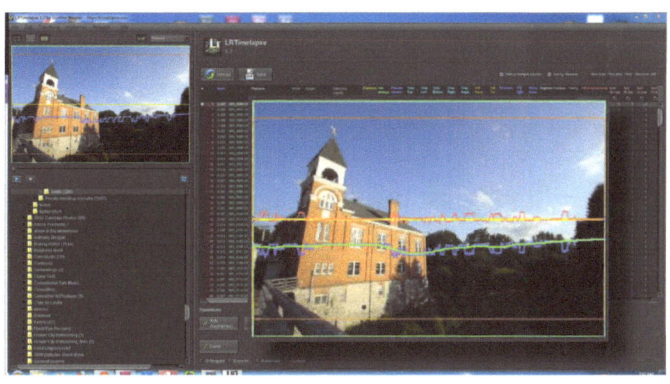

This powerful application, while simple to use in basic modes, provides a host of advanced features and functionality. The standalone flavor of the app can also be used as a very helpful

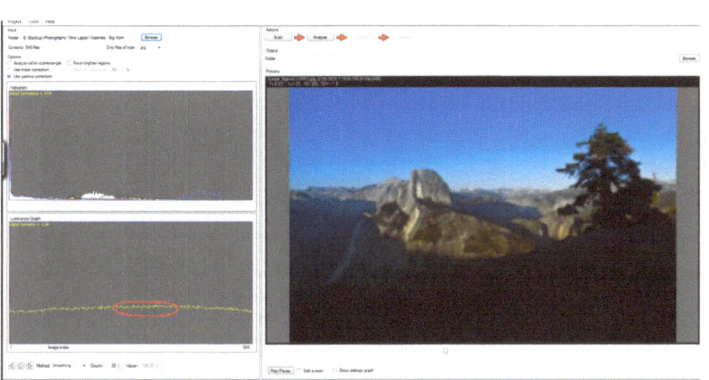

sequence analysis tool to diagnose problems and improve your flicker prevention skills for the next shoot.

Looking for more info?

We'll cover each but for more detail on advanced features and use be sure to visit their websites.

MOVIE FILES

Movies are big. I'm not just talking about worldwide gross, I mean they take up a ton of memory. In order to effectively share our time-lapse movies on the web or to pipe it to our TVs etc. we usually need to find a way to squeeze the footage down to a smaller size without compromising much quality. Like a suitcase filled with your favorite clothes, it matters how you pack.

CONTAINERS VS CODECS:

The file format you choose whether it's .avi, .mov, .mp4, etc. is really just the type of container or wrapper that the video uses for transport. Is it a red suitcase? A brown hard-shell one with wheels and a handle? Type matters, but it doesn't really affect the quality of the items within.

Codecs on the other hand are software used to adjust the amount of space videos take up. They're the algorithms used to first compress the video information and then decompress it (codec = compressor + decompressor). Codecs largely determine the file size and quality of the video when it comes time to play it.

Choosing a container and codec: Sometimes it can be a little tricky and it's a bit of an art and a science. Our goal will be to choose the right format for the end destination and also balance quality and file size based on our goals for playback and use.

Where to begin? A good way to figure this out is to start at your end destination and work backwards. For example if we are exporting to the web, say to Vimeo or YouTube, start with their recommended video compression guidelines. If we just want to play the video back on our home computer and don't mind a larger file size or if we want to create a master uncompressed archive file, pretty much exclusively for use in a video editor, we have other options.

Common codecs and formats for common goals: There are many codecs out there and I've kept this recommended list very very short. I encourage you to experiment, compare, and read more about the different export and render settings your software makes available.

 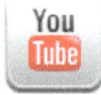

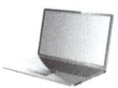

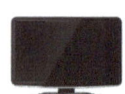

Web/sharing
H.264 (usually in format
.mp4 or .mov, .wmv)

**Home/further
editing**
PhotoJPEG (format .mov)

Archive/Master editing
DNxHD, ProRes 422
Uncompressed AVI
TIFF Sequence

WHAT FRAME RATE TO USE?

The second important rendering decision is the video playback frame rate. I have produced time-lapse sequences at 24fps, 25fps, and 30fps and can say that I like the look of 24 better, but I challenge you to try different rates and see the results. You'll get a better sense of how the frame rate will change both the speed of the action taking place in the time-lapse and the "look" of the movie on screen. It's your story, tell it how you want to.

What about 23.976? (fractional frame rates)

Unless you are rendering specifically for TV the whole issue of fractional frame rates might be only of historical interest. Most of our work is specifically tailored for computer and digital consumption so we'll stick to 24, 25 or 30 frames per second.

BIT RATES: A file with a higher bit rate will have superior audio/visual quality, but it will cost you in terms of size. YouTube, Vimeo and other online sharing sites will have recommended bit rates (usually pretty low) as well as their own compression algorithms to take whatever you provide and "compress", (ahem) I mean *optimize* it for playback. Of course it's up to you (and your upload patience and/or hard drive limits) as to what rates you choose but I usually try to aim between a 15 and 30 mbit/s for HD video.

RESOLUTION: Large frames mean better looking videos when they are shown on bigger screens. Shoot for 1920x1080 in HD (or less commonly at 1280x720).

PIXEL ASPECT RATIO: Aspect ratio is a number to describe the relationship of the width of a picture to the height of the picture. Mismatched aspect ratios can make your footage look stretched or squished and that's not good. Since the goal of most of our projects will be to export video for computer and use online in true HD, create movies with a 1.0 square pixel aspect ratio.

It's a balancing act

A lot of these choices might depend on your computing power, hard drive space, upload speed, artistic feel, in other words there might not be a perfect answer every time. I do encourage you to experiment but I also encourage you to be practical. I know a lot of people who never watch HD video clips online, they simply switch it off and prefer quicker viewing times. That's okay.

Render time might become an issue depending on your computing power (RAM and processor). Sometimes I wait until bedtime to hit render, it's just easier than tying up my computer for an hour (or a few).

Take note of the results as well as the sacrifices to get them. Remember who your target audience is.

TIME-LAPSE SOFTWARE WORKFLOWS

Here are three basic workflows that touch all major parts of the time-lapse creation process.

If you are creating your own workflow for the first time take a spin through these applications, learn more from the sources themselves, and begin to match your needs with each programs results, features, and costs.

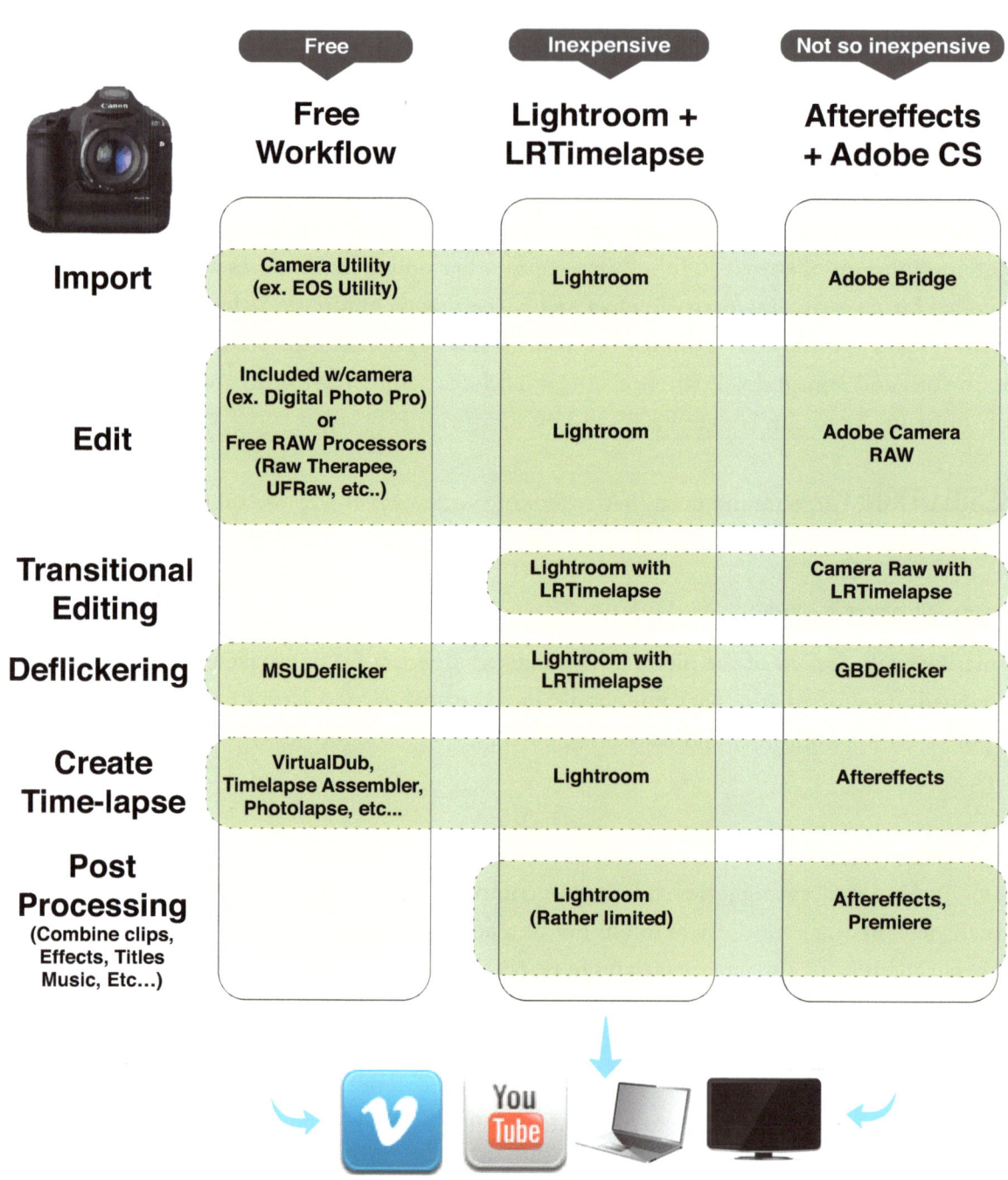

	Free Free Workflow	**Inexpensive** Lightroom + LRTimelapse	**Not so inexpensive** Aftereffects + Adobe CS
Import	Camera Utility (ex. EOS Utility)	Lightroom	Adobe Bridge
Edit	Included w/camera (ex. Digital Photo Pro) or Free RAW Processors (Raw Therapee, UFRaw, etc..)	Lightroom	Adobe Camera RAW
Transitional Editing		Lightroom with LRTimelapse	Camera Raw with LRTimelapse
Deflickering	MSUDeflicker	Lightroom with LRTimelapse	GBDeflicker
Create Time-lapse	VirtualDub, Timelapse Assembler, Photolapse, etc...	Lightroom	Aftereffects
Post Processing (Combine clips, Effects, Titles Music, Etc...)		Lightroom (Rather limited)	Aftereffects, Premiere

A FEW WORKFLOW OPTIONS

There are many different applications that can be used to assemble your images into a time-lapse movie. We'll walk through three workflows that touch different ends of the cost, functionality, and time-to-learn spectrum. Take a look at a few summaries below then launch into the combination that suits you best.

OPEN SOURCE/FREE WORKFLOW

1 *Free / Donation*

More and more software developers are following the open source philosophy of free and public software, and photography users are among the many groups to benefit. Mix in an application or two that came packaged with your DSLR camera and we've got ourselves a free and pretty powerful time-lapse creation workflow. Download links provided in the workflow section. Mac and Windows applications included.

Learning curve: *Moderate.* Each application by itself is pretty easy to pickup quickly, but having to patch together several independent applications each with very different interfaces adds some friction.

Cost: *FREE/Low.* These applications either came with your camera or can be downloaded for free. (*Free yes, but if these apps become your go to workhorses I always encourage supporting the authors and their further open source innovation with donations*)

Functionality: *Good.* Some applications have a wider reach than others within their respective workflow sections. Depending on your needs you might find yourself moving to more feature rich applications.

2 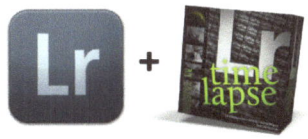 ## LIGHTROOM AND LRTIMELAPSE

Lightroom by Adobe is a powerful photo management and editing application/database. We'll use Lightroom to batch process changes and corrections to our image sequence (in concert with LRTimelapse) and render the movie itself by using the slideshow export feature.

LRTimelapse is a Java based companion for RAW processors written exclusively to take advantage of the features and functionality of Adobe Lightroom. Developed by Gunther Wegner, a photographer, filmmaker and designer from Hamburg Germany, LRTimelapse is a powerful image metadata editing tool that allows us to gradually and smoothly change exposure parameters over the entire time-lapse sequence using keyframes. LRTimelapse also allows us to quickly make Ken-Burns effects (pan/tilt/zoom) and deflicker.

Learning Curve: *Low*
Lightroom is very intuitive and simple to learn. LRTimelapse, while the interface might look a little daunting it's very easy to use.

Cost: *Moderate*
Even though LRTimelapse is free (*donationware*) it's best companion and most powerful tool Lightroom costs around $120 (*$70 for teacher/student license*).

Functionality: *Great*
Lightroom makes editing time-lapse images easy and LRTimelapse adds the vital transitional editing tools to get the job done. A great pair.

3 AE ADOBE AFTER EFFECTS AND THE ADOBE CREATIVE SUITE

The Adobe Creative Suite is a popular high-performance collection of powerful software. The applications can be used to edit, enhance, design, publish, and create just about any form of digital media you desire with incredible control and flexibility.

Sold as standalone industry specific products or in several different bundles, time-lapse photographers will mostly be concerned with **After Effects:** Adobe's digital motion graphics and compositing application which we will use to render our time-lapse movies. **Premiere Pro:** Adobe's real-time, time-line based video editing application as well as image editing tools provided by **Photoshop or Photoshop Elements** may also become important components of your pre and post-rendering workflow.

Learning Curve: *Moderate*
Navigating and learning the basics of Adobe's products such as After Effects can take a little getting used to. It's easy to learn but fully mastering them is near impossible; *you'll find that you can never really know everything about the application, you only keep learning.*

Cost: *High.*
After Effects as a stand-alone application breaks the bank at around $999 but the entire production premium which includes Photoshop, Premiere, and many more powerful applications costs about $1,500. If you are a student or involved in education the price is reduced to **$449.** Individual titles like After Effects can be **leased on a monthly basis for around $49 each**.

Functionality: *Extensive.*
After Effects is a powerful digital motion graphics application and our basic time-lapse rendering process will only utilize a very small portion of its full potential.

The main advantage this application has as part of the larger Adobe Creative Suite is its ability to seamlessly work together with other applications to accomplish all tasks of a high-performance video production workflow.

LRTIMELAPSE & LIGHTROOM: EXAMPLE

(+Batch editing, Ken Burns movement, and deflickering)

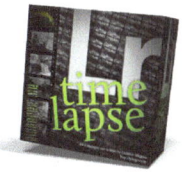 LRTimelapse is a great application (lrtimelapse.com). Newer versions continue to add helpful advances to its already quite exhaustive feature list and I'm excited to follow Gunther's progress.

In a nutshell LRTimelapse takes changes and corrections you make in Lightroom and then smoothly applies them throughout the entire time-lapse sequence. By altering either the first and last image, or several images throughout the sequence, LRTimelapse can quickly fade the changes we need to only the parts we want. Deflickering can also easily be accomplished in the exact same way by flattening out big exposure jumps.

Here's a simple workflow for editing time-lapse images and rendering a movie using Adobe Lightroom and LRTimelapse.

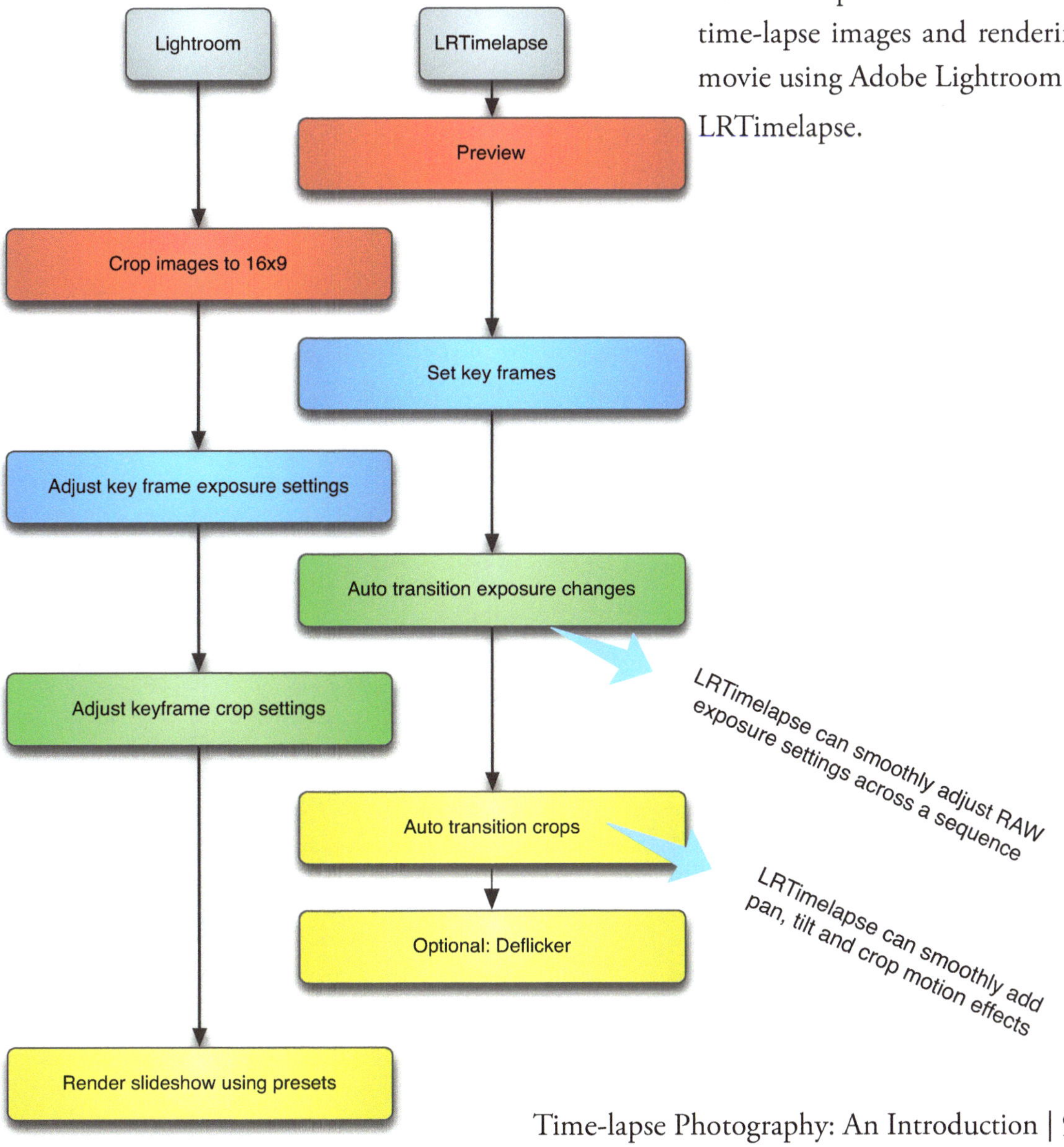

Lightroom	LRTimelapse
	Preview
Crop images to 16x9	
	Set key frames
Adjust key frame exposure settings	
	Auto transition exposure changes
Adjust keyframe crop settings	
	Auto transition crops
	Optional: Deflicker
Render slideshow using presets	

LRTimelapse can smoothly adjust RAW exposure settings across a sequence

LRTimelapse can smoothly add pan, tilt and crop motion effects

STEP 1 : PREVIEW IN LRTIMELAPSE

Open LRTimelapse and navigate to your folder of time-lapse images. Allow previews to load (this may take a few minutes) then press play or pan through your sequence and get a feel for how things turned out and what kind of exposure changes you might want to make in Lightroom. *(keep in mind these previews will always reflect your source images and not development settings or changes you will make in Lightroom)*

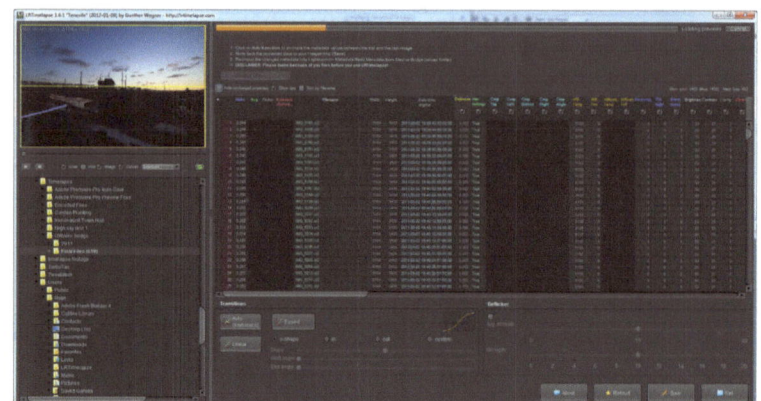

Click "yes" to the dialog asking to initialize metadata, or select all the images in the listing panel, right click selecting "metadata > initialize metadata". Click "save".

STEP 2: IN LIGHTROOM CROP TO 16 X 9 ASPECT RATIO (OPTIONAL)

If you are exporting for HD video open Lightroom and start by cropping your images to a 16x9 aspect ratio. Navigate to the same time-lapse sequence folder, select the first image, choose "develop", and select the crop tool (shortcut "R"). Select the drop-down next to aspect and choose 16 units by 9 units.

Arrange the crop how you would like it and select done or press "R" again. Now sync this new change across all images in your sequence. Select all image and then click the "Sync..." button at the bottom right. Make sure "Crop" is checked then press "OK". Save the changed metadata to the files by pressing "Save".

STEP 3: EDITING YOUR IMAGES USING KEYFRAMES

LRTimelapse utilizes keyframes to fade in exposure changes across a time-lapse sequence. In

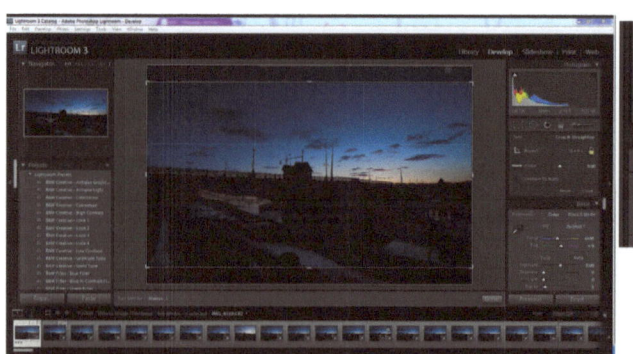

fact that's pretty much the definition of keyframes, the starting and ending point of a transition.

LRTimelapse accepts two or more keyframes, looks at the changes you made in each, and then allows you to automatically spread some or all of those changes smoothly between them. Here's how to do it:

Start by setting your keyframes in LRTimelapse

Take a look at the preview window. Our goal here is to determine two or more points where we would like LRTimelapse to smoothly incorporate our changes.

We will need at least one starting and one ending keyframe, but we could create as many as we want depending on the changes or corrections we would like to make in the scene.

Scroll through the preview window and create some keyframes by clicking the diamond symbol in the file listing panel or right click on the file listing panel and select "keyframes > create a set number of evenly spaced keyframes". Save your metadata.

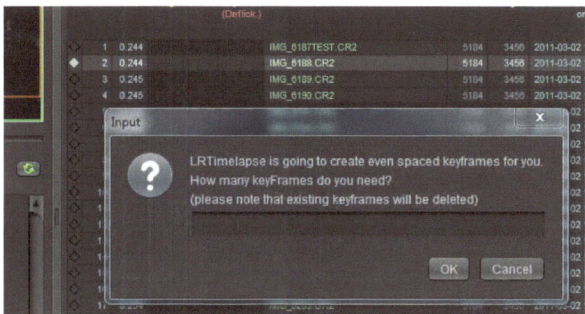

In Lightroom edit the key frames

Back in Lightroom, reload the metadata for all the images ("metadata > read") then quickly find the keyframes by filtering for images with a single star designation (LR-Timelapse edited the metadata for these images to include a star rating so we could quickly find them).

Select and edit the first keyframe image. Keep in mind how the time-lapse will be changing and how the edits you are applying to this image might look gradually applied to the images between the next keyframe.

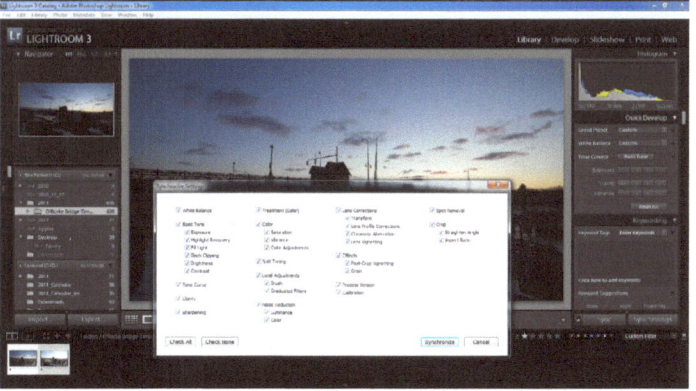

Once this image is edited, sync its changes to the next keyframe by selecting both this image and the second keyframe (hold shift) then press "Sync..." making sure the changes you made will be passed along via the checked sync settings.

Now edit the second keyframe keeping in mind that any changes made to this image will be faded into all the images between them.

The more frames between the two keyframes the slower the fade, the fewer the faster those changes will occur. Continue this process of making changes and syncing them from the current keyframe to the next in the sequence. Once finished be sure to select all the keyframes you edited in Lightroom and save the metadata.

STEP 4: SMOOTHING THE CHANGES IN LRTIMELAPSE

Back in LRTimelapse, reload the images. This will import the changes to the 2 or more keyframes that you made in Lightroom. Now select "auto keyframes" to automatically fade those changes into the entire sequence's metadata.

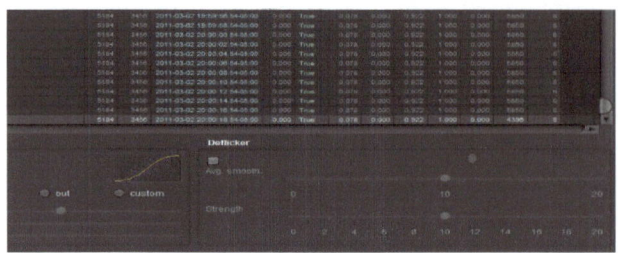

Now that the changes have been applied to all the images, select save again in LR-Timelapse.

Back in Lightroom, deselect any filters so you can see all the images in the sequence, make sure all images are selected, then read in the changed metadata again. After the thumbnails update, you'll see that all the images have been modified to slowly fade any changes you made between each keyframe across all images between them.

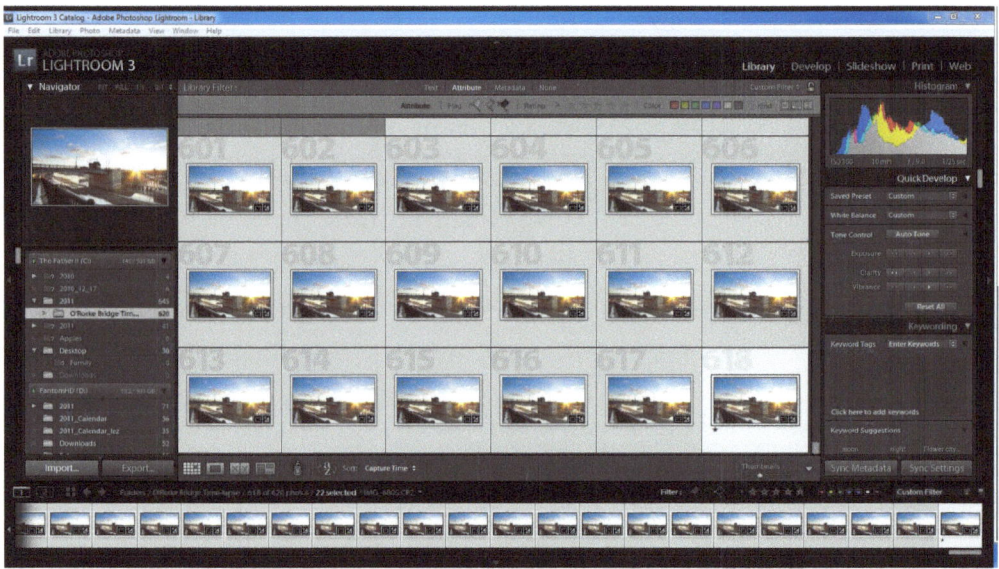

You're now ready to export the images as a time-lapse movie using Lightroom's slideshow feature and handy LRTimelapse presets... or if you want you can make things really interesting and add some automated movement in the sequence. That's what we are going to tackle next.

STEP 5: ADD KEN BURNS EFFECTS - MOVEMENT (OPTIONAL)

Just like using keyframes for exposure changes, we can also fade between different crops and image orientations. In other words we can achieve Ken Burns panning and zooming effects in a time-lapse by slowly changing how each image fills the screen. Here's one way to do it using LRTimelapse:

Create new keyframes in LRTimelapse

Clear any old keyframes that are left over from image editing (right click in list panel and select "Keyframes > remove all"). Now create 2 or more new keyframes at the beginning where you want the movement to start (usually the first frame of the time-lapse) and where you would like the movement to change or end (usually the last frame). Once again it's easier to do this in LRTimelapse using the preview window, save the keyframe changes, then re-read the metadata in Lightroom.

Create the initial zoom/crop perspective

Search for the first key frame (using star rating), and apply the first zoom or crop (press the "R" key). This new view, in the example below a zoomed and slightly rotated perspective, will be the new changed beginning perspective.

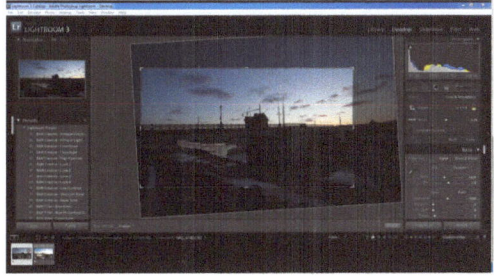 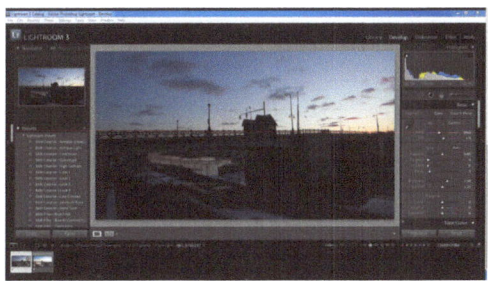

Once this new beginning perspective is set, select the current and the next keyframe and sync ONLY the crop changes by deselecting all other parameters in the sync selection dialog box shown below.

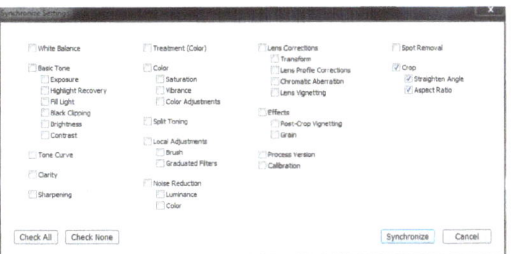 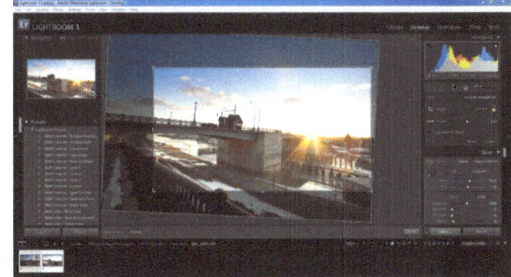

Create the next/final crop perspective to shift to

Now select the next key frame and apply the new perspective that you would like LRTimelapse to slowly shift to using the previous keyframe perspective as the starting point. Press "R" to crop, then choose done or press "R" again to accept the new view. Now select the two or more cropped key frames and save the metadata.

Auto transition between the crops in LRTimelapse

Head back to LRTimelapse and hit reload to accept the changed keyframe metadata. This is important: select only the 5 light blue crop settings columns, making sure everything else is

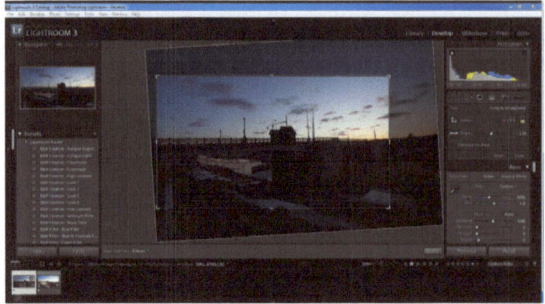

deselected. The crop changes are the only information bits we would like to pull from those keyframes, not exposure data.

When only the crop columns are selected, choose "auto transition" to apply the crop transformation.

You'll now see an orange box and pattern in the preview window. Scrub through the preview and check your work. If the crop looks good, save the metadata in LRTimelapse and head back to Lightroom for rendering.

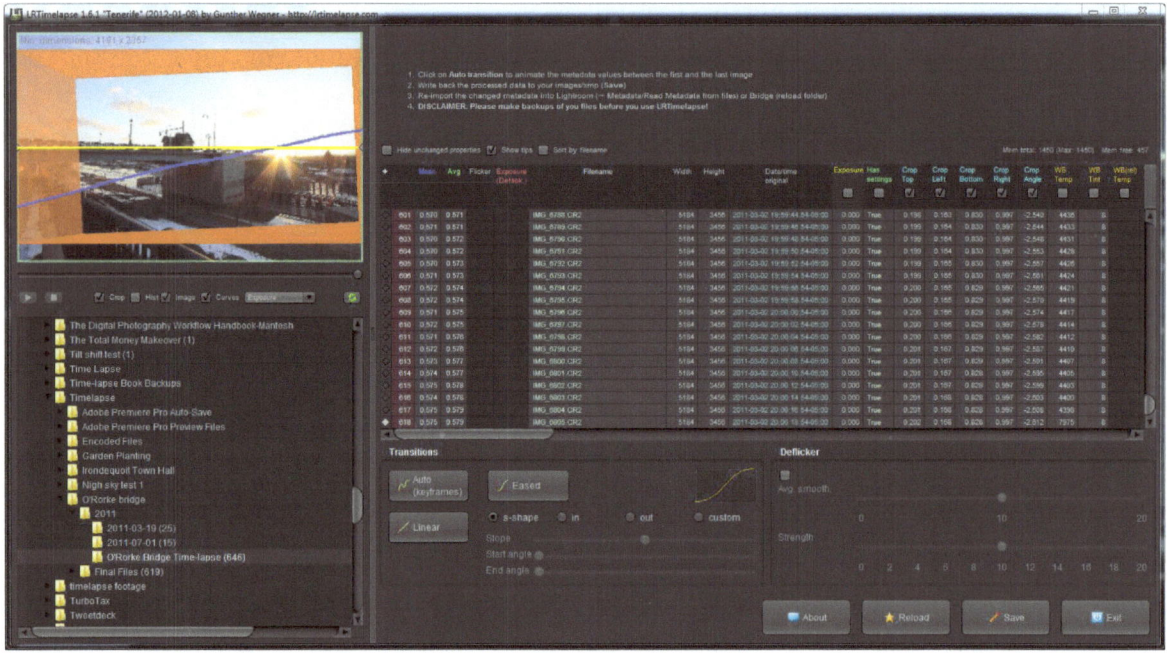

STEP 6: DEFLICKER USING LRTIMELAPSE (OPTIONAL)

De-flickering in LRTimelapse is really simple. Take a look at this preview from a different time-lapse filmed in aperture priority mode.

The blue line indicates how bright every single image is. The more jagged the curve (like this one) the more flicker that is present.

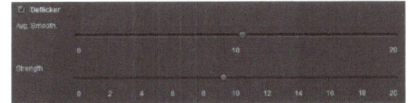

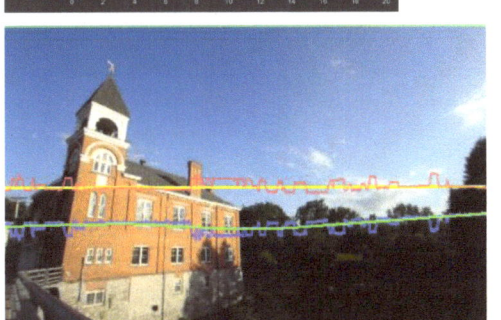

LRTimelapse now calculates the difference between the blue (brightness) and the green(flicker adjustment) and the result is the red curve (the new exposure value).

Save metadata with these new changed exposure settings and read in those changes inside Lightroom.

2-pass deflickering

If you still experience flicker when you render your time-lapse movie you can bring the images through for another pass. Go ahead and deflicker once as normal except instead of rendering the movie export the images as JPEGs at max quality to a separate folder (check "add to this catalog" and "minimize embedded metadata").

Now open this new folder in LRTimelapse and repeat the deflickering process one more time. This second pass should substantially reduce any leftover variances.

STEP 7: RENDER THE TIME-LAPSE IN LIGHTROOM

Head back to Lightroom one final time and read in the sequence metadata. Our time-lapse images have now been corrected and enhanced, we've possibly added movement and Ken Burn's effects, and we've corrected for any time-lapse flicker. We are now ready to export to a movie.

Install the time-lapse slideshow presets

If you haven't done so already make sure to install the Lightroom time-lapse templates available at lrtimelapse.com/download. These templates allow quick export to 720p and 1080p 16Mbps at 15, 24, 25, and 30 fps. PRO slideshow templates are also available for purchase allowing up to 3k and 4k resolutions and bitrates up to 70 Mbps as well as professional framerates at 23.976 and 29.967 fps.

Select Slideshow and export

Switch to the slideshow view, double check any playback settings on the right-hand window, then select "Export Video." Select your desired resolution and frame rate. That's it.

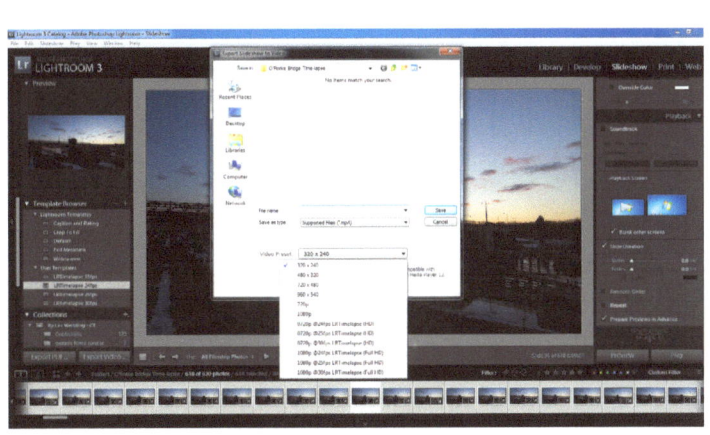

VIRTUALDUB (WINDOWS): WORKFLOW EXAMPLE

VirtualDub is a JPEG capture and processing utility for 32-bit and 64-bit Windows platforms licensed under the GNU General Public License. It's quick, streamlined and not very pretty, but it gets the job done.

VirtualDub homepage: virtualdub.org/index.html (32 or 64 bit versions)
H.264 Compression Codec: sourceforge.net/projects/x264vfw/files (32 bit version only)
MSU Deflicker filter: compression.ru/video/deflicker/index_en.html
More optional filters are available.

STEP 1: INSTALL (WITH CODECS AND FILTERS)

Download and install VirtualDub. I recommend downloading and installing the H.264 codec (for the 32-bit version of VirtualDub only). Running the install for H.264 will automatically make it an option inside VirtualDub. I also recommend the MSU Deflicker filter plugin. Follow the instructions during install to unpack them into the VirtualDub plugin folder.

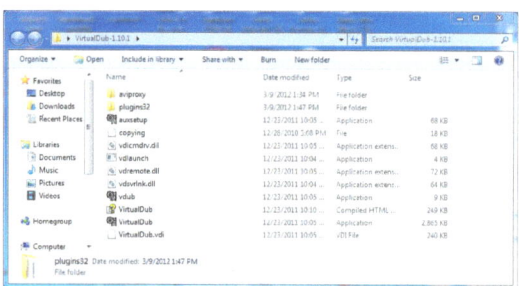

STEP 2: PREPARE YOUR IMAGES (EXPORT TO JPEG)

VirtualDub is a bit more limited in the different types of files it recognizes so you might have to perform an extra conversion step if you captured your time-lapse images in the RAW format. I usually do, so here's my process of quickly preparing the images:

1. Make changes to your sequence of images using a batch processor (optional)
2. Export all images to JPEG format in a separate folder.
3. Be extra careful naming your files, VirtualDub needs them to be 100% sequential (ex. IMG_4585.jpg, IMG_4586.jpg, or cape_cod_sunset(1).jpg, cape_code_sunrise(2), etc.)

How to quickly rename hundreds of files in Windows 7?

Most of the time you won't have to worry at all because the original file names set by your camera or the image editor should set you up perfectly, but what if for some reason your images are in the right order but the file names are such that VirtualDub doesn't think they're all a linked sequence? *You'll be able to tell because when you load the sequence the software either only takes in a single frame or a portion of them seeming to stop somewhere in the middle of your images.* If this happens you'll need to rename them. Again no worries here's how to quickly do it:

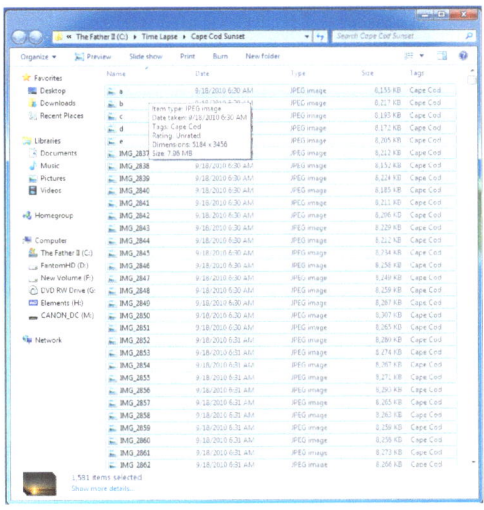

1. Select all the images in the sequence

2. Right click on the first file in the sequence

3. Select "rename"

3. Choose a descriptive name

4. Press "enter"

Windows will then go through and rename all the images to what you selected followed by a sequence number in parenthesis.

Before: A.jpg, B.jpg, C.jpg.....

After: cape_cod_sunset(1).jpg, cape_cod_sunset(2).jpg, cape_cod_sunset(3).jpg

STEP 3: IMPORT YOUR SEQUENCE

When your images are separated in their own folder *and* are named sequentially, launch VirtualDub.

Import the time-lapse sequence by choosing "File > Open video" file and select only the first image in the sequence. **Make sure "Automatically Load Linked Segments" is Checked.** VirtualDub will recognise that it's a connected collection of images and pull them all in.

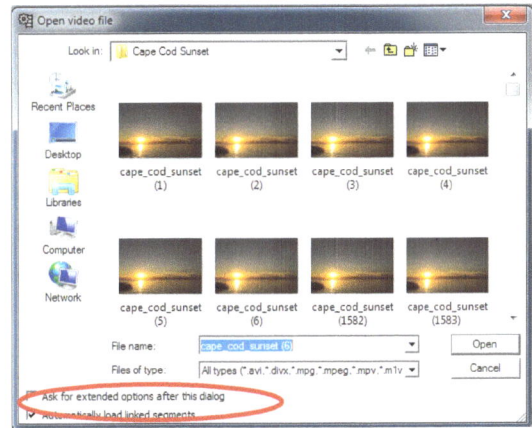

The next screen you see will be a zoomed in preview of that first image. Right click on the photo and select a smaller zoom, maybe 12% or 25%.

That's better. We're now able to see the first frame.

STEP 4: RESIZE YOUR IMAGES (OPTIONAL)

Take a second to think about what you will be doing with this movie file once it's created.

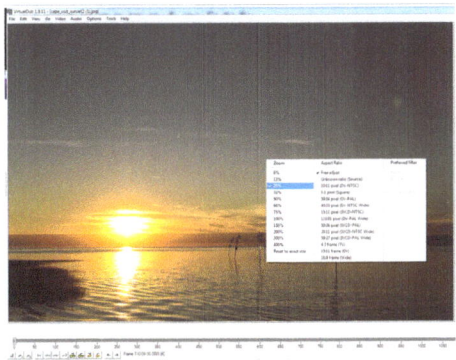

Will you be doing more editing using a video editor (combining with other clips, panning or zooming into the image, etc.) then resizing the clip in a second and final render? If so you might want to keep the image resolution as big as you can.

If you will not be doing further editing and want to share to YouTube or Vimeo for example, then you will need to resize the images to a standard format like HD. You can use the Virtual-DUB filter to resize or a host of free automatic image resizing applications or choose to resize when you export the files from your image viewer/editor.

Here's how to easily apply a resize filter.
Click the "Videos" drop down and select "Filters". Now choose "Add." Press "R" to jump to the bottom of the list and find "resize."

Click "OK" and you'll now see the size options box with your current images sizes already pre-filled. To resize to standard HD, select absolute pixels and enter 1920x1080 (or 1280x720).

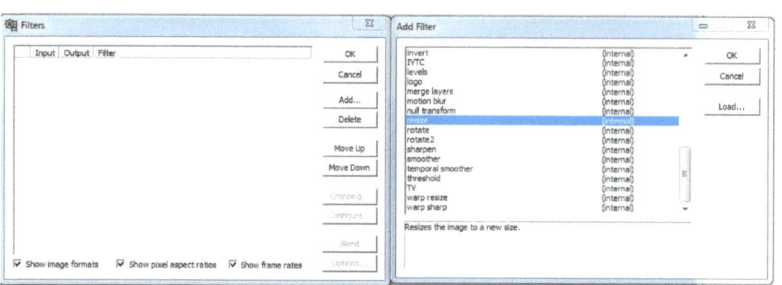

You can disable aspect ratio calculation because you are defining your own 16:9 ratio. The "Lanczos3" filter mode comes recommended.

Click "OK".
You've now defined a resize

filter that will run as part of the video rendering process. You'll see the added filter in the filters window.

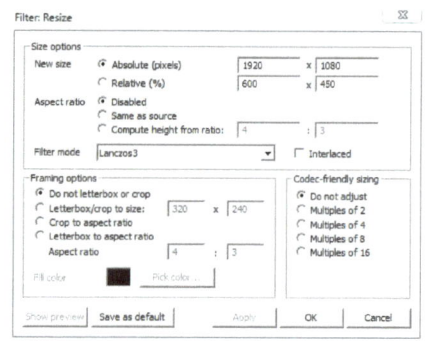

The plug-ins folder under VirtualDub is where you put any of the filters (deflickers etc., files with .vdf extension) you may download from the site I linked to above.

STEP 5: CHOOSE A FRAME RATE
Choosing a frame rate is simple. Select "Video" > "Frame rate..." and choose the rate you would like.

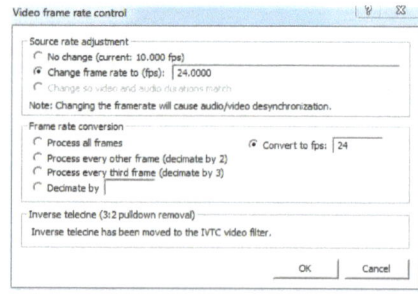

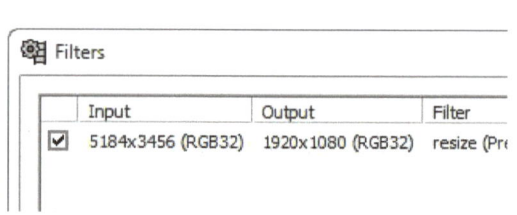

In this example I am going to select 24 frames per second.
Click "OK".

STEP 6: CONFIGURE COMPRESSION SETTINGS

The final step is to define compression settings. By default VirtualDub exports to an uncompressed .AVI file which will be pretty large in size. \We talked about some of the different compressors, or codecs and many are available for VirtualDub.

At this point you have a few options:

1. You can render your time-lapse as a large and uncompressed .AVI video file. This could be thought of as a master file which you could use in an editor or compress it later using different codecs for the web.

   A simple way to "compress later" would be to download MPEG Streamclip video converter for Windows. It's an easy application that provides many export options including this example's goal which is the h.264 codec.

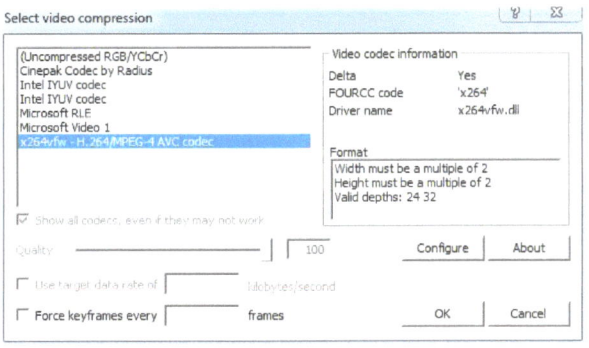

2) I recommended installing direct H.264 support for VirtualDub and rendering using this codec format for most web destinations.

To configure go to: "Video > Compression" and select x264vfw - H.264/MPEG-4 AVC Codec. Now choose the "Configure" button. Here's where you can select the speed/size/ and quality settings.

Here are a few recommended starter settings:

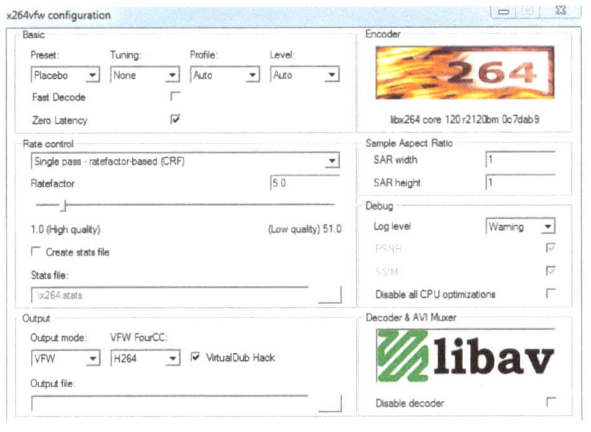

Preset: Placebo (or medium for slower comp)
Zero Latency: Check
Single Pass - ratefactor based: set to high quality
Make sure VirtualDub Hack box is checked: it helps overcome some multi-threading limitations inside the application.

Select "OK" and that's it for the main video settings.

STEP 7: DEFLICKER USING THE MSU DEFLICKER FILTER (OPTIONAL)

Configuring the deflickering filter is just about as simple as using the resize filter.

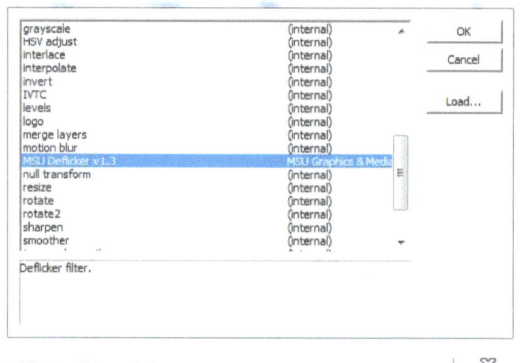

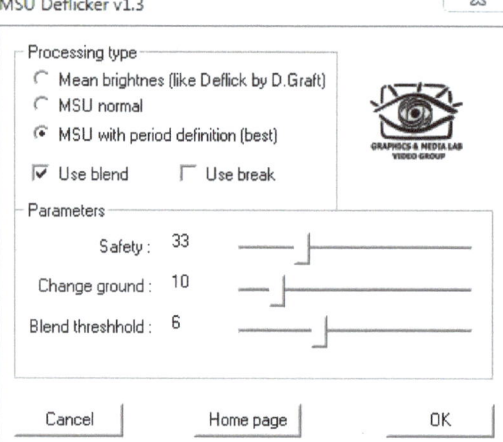

Click "Video > Filter... > then Add"

Find and select "MSU Deflicker". A dialog box will popup with de-flickering settings. The default settings should work well most of the time but you do have the ability to change settings.

I'd stick with blend mode, which compares the current frame with previous ones using the threshold parameters and adjust the strength settings (Safety and Change Ground) and the abruptness of adjustments (blend threshold) settings as necessary.

Save the configuration:

If you find this or other collection of filters and settings to be effective make sure to save your processing settings in the file menu, that way you'll only have to do this dance once.

When everything is set press the play button to preview a few slow frames or drag through the timeline

Save

All that's left is a quick "File > Save As AVI..." write the name of time-lapse (write .avi at the end) and then a slightly a slower render time.

Adding Audio:

If you wanted to add audio to the clip, click "Audio > Audio from other file...", choose Wav or Mp3, leave "**Auto detect bit rate**" selected. Click "OK". (tweaking video and audio is much better left to a NLE though)

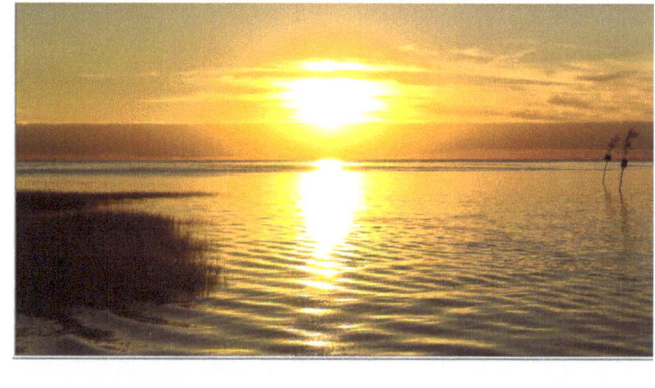

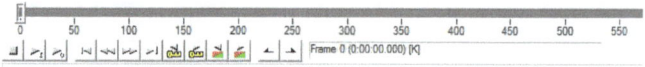

A little roundabout but it gets the job done. VirtualDub has found a place in many photographer's time-lapse workflows.

TIME LAPSE ASSEMBLER (MAC)

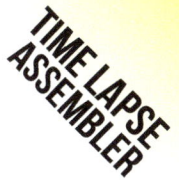

Time Lapse Assembler is a donationware Mac application that allows you to create movies from a sequence of JPEG images plain and simple.

Time Lapse Assembler homepage and download link: dayofthenewdan.com

STEP 1: INSTALL TIME LAPSE ASSEMBLER

Download and install Time Lapse Assembler following the instructions on the website.

STEP 2: PREPARE YOUR IMAGES

Like VirtualDub, Time Lapse Assembler requires your images to be in JPEG format, sequentially labeled and in a separate folder. If your images are in RAW either batch export from your photo editor/viewer software to JPEG or use one of several free batch RAW processors like Raw Photo Processor (found at raw-photo-processor.com).

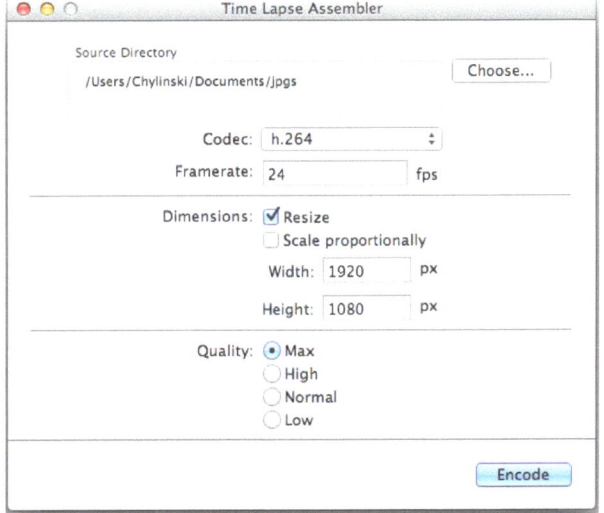

STEP 3: CONFIGURE RENDER SETTINGS

Wow that was quick! we're already configuring final settings. Choose a codec and frame rate. Depending on your destination you can choose to resize or leave the images in their native resolutions.

STEP 4: ENCODE

Quick easy and great results.

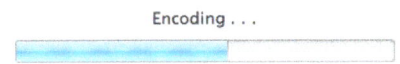

ADOBE AFTER EFFECTS: WORKFLOW EXAMPLE

After Effects (AE) is a big program. One of my favorite things to do on a rainy Sunday morning, coffee and steel cut oats at my side, is to follow along with one of hundreds of visual effects tutorials out there and take a stab at a cool new manipulation. *OK, it doesn't have to be a Sunday... or rainy,* but anytime I work on a project I learn something new.

Digital effects work in AE is extremely powerful and creating a complex outcome for the first time can be a good challenge. The great news is that rendering a time-lapse movie and applying basic pan/tilt/or zoom effects after a quick walkthrough isn't much of a challenge at all.

At first glance the interface might look a little daunting, but we'll only be concerned with a few of the main panels. Here's what we'll be using:

Project Window: Allows you to bring items into the program (this is where you will import your image sequence).

Composition Window: This is where we can preview what the rendered video will look like, it's size, any effects, movement, etc.

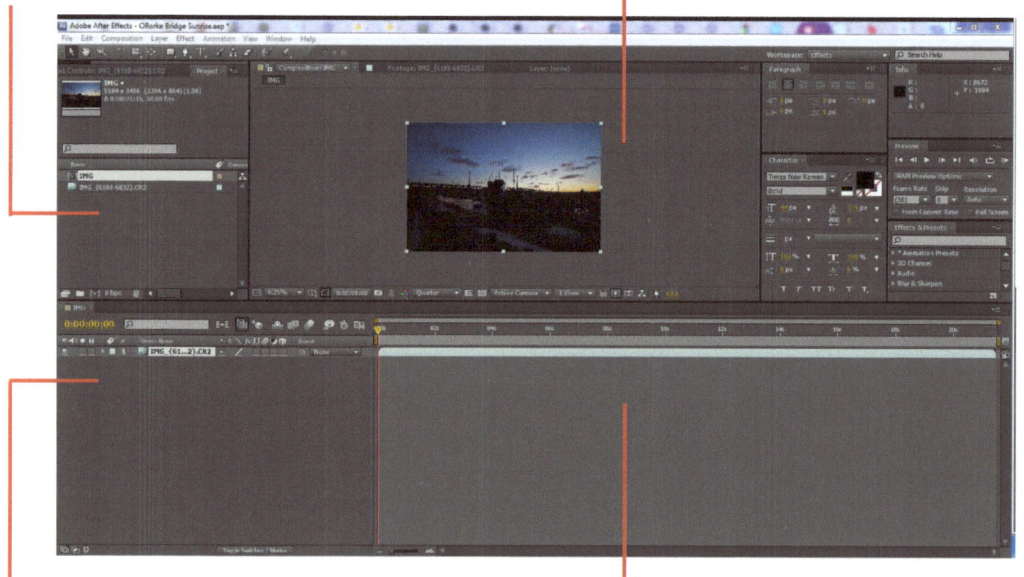

Timegraph: This is where each layer, in our case the bridge time-lapse sequence, is shown as a colored duration bar, where the length is signified directly above by a timer ruler denoting seconds of video at your set frame rate.

Timeline Panel: This is where layers of video, graphics, etc. are stacked to be manipulated on the timeline. This is also where we can easily apply keyframes and a sense of motion in our video. More on that in the next few pages.

STEP 1. IMPORT THE IMAGES AS A SEQUENCE

Open a new After Effects project (it's a habit of mine to immediately title and save it) then right click/command click inside the project window or select "File

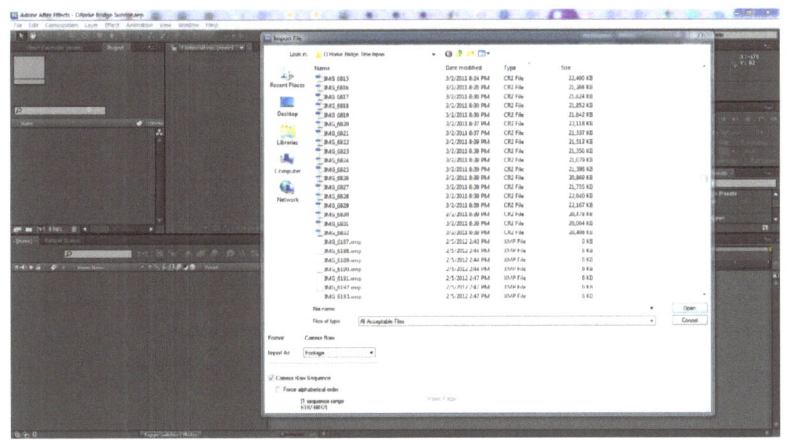

> Import > Files" to open the import files dialog box.

Navigate to your time-lapse directory and to the specific sequence you want to render.

Depending on any RAW processing work you may have done and what file format you are importing you may need to sort by name to separate the RAW files (.CR2 in the case of Canon, .NEF for Nikon) from the .XMP sidecar files.

Select the first image then hold shift and click the last image highlighting the entire sequence. Make sure the sequence box is checked.

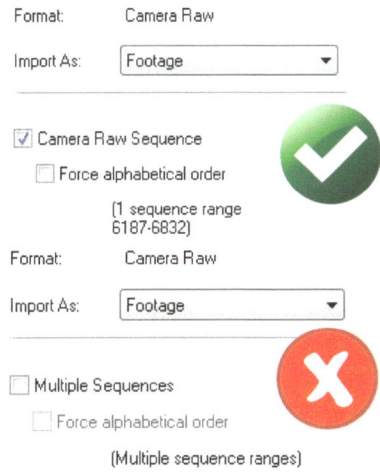

If after selecting the entire sequence of images the box reads "Multiple sequences", AE doesn't like how the files are named and doesn't think they belong together. You can quickly fix this by either batch renaming the files in your image editor or right inside the folder view in either Windows Explorer or Mac Finder.

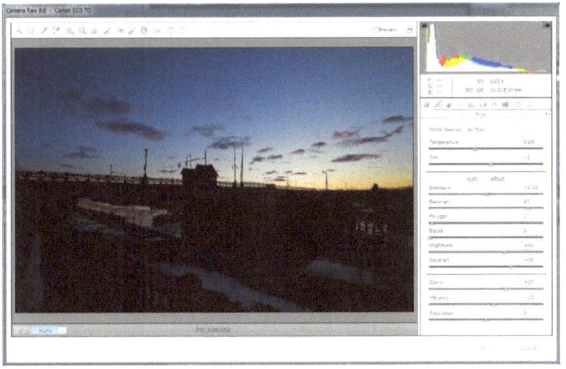

If you are importing a sequence of RAW images you will be presented with an opportunity to batch edit your images before squeezing them into a sequence. *Isn't that handy?*

Now if you've already edited your RAW images before importing them here those changes should be reflected in the preview and there's nothing that you need to adjust. If you are happy with how things look select "**OK**".

If you feel the need to make any adjustments just be doubly aware that these changes will be made across all images in the sequence. Small logical changes to the beginning of a sequence, for example the brightening up a pre-sunrise foreground, might become severe towards the end of the scene as things become brighter and potentially blown out. With this in mind if you are happy with how things look select "**OK**".

The image sequence is now loaded into your project window and is ready to be placed on the timeline. It's also helpful to look at the size of the sequence and how many frames per second (FPS) the project is set to. We'll have a chance to adjust both before rendering.

STEP 2. CONFIGURE AND CREATE THE COMPOSITION

What is the goal for this rendering? Where is the video destined to end up? How big (both file size and resolution) do you want the movie to be? Using some of the time-lapse rendering considerations we spoke about at the beginning of the chapter, this is where you design your video's characteristics.

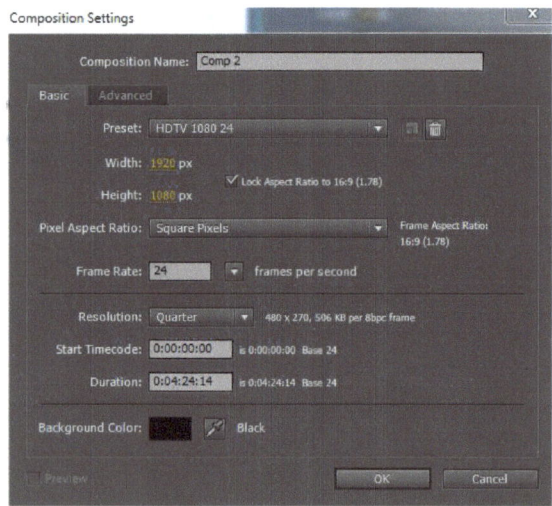

Choose "Composition > New Composition" and enter the settings to match your destination goals. Here's what I find I commonly use:
Resolution: Likely HD 1920x1080
Pixel Aspect ratio: Square pixels
Frame Rate: usually 24 or 30
Now add the image sequence to the timeline by clicking and dragging into the timeline panel below. You'll see a colored bar matching the length of the time-lapse sequence in seconds.

Adjust resolution and think about movement

There are different ways of getting the time-lapse sequence into the composition but I like to drag and manually resize. It reminds me just how big my original resolution images are and what kind of freedom I have to move the images within the much smaller HD window.

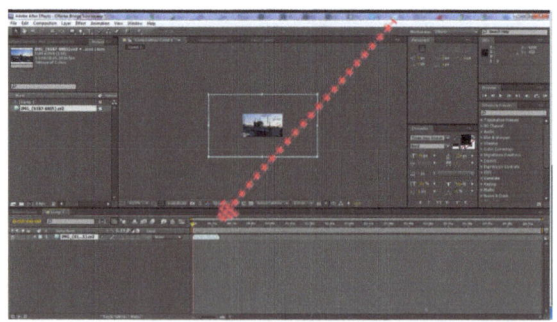

The blue outline in the composition window shows the sequence's actual size while the smaller preview box in the middle is the size of the output resolution as defined in our composition settings. We've got a lot of room to crop, pan, tilt, or just shrink proportionally to match the 16:9 aspect ratio.

STEP 3: PANNING AND TILTING (OPTIONAL)

Let's configure a left to right pan and a slight upward tilt in the time-lapse. Go ahead and shrink the image sequence a bit by making sure to click the corner and then **hold the shift key to resize proportionally.** Then move the larger sequence to the left to give us room for the move back to the right. Make sure to watch your edges or else you'll have black space in the final video.

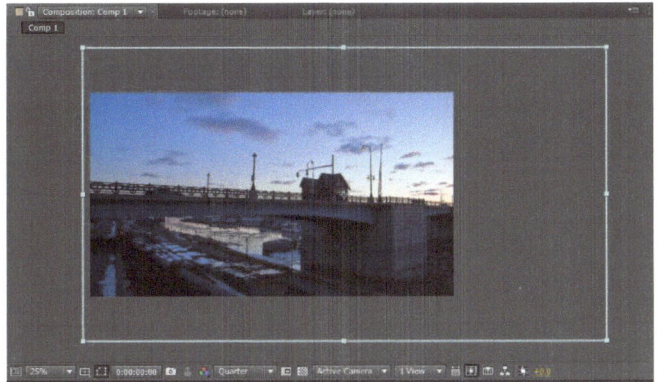

Find the position property:
Expand the transform options by swinging the options triangles down until you see the "Position" option within the transform category or press "P" to solo the option.

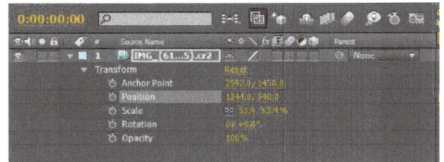

Set the first keyframe:
Make sure the time-lapse is positioned how you would like it to start in the composition window and move the cursor in the timeline to where you would like the movement to begin (usually at the beginning). Now click the position property clock icon to set the first keyframe. This is now our starting point and AE will move from this keyframe to the next keyframe we define.

Set the next keyframe:
Now move forward along the timeline to when you would like the movement to stop or change (usually at the end) and adjust the time-lapse position in the composition window to reflect where you would like it to move to. I am going to move it all the way to the right until I run out of width and slightly higher to see more of the sunrise. You'll see that AE automatically creates the next keyframe and attaches a little chain to your last position letting you know where it will be moving from. (screenshot on the next page).

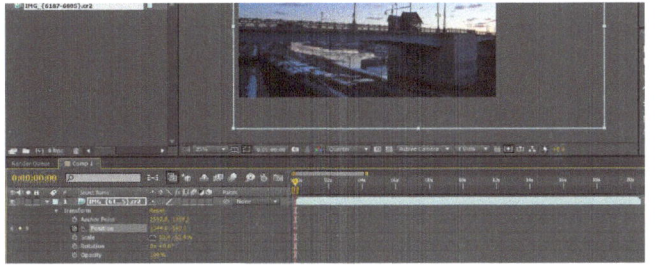

If for any reason you aren't happy with the keyframes and want to redefine the movement from scratch, just click on the position clock icon to erase and start over. After Effects will now move from one keyframe to the other. The closer the keyframes are and the bigger the movement or changes between them, the faster AE will need to change from one to the other.

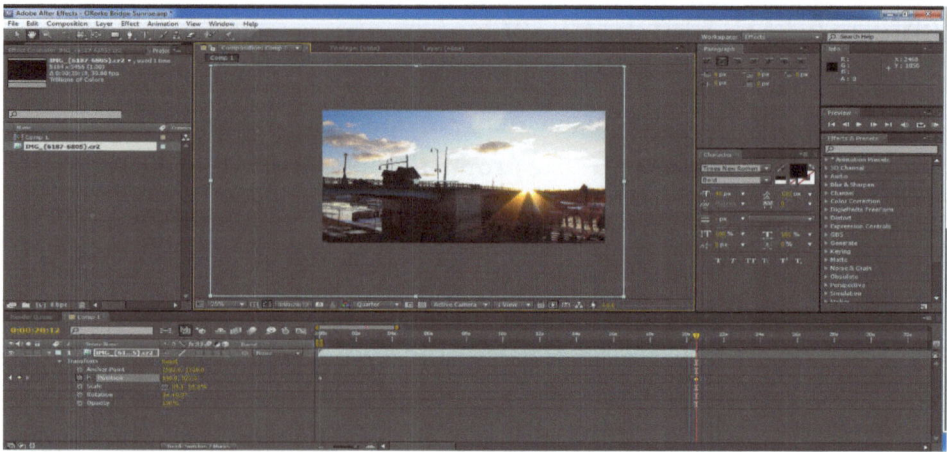

STEP 3: DEFLICKERING (OPTIONAL)

I've been using GBDeflicker as an added plugin for After Effects for about a year now and am very impressed with the results. It's simple to use and very effective. While there are many advanced options inside the add-on, the default settings with small changes to the smoothing method will quickly provide great results after rendering. Here's how I setup the basic configuration:

With the plugin installed and the time-lapse loaded in the timeline, add GBDeflicker as an effect by selecting "Effects" from the top menu then "GBDeflicker".

You'll now see a new configuration panel with the plugin's options. The histogram graph shows all the color channels for the current selected frame as well as the overall luminance graph in white. The lower graph is blank at startup but if you want to see a preview of the yellow luminance values for the entire clip you'll have to preview your sequence (this takes a long time so I usually skip the visual).

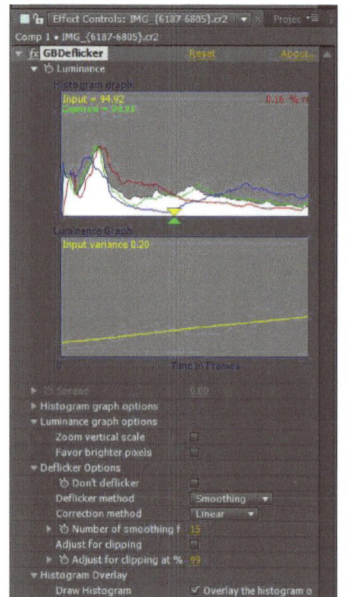

As you can see in this sunrise clip the luminance steadily increases from start to finish and since it was filmed in full manual mode it doesn't look like I have much flicker. If there was flicker in the clip you'd see sharp peaks and valleys in the luminance graph line.

The smoothing method, or changes based on the moving average of the input luminance, is set by default and is very effective for most scenes. We'll go ahead and leave that set as well as the other default settings.

With our time-lapse sequence resized, panning motion using keyframes programed, and deflickering configured we're ready to render the composition.

STEP 4: SELECT RENDER SETTINGS AND RENDER

From the composition menu select "Make Movie". After choosing where to save the composition all your timeline changes and effects will be moved to the render queue ready for final output.

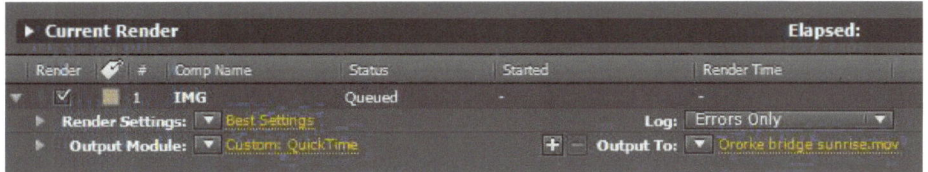

By default After Effects usually shows a Lossless rendering configuration which might be good for archival or a master copy to edit elsewhere but in this particular example we are going to be

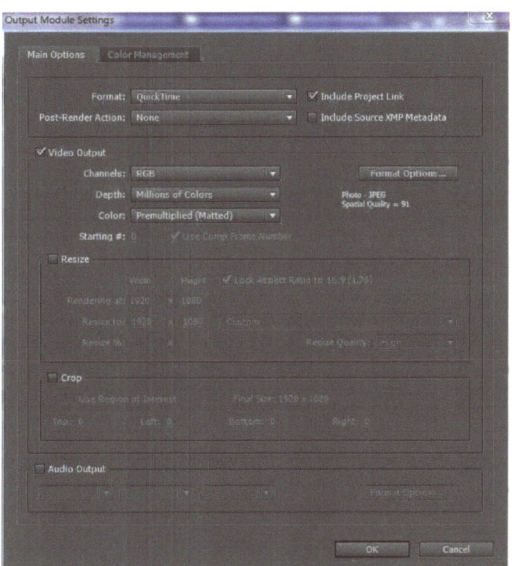

exporting for Vimeo. A good codec to experiment with is H.264.

Click on the output module text to bring up the Output Module Settings.
Choose Quicktime as the format. Then click format options to chose the H.264 codec from the choices available.

Keep the quality settings nice and high 90-95 but no need to go to 100 as you get diminishing returns with quality and large file sizes.

Click "OK" twice to save the settings to the render queue.

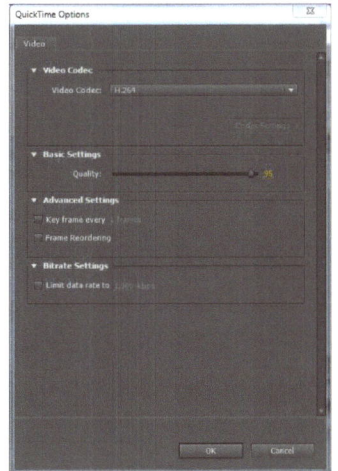

Lastly click on the "Output To:" option and choose a movie title and save location.

That's all for configuring. You are now ready to render the time-lapse. Click render and in anywhere from 10 minutes to several hours your movie will be complete.

USING NON-LINEAR EDITORS

Some of the most interesting time-lapse clips usually include a lot more than just time-lapse sequences. A great story can blend music, full motion video, transitions, titles and texts, color grading and correction, the list goes on and on. Depending on which software application you use to create your time-lapse movies, editing and combining clips might come as a natural next step and might even be done in the same application. However it's likely that you will need to transition to a dedicated nonlinear video editor or NLE.

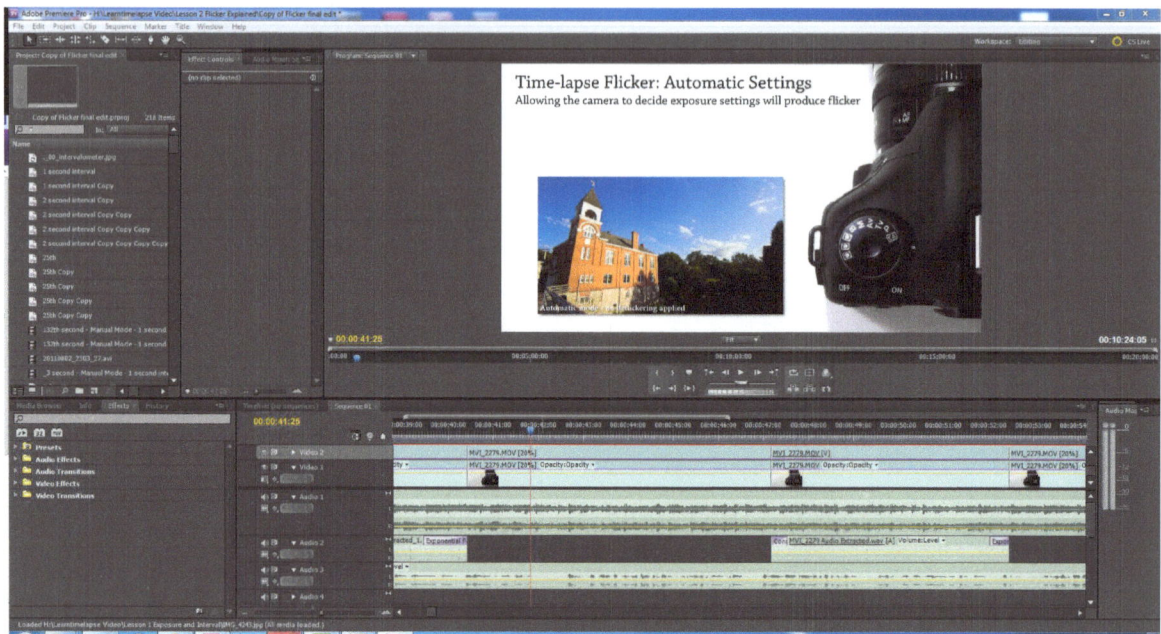

There are many NLEs on the market and while it would be foolish for me to recommend any single application I can implore you to do a little experimenting with the big guys. Most applications offer a 30 day full feature trial to give them a spin, Adobe Premier Pro or Elements, Final Cut Pro, Sony Vegas, etc. All very powerful applications that will place few limits on your creativity.

Alternatively if you are looking for something simpler (and cheaper) try out movie makers and home video editors designed for less intensive time-line operation like Apple iMovie or Avid Pinnacle Studio or Dazzle.

Resources will be your friend

No matter which application you choose I encourage you to run through a few tutorials as you begin to get your feet wet. For larger applications like After Effects, Premiere, or Final Cut it's well worth spending some time viewing tutorials on YouTube, Lynda.com or Videocopilot.net. You'll easily earn back the time spent not having to hunt for options and features through the creation of an efficient workflow. Get creative and have some fun with your videos.

WHERE TO FIND FREE MUSIC

It doesn't happen all the time but when a scene clicks with the right music, wow! It can really heighten the emotions. Pairing music and video is tough but finding good creative commons and free music to use is even tougher.

Here are a few of my favorite places to begin your search for royalty free and creative commons music both free for commercial and non-commercial use. Always double check the licensing before use. Learn more about creative commons licensing at creativecommons.org.

CC Mixter: ccmixter.org
Free Music Archive: freemusicarchive.org
Soundcloud: soundcloud.com
Music by Moby: mobygratis.com
Production Music: freeplaymusic.com
Public Domain Sounds: pdsounds.org
Internet Archive: archive.org

Searches for royalty free or stock music/sound effects will bring up a host of free and paid sites featuring all kinds of music genres, be sure to always read the fine print before downloading.

If you have a favorite song in mind but aren't sure if you can use it, send the artist an e-mail beforehand. Chances are they'll be happy to hear from a fan and be excited to be part of your project.

PLACES TO SHARE YOUR TIME-LAPSE MOVIES

One of the most rewarding aspects of time-lapse photography is receiving great feedback from viewers all over the world, and the best place to share your clips is probably the same place you go to watch them. Creating contributor accounts on YouTube and Vimeo is quick and easy and will allow simple sharing on Facebook, Twitter and through e-mail. While YouTube has by far the world's largest audience, Vimeo is more tailored for the video artist in all of us.

SELLING TIME-LAPSE MOVIES AS STOCK FOOTAGE

If you find yourself with a growing collection of great clips and you are looking to have a little fun in the stock photography/video space check out these sites. While you probably won't pay for your camera overnight, building your portfolio content overtime does add up. I'll share that I have had tons of fun earning hundreds from a very small portfolio of images and videos.

Overview of the photo and video microstock marketplace: microstockgroup.com

iStockphoto: istockphoto.com
Pond5: pond5.com

Fotolia: fotolia.com
Panthermedia: panthermedia.net

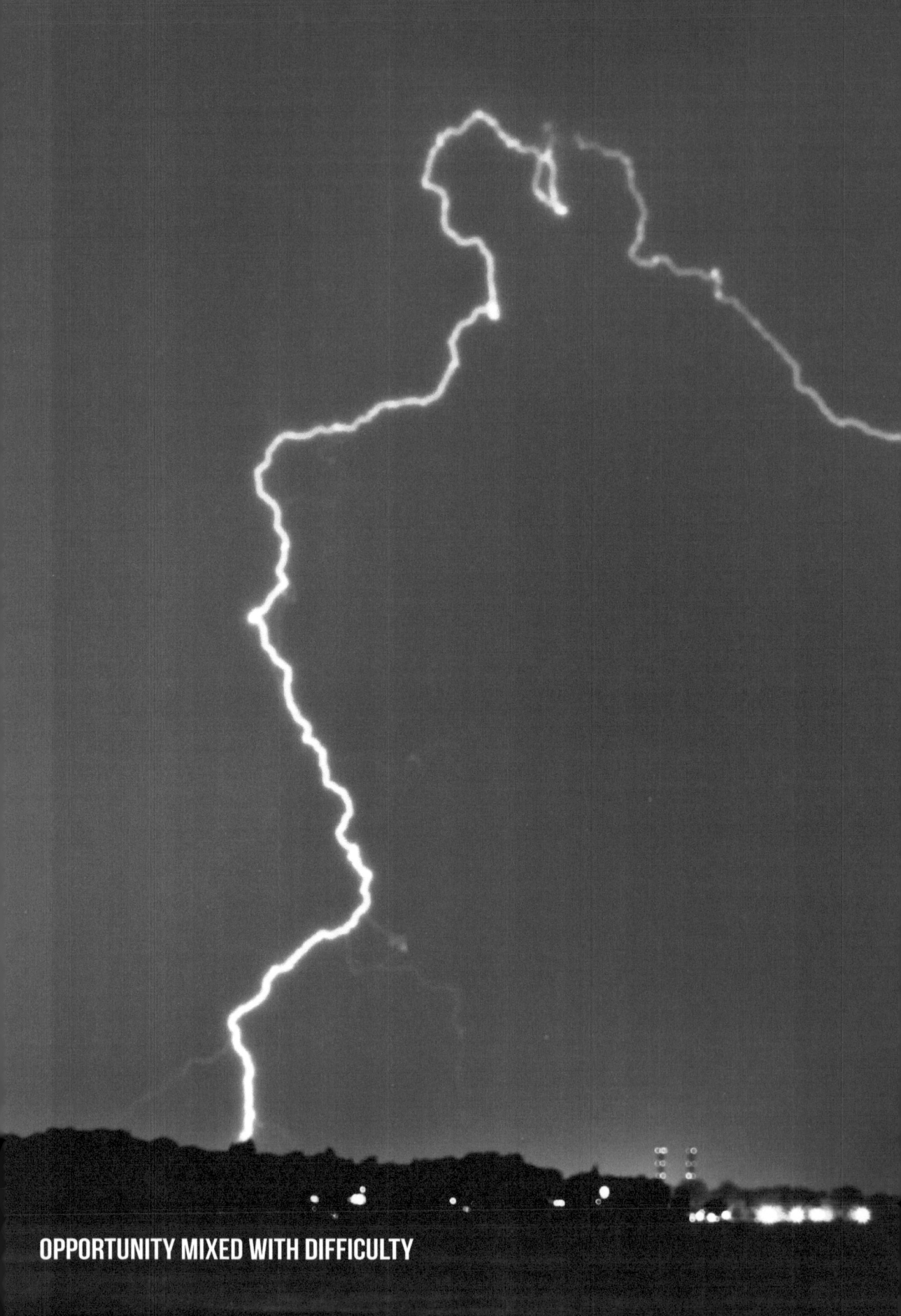

OPPORTUNITY MIXED WITH DIFFICULTY

6 TIME-LAPSE CHALLENGES

Experience will be your best guide and the best way to gain experience is to test the limits of your understanding.

I've organized four challenges to test our planning, shooting, and processing skills--and while we'll walk through a few introductory ways to accomplish each, I hope these scenarios spark questions and a fascination on how these techniques can be applied to different situations.

We'll attempt:

- An Astrolapse
- The Time-lapse Holy Grail
- High Dynamic Range (HDR) Time-lapse

We'll also take the first step in considering how motion control devices can be used to create amazing time-lapse effects.

Before we begin promise me one thing: that you'll come back, ask questions and share your works with the time-lapse community. "OK", you don't have to promise, but just know that the community thrives on the sharing new ideas, new technology and new ways to tell time-lapse stories.

We'd love to see you there.

"HOW LONG SHOULD YOU TRY? UNTIL."

- JIM ROHN

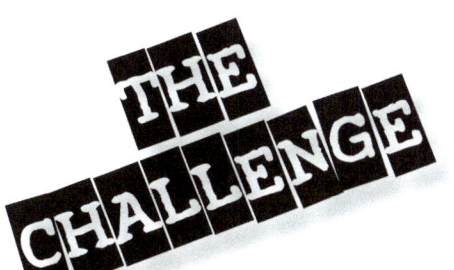

ASTROPHOTOGRAPHY TIME-LAPSE

"The treasures hidden in the heavens are so rich that the human mind shall never be lacking in fresh nourishment." - Johannes Kepler

Photographing a night scene is one of the most unique and rewarding subjects possible. Not only can we capture astronomical phenomena within a single long exposure but as time-lapse photographers we can experience many different celestial events within a single night's time-lapse.

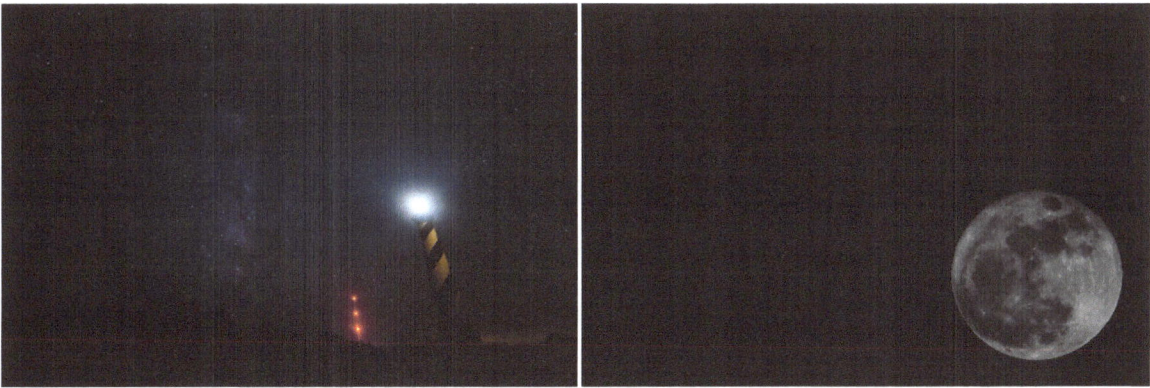

Achieving a good exposure for night photography requires a better than average understanding of exposure settings and exposure times. We'll walk through an example setup, share some tips and tricks, trudge through some trial and error and be amazed by the realm of new possibilities.

Time-lapse Challenge:

Night photography can be tough. Sometimes it's hard enough just to get away from the city lights to see the stars with a long exposure. It's also time consuming. No worries though, just blame the baggy eyes, cold toes, and run-ins with park police (who think you are doing everything *but* filming the night sky at 3AM) on me. I assure you that when you're humbled by your first shots of an alive night sky, it will all be worth it.

Here's our game plan:
1. Resources - Find dark sky and predict what's going to happen up there
2. Special Settings - Some tips on how to get good shots
3. Processing - Some special attention to noise reduction, etc.

Let's go.

RESOURCES FOR NIGHT SKY PHOTOGRAPHY

The first thing you need to do is find some night sky to shoot and believe it or not this could be more of a challenge than you think. Experiment with your home location but if you find that the sky is just too bright to capture stars at long exposures you will need to move (your camera that is). Here are a few good online sources to give you a head start. Don't forget to check with your local observatories or star gazing clubs as these folks can be a great resource (and loads of fun to join).

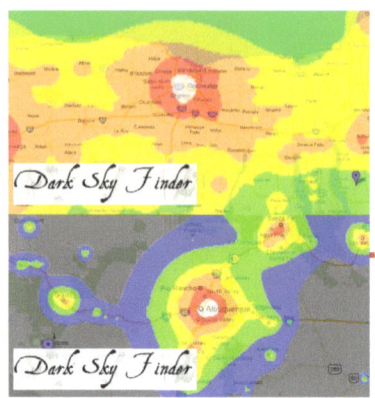

Dark Star Finder: jshine.net/astronomy/dark_sky/
Clear Sky Chart: cleardarksky.com/
International Dark Sky Association: http://www.darksky.org/DSDestinations
City lights map data: blue-marble.de/nightlights/2010

I live in Irondequoit, NY a suburb of Rochester, it's way too bright near my home (just borderline even if I shoot out over the lake). The map at left shows city light pollution high and low points. The cooler the color the darker the sky. Aim for at least a green zone if you can, you will be amazed of the difference. 35 miles East to the Sodus Bay area is a the nearest green zone for me. Just for comparison take a look at the midwest. Quite a difference, eh? Lucky bums.

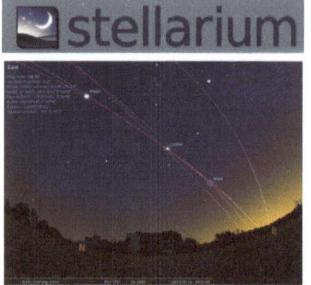

SKY MAPS

Knowing what's going on up there, where it's located, and when you will need to start shooting to capture it is very important. Any time-lapse of the night sky is pretty cool, but take this opportunity to learn a little more and maybe even target a specific constellation or the Milky Way.

Stellarium.org

Stellarium is one of the best tools for night sky time-lapse photographers. Enter your future location, date, and time, and press play to see essentially what you can capture over a long night. Pan around to see which direction is the best to shoot. I cannot recommend the resource enough.

SMARTPHONE APPS

Being able to chart the sky in real-time is amazing. I could spend hours on a clear night just playing with these. (It should be a default application on all smartphones).
Android: Google Sky Map **iPhone:** Skywalk

LONG EXPOSURES

Astrophotography is a big subject and is easily a book on its own, but that certainly won't stop us from exploring some fundamentals. Combining a good understanding of long exposures, lenses, sensor noise, and timing (while not forgetting that we are on a spinning platform) is all part of the challenge that makes this so rewarding.

Star Streaking and the rule of 600: There's one thing that really helps in astrophotography and that's a fast wide-angle lens. Here's why: to get good photographs of the stars and the Milky Way we'll need to collect a lot of faint light. Two things allow us to collect weak light: long exposure times and wide apertures. The wider the aperture the more light we can collect in less time. The smaller the aperture the longer we will need to keep the shutter open for the same exposure. If we keep the shutter open too long however the stars will begin to streak and instead of star points we get little lines (remember that whole spinning earth thing).

There are such devices that help us compensate for the earth's rotation but for most of us we will have to work with what we've got. Now depending on the focal length of your lens most of us will be able to shoot anywhere between 8 and 30 seconds without noticeable star trailing, but that's a pretty big spread. A good rule of thumb to calculate the max time you can shoot without streaking is to divide 600 by the effective focal length of your lens (taking into account a cropped or non-cropped sensor). For example: A wide-angle features a 10mm x 1.6 crop factor = 16mm effective focal length. 600/16= 37 seconds. A standard kit lens features a 28mm x 1.6 crop factor = 45mm effective focal length. 600/45= 13 seconds. Big difference. Using my wide angle lens and I should be able to shoot around 25-35 seconds maximum.

APERTURES AND SHUTTER SPEEDS:
A long shutter speed might be great but if our aperture isn't very wide we might not collect enough light. That's why very wide aperture lenses are called fast lenses, they collect a lot of light in a short amount of time. Fast lenses are also expensive. No worries if you don't have the ideal lens, you'll still get some great shots but if you get the chance think about renting a really wide and fast one next time you head out to a purple zone.

ISO:
Each camera's maximum ISO limits will be different and each camera's ability to produce good shots at its highest ISO will also be different. Our common ISO setting will probably be around 2000 or 3200. Don't worry if your camera maxes out at a lower number, you'll still be able to capture some stars. Always use the lowest possible ISO setting that will still allow the other exposure variables that you need. A higher ISO will result in more image noise.

LONG EXPOSURE TIME-LAPSE WORKFLOW:

A shot in the dark: Scouting

"It's dark, I can't see anything!" - Plan ahead when it's daylight but in a bind you can also use your camera for night vision and scope out a good composition. Setup your tripod, expose for 30 seconds, wide aperture, manual focus to infinity. Don't worry about getting a good shot just yet, move around until you find an interesting composition using your snapshots. Once you find a good scene, lock down you camera and tripod using extreme vigor.

Focusing on the stars is tough, here's how:

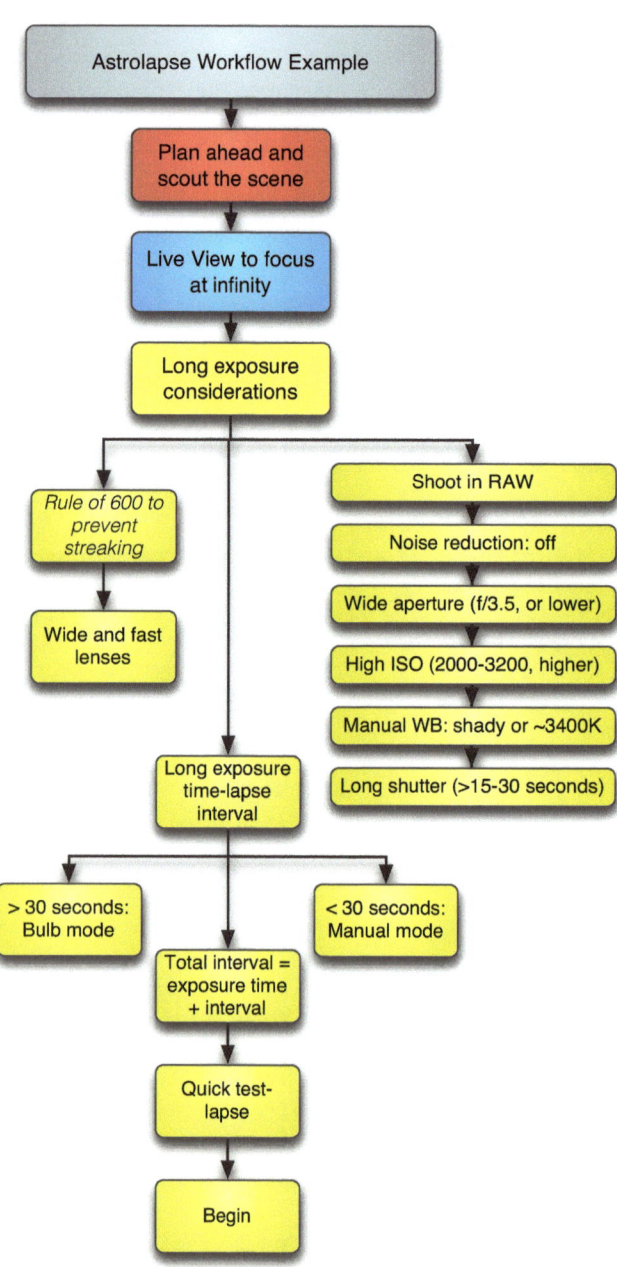

Switch your lens to manual focus and move the dial to infinity. This should get you close but you will need to make some fine adjustments. The problems is, there isn't anything visible in the viewfinder to adjust to.

Try this: Switch your camera into movie mode then press the zoom button to zoom in to 5x. Using the control stick to move left and right, pan around until you see a bright star (or planet) in the main center white box. If you still cannot see anything you may need to press the zoom button again and now pan at 10x. When you do locate a bright star (making sure you are now zoomed in to the maximum 10x) slowly manually adjust the focus on the lens until the hazy speck becomes as crisp of a point as possible.

You should now have a properly focused exposure. Disable Image Stabilization (IS) on the lens. Attach lens hood. **Shoot in RAW.** You will have many more options in post production. **Noise reduction:** OFF. We'll do any noise reduction in post production and don't have time for the camera to do it automatically for each photo.

Night sky photography is a balancing act. Our goal is to capture as many stars as we can while at the same not letting our exposures go so long we get star streaking or setting our ISO so high we get loads of image noise. You'll likely have to experiment with different exposure combinations based on the gear you have but here are a few starting recommendations:

Aperture: Wide open (Lowest f-stop) ~ f/2.8, f3.5, or lower
ISO: High. Start at 2000 or 3200 (but experiment higher, or lower)
White Balance: Manual setting, shady or custom around 3400 K

Shutter speed: Start at 30 seconds or the maximum time your focal length will allow without streaking the stars. Dial up or down to test the exposure. If you find yourself exceeding 30 seconds switch to camera bulb (B) mode and use intervalometer bulb timer to continue experimenting.

Setting your time-lapse interval.

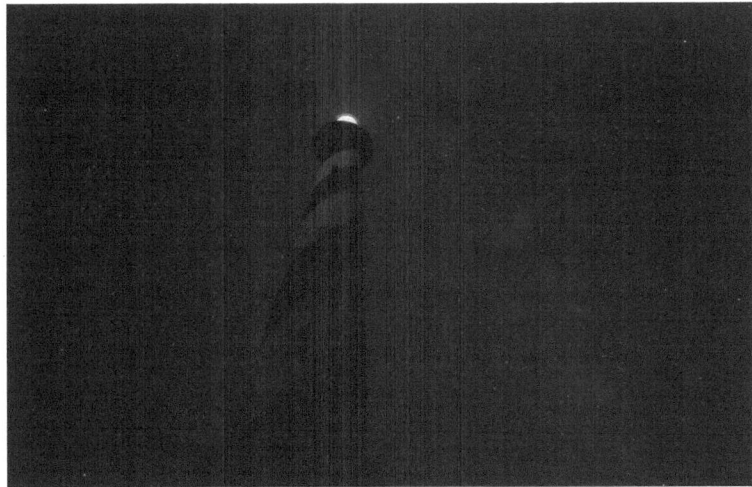

To see the stars and the Milky Way move across the sky you want to have only a 2 or 3 second interval between each 20 to 30 second long exposure. How we program this into the intervalometer depends if we've crossed that 30 second mark or not. We'll show two different interval examples on the next page, one using Bulb mode, the other manual mode.

POWER AND PROTECTION: You'll be shooting for several hours or more so you'll need a lot of juice (for both camera and photographer). Think about getting a 2-battery camera grip and two freshly charged batteries. Dew and moisture might also become an issue staying out all night so it may be a good idea to invest in a rain cover or just tape up a plastic bag with holes for each end of the camera. You might also want to look into a small lens heater to keep dew from forming on the end of the lens. Battery powered setups exist or just rubber band a hand warmer to the top of the lens.

Intervalometer programming for
BULB (>30S EXPOSURE):
Example: 32 second exposure value

Intervalometer programming for
MANUAL MODE (<30S EXPOSURE):
Example: 20 second exposure value

If you are setting up the shot to begin at some crazy hour for which you will not be awake, program the delay time in hours:minutes:seconds. Otherwise leave it at zero. For example a 2.5 hour delay:

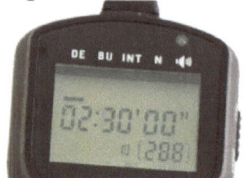

If you are setting up the shot to begin at some ungodly hour for which you will be awake, program the delay time to be zero

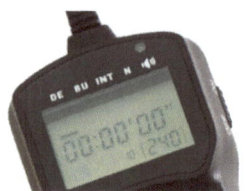

The number you program for bulb mode is essentially how long the intervalometer electronically holds the shutter open. Program the bulb (B) setting to 32 seconds.

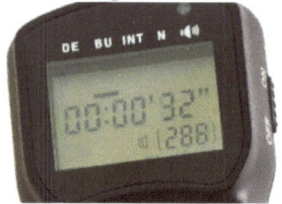

Since our exposure is < 30 seconds we can program that on the camera but we still may want to use bulb for more timing options. For this example program the (B) setting to zero.

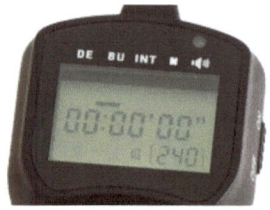

The total interval is the gap between shots that the camera will not be recording an image. Total interval time = exposure time + interval. I want a 2 second interval for example so my total interval is 32 + 2 = 34 seconds.

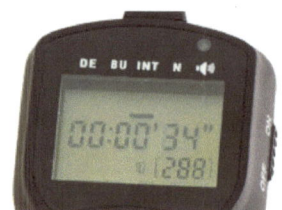

The total interval is the gap between shots that the camera will not be recording an image. Total interval time = exposure time + interval. I want a 2 second interval for example so my total interval is 20 + 2 = 22 seconds.

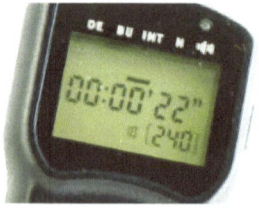

Last program the number of shots. I want a 10 second clip played back at 24 fps. 10 x 24 = 240 images minimum.

Last program the number of shots. I want a 12 second clip played back at 24 fps. 12 x 24 = 288 images minimum.

288 shots each taking 34 seconds = 219 minutes or about 3.5 hours.

240 shots each taking 22 seconds = 88 minutes or about 1.5 hours.

Record a quick test, format then, begin:
Start the time-lapse and let it run for 10 shots or so. Stop and scroll through the images on screen. Taking a few minutes to fix an error in the framing or exposure now, instead of 4 hours from now, is really worth it. Trust me. Format your card or delete the few shots then press start and relax.

If you are trying to keep your shot pristine make sure to keep all light way far away from your camera and the portion of the scene it can see. I have messed up a few shots thinking it was safe to check my cell phone only to have it show up as bright flickers reflecting from the trees and foreground. DO NOT underestimate what light a long exposure will pickup. Sometimes it is fun to have activity in the shot, lights in a tent, a campfire, etc, but if you want a clean shot be careful.

A few tips for batch processing astrophotography:: Here are a few special batch processing considerations for when you get home and are rested, wait... who am I kidding, for the same morning you get back. I do encourage you to check out some of the great processing resources by some amazing astrophotographers in the resource section.

Start with color:: Adjust your color temperature to create the night sky feel you are going for. In this example mine appeared too cool so I increased the temperature a bit and got a nice black night sky.

Saturation of individual colors:: Adobe Lightroom and Photoshop also allow you to quickly adjust the saturation of individual colors. I pulled a little of the distracting orange out of the city lights.

Exposure/brightness/contrast:: Play with the exposure and brightness settings to pull out a few dimmer stars. Adjust the contrast to darken up the background light levels.

Noise reduction/lens correction:: You'll likely want to adjust the noise reduction settings to make a much cleaner looking photo. Don't go too high or you'll start to loose some of those faint stars you worked so hard to capture. If your editor has a lens correction profile, consider applying the fixes.

Stacking, the next frontier: A stacking application merges multiple images and substantially reduces high ISO image noise while at the same time really enhancing detail. DSS (Deep Sky Stacker) is a free application and a good place to start. That's it for this challenge. Follow the normal export and render process.

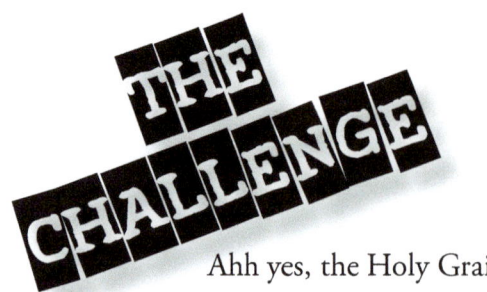

TIME-LAPSE FROM FULL DAY TO NIGHT

Ahh yes, the Holy Grail.

"Choose wisely, for while the true Grail will bring you life, the false Grail will take it from you."
- Grail Knight: Indiana Jones and the Last Crusade (1989)

This challenge is all about choosing... (wait for it) **"wisely"** but really all the methods discussed here get the job done. Each solution has a its own set of advantages, costs, and challenges but when you render that amazing sequence it all becomes worth it. The results can be mesmerizing.

Day-to-night or night-to-day continuous flicker-free shots are more achievable than ever before. Hardware and software tools, some of which have just recently been made available, will guide our path. We've got a lot to learn, so let's go!

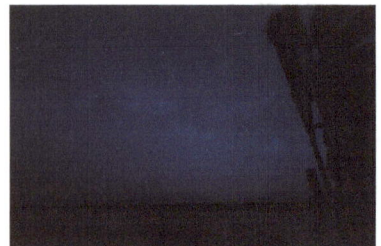
Stars and Milky Way

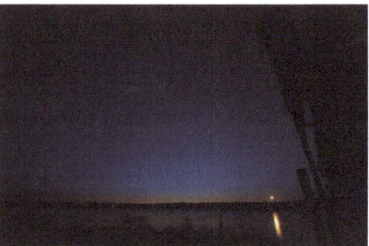
Brighter moon and Stars

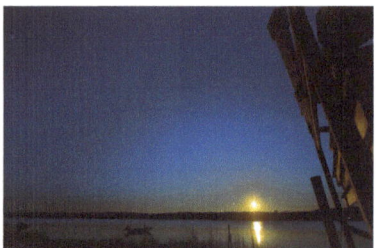
Sunrise

There is a huge difference in the amount of light between night and day, sometimes up to 20 stops or more. GBTimelapse, one of the solutions we'll explore shares this analysis of the problem: Since each stop is a factor of two, twenty-one stops or 2^{21}, literally means there are over *2 million times more light in the daytime than at night.*

Time-lapse Challenge: In order to span that wide of a gap our exposure settings must change *a lot*, but in order to create a flicker -free time-lapse they must also change very gradually. We learned all about the problems DSLRs face in the Chapter on Flicker and we'll face them all during this challenge.

Not only will the Holy Grail test your camera's control ability, it will also test your knowledge of the heavens above. Sunrise, sunset, nautical twilight, the moon, the Milky Way, depending on where you are on Earth and what time of year...all these factors must be balanced and planned for. Viewers will just think that you got lucky. For which you can reply, "It's not luck."

It all comes down to bulb ramping or "bramping"

Since your camera cannot make the flicker free gradual changes needed to cover such large changes in brightness we will need to assist it in one of two ways (or a combination):

Physical Bulb Ramping During Recording:

By utilizing a specialized external camera control device we can either program the gradual changes to occur over a set period of time or we can use a more advanced computer driven application to analyze brightness environment changes and gradually shift exposure settings up and down automatically.

Simulated Bulb Ramping After Recording:

A different approach would be to allow the camera to make abrupt exposure changes in aperture priority mode, even add and remove ND filters mid time-lapse, then use software and a little elbow grease to smooth out those jumps and achieve similar results.

The Tools:

GBTIMELAPSE: GRANITE BAY SOFTWARE

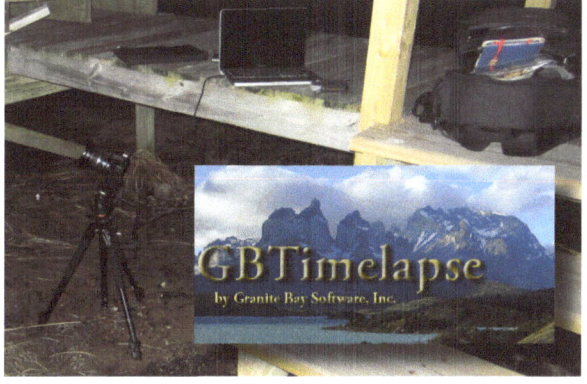

or

ADVANCED EXTERNAL CONTROLLERS

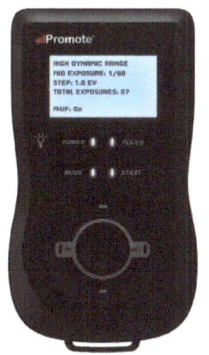
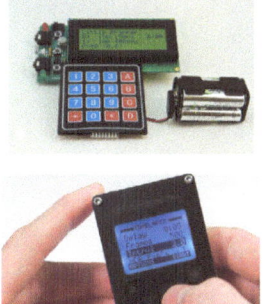

The Tools:

LRTIMELAPSE

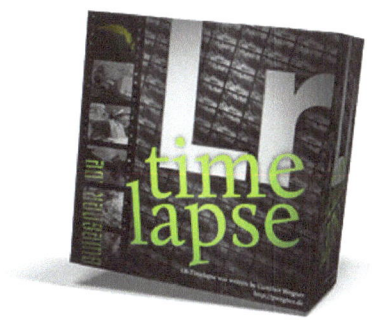

and

ADOBE LIGHTROOM

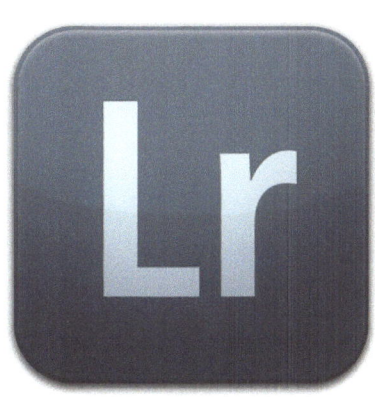

Let's stamp down a few terms:

Bulb mode: We've used it before but to cement in understanding it's the only camera mode where the camera doesn't know the exposure duration ahead of time. Traditionally the shutter would remain open for as long as the photographer held down the shutter button, but for DSLRs this can also be controlled electronically.

Bulb ramping: This is where the solution to the Holy Grail lies. We will be varying, ever so gradually, the length of time the camera shutter remains open, much more gradually than the camera can do on its own in normal modes such as shutter priority or aperture priority.

Interval ramping: As our exposure times increase the time-lapse interval will also need to increase, otherwise a collision will occur and we will end up skipping shots. Some of the solutions we discuss incorporate interval ramping allowing for long exposure night shots and short exposure day shots.

Planning your Holy Grail attempt: Here's a fast recipe to plan for both night and day activity
1. Use Google maps/Google earth to locate the coordinates of possible shooting positions
2. Enter the coordinates in Stellarium night sky simulator and change the viewing direction and time of day to find and plan for interesting activity
3. Fast forward in time to find out where and when the Sun or Milky Way will rise/set
4. Jot the times down and get out there plenty early to set up and test

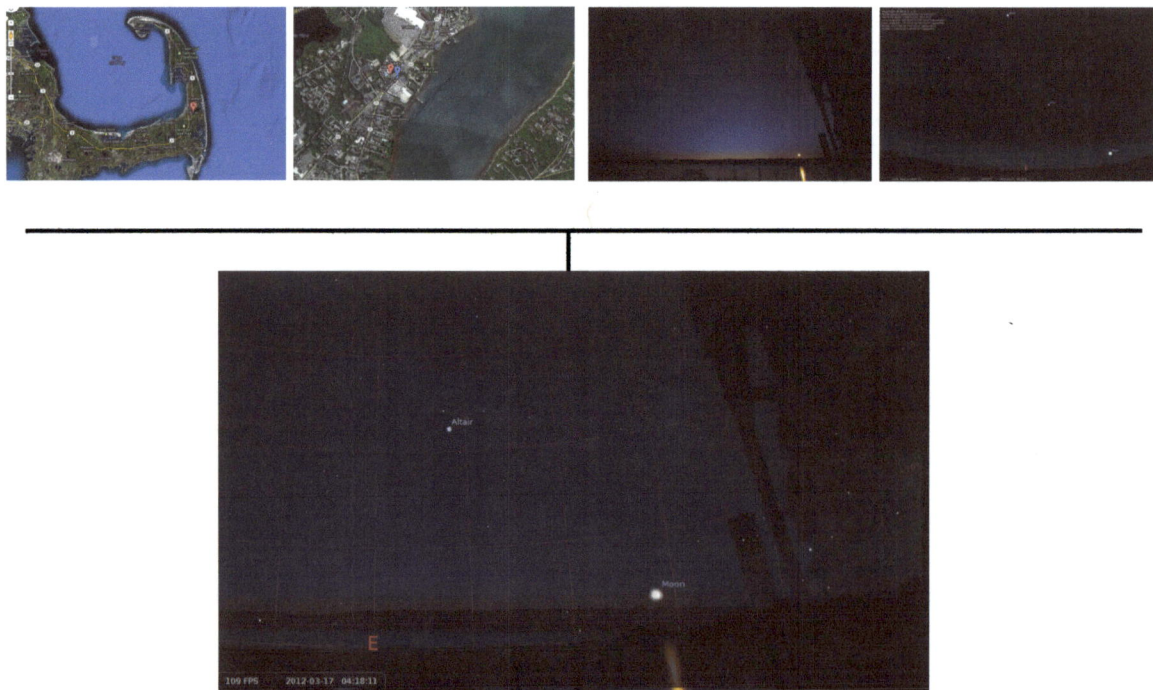

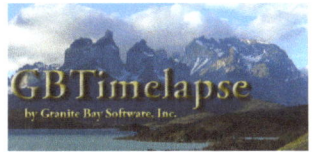

TIPS GBTIMELAPSE

GBTimelapse by Mike Posehn at Granite Bay Software is a very powerful time-lapse tethering application for Windows that gives you phenomenal automatic control of your exposures. It's fairly easy to use and if you can manage to lug a laptop out into the field and keep it powered, produces amazing results.

Featuring scripted and automatic exposure ramping capabilities for time-lapse and HDR photography as well as new motion control capabilities for time-lapse dollies, GBTimelapse is pretty incredible. I've had great success with the application and am amazed by its features. GraniteBaySoftware.com (~$99)

What is the workflow: This challenge is all about many gradual exposure changes over extreme variances in lighting conditions. One way to use GBTimelapse is to combine the use of ND filters (affixed at the beginning in bright daylight, then removed as the sun sets) and initiate it's automatic brightness control feature AutoRamp. GBTimelapse will adjust the exposure variables smoothly overtime and also compensate for the use and removal of the ND filters once certain programmed exposure limits have reached. The result is a smooth luminance curve over the length of the time-lapse sequence even with abrupt physical camera changes and the changing of aperture and ISO settings.

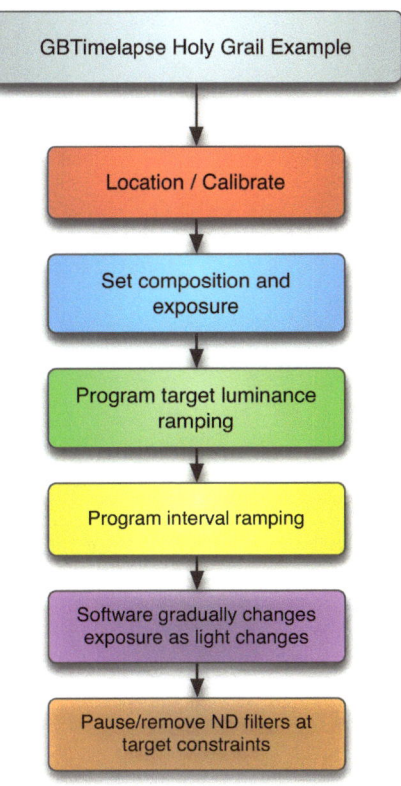

Input GPS coordinates (optional) to automatically calculate rate of brightness changes. Calibrate ND filters and lens following the software's instructions.

Create your composition, focus manually and switch to camera bulb mode.

Set exposure and time-lapse interval parameters for sequence (max and minimum autoramping settings) and the initial shot, ISO, aperture, color temp, etc. as well as when the software should make a shift (ex. shift aperture when bulb time gets to 1 sec.).

Set a target luminance for GBTimelapse to maintain (a good baseline is 100).

Begin time-lapse, GBtimelapse will gradually change exposure settings to keep the image near the target luminance. Monitor occasionally and remove filter when programmed constraint has been met (wait for exposure to end, uncheck filter in software, it will then pause and allow you to quickly remove it).

ADVANCED INTERVALOMETERS:

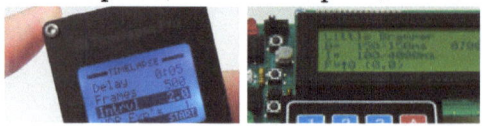 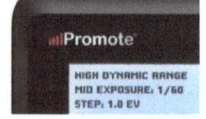

Time-lapse+, Little Bramper (Canon only), Promote Controller, these devices and others allow for that most important Holy Grail achieving feature: ramping.

What is the workflow:

Just like we discussed before it's still all about small and gradual changes over time, but unlike GBTimelapse and it's ability to collect luminance feedback from the camera, advanced intervalometers execute ramping based on a programmed script we configure ahead of time or manually change by allowing us to dial up or down exposure variables. Think prediction or reaction instead of automation. Depending on the device you use each will have a different configuration and control process but at a high level each device's workflow looks similar to this:

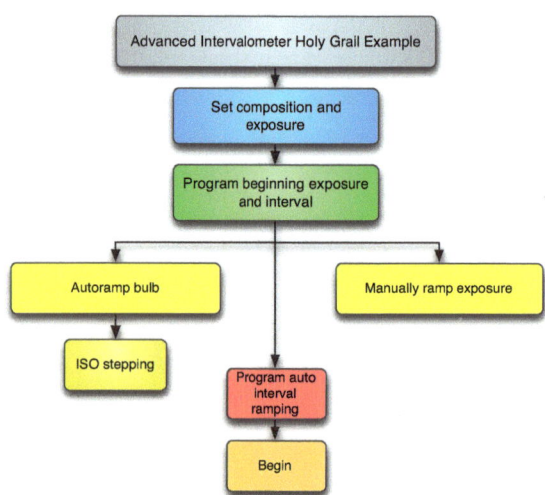

1.   Set composition and exposure:
Depending on your device you'll probably need to take a few trial photos. Either in M mode (Promote) or B mode (Little Bramper) set the desired aperture and make note of a good exposure with a shutter speed that's less than 1/20th of a second (bulb mode limit). You might need ND filters to get low enough. This will be your initial and most important setting/commodity.

2. Program initial exposure:

Switch to camera bulb mode and program the initial exposure based on test shots. Set all other settings manually. Manual focus.

Some devices allow **optional manual bramping control** throughout your sequence. If this is the case, turn your histogram view on and preview each photo as you snap away over time. As it becomes too dark or too bright ramp up or down the exposure using the controller.

Most devices also allow (some exclusively) programmed bramping. After you set the initial exposure program how fast and how significantly the device should change the settings over a given time. For example sunset and sunrises are best photographed with a +2Ev or -2EV change per 10 minutes respectively. Programmed ISO- stepping (Little Bramper) can also be used to increase the your bulb ramping range. Set the interval to either ramp automatically after a set number of shots or configure manual interval control.

LRTIMELAPSE AND LIGHTROOM:

While a correction solution and not a preventative solution, LRTimelapse will allow us to correct for flicker and exposure changes we make manually (bumping up or down exposure settings by hand, or adding or removing ND filters) throughout the sequence.

What is the workflow? We can get pretty darn close to the Holy Grail by shooting changing scenes in aperture priority (AV) mode and then correcting the resulting flicker by using LR-Timelapses and Lightroom. We can even add or subtract ND filters throughout our sequence and then in post production smooth out the big (very big) exposure jumps to a pretty acceptable level.

Shooting the time-lapse: Attach one or more ND filters to the camera and choose aperture priority mode. Lock down all other settings (white balance, ISO, etc.) and enable image previews so you can view each image as it's taken.

As the sun begins to set and the light fades the shutter speed length will increase to keep the same exposure value. As the shutter continues to get longer and before it gets too close to our interval time (or at a time you see fit), pause the time-lapse and remove an ND filter. The shutter speed will now shorten substantially to compensate for the added light that the removed filter is no longer blocking. The camera now has more "room" to adjust the shutter again in the same fashion. You can repeat this method with a second ND filter or by changing ISO values instead, each time pausing and quickly making the change before resuming.

Correcting the big jumps: We'll follow a similar workflow as we did for standard sequence correction with LRTimelapse, however we'll need to pay special attention to those big physical changes like that ND filter removal ISO adjustment.

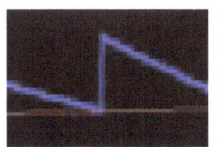 Follow the normal LRTimelapse transitional editing workflow except now lookout for steep brightness jumps in the LRTimelapse preview windows (look for steep jumps in the blue brightness graph). Use the preview slider to find the exact frame where the change occurs then create one keyframe just before and one keyframe just after the jump. When you are working your way through adjusting your keyframe images in Lightroom and you get to one of these "before and after" keyframe sets pause and make some meticulous adjustments.

Using your exposure adjustments match the "after" keyframe as best you can to the "before" (setting both up in the lightroom side-by-side preview is helpful). If you can make a very close match, LRTimelapse will fade away that big jump.

THE CHALLENGE

HDR TIME-LAPSE

"You cannot depend on your eyes if your imagination is out of focus."
- Mark Twain

Your eyes can see around 18 stops of dynamic range (after a minute or two of adjustment), which is a pretty wide range brightness. Your camera on the other hand can only pick up roughly 10-12 stops of dynamic range, almost half the range that your eyes can see. Have you ever taken a photo of a dynamic scene and then later been disappointed that the image appears flat and dull? HDR photography combines several different exposures of the same scene to allow us to capture much more detail than we could in a single photo.

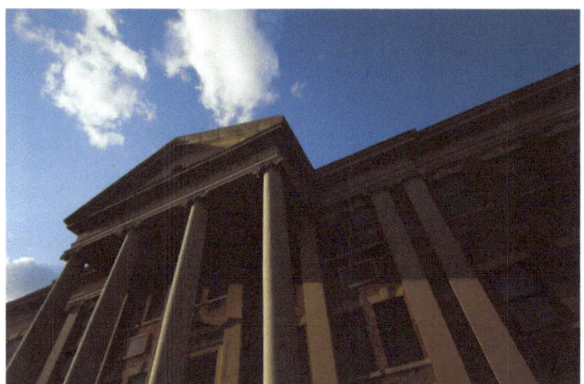 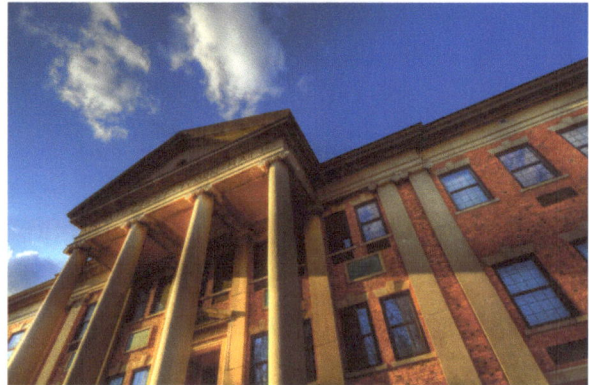

HDR effects can be subtle or they can be surreal. You either like them or you don't. Personally I think the effect can be phenomenal in some situations and I've used it to make a dull or ordinary scene come alive with interest. Now maybe that's my fault for shooting a dull scene, but I think if it adds to the shot, if it helps you show what's there, if it adds interest, well, isn't that what it's all about? HDR works for me.

Time-lapse Challenge:

Getting HDR photography right can be challenging and HDR time-lapses can take that challenge and multiply it. We'll talk about two approaches you can take to achieve the HDR effect and what you need to do to batch process (preferably overnight, as this is a computer cruncher) hundreds of photos into tone adjusted HDR images.

Here's our game plan:

1. Settings - Two different ways to achieve the HDR effect: single RAW photos and multiple RAW photos
2. Processing - Tips for HDR batch processing
Let's go.

Single vs Multiple Exposure HDR

TIPS HDR imaging was originally used for 3D image processing but is now in full force as an effect for regular photographers.

Normally an HDR image is created by taking multiple exposures, usually three but sometimes up to nine, and blending them together into a 32 bit image. We then take that 32 bit image and tone map or cherry pick colors and detail and bring that huge space back down to something our screens and printers can handle in the 8 or 16 bit world.

HDR time-lapse using single exposures

The power of RAW images allow us to take one photo and expose it differently multiple times then combine those exposures back together to form a 32 bit image. While there's a debate wether or not you can get a true HDR image from a single photo, this pseudo-HDR technique provides pretty good results with much less work requiring one photo per HDR frame instead of three.

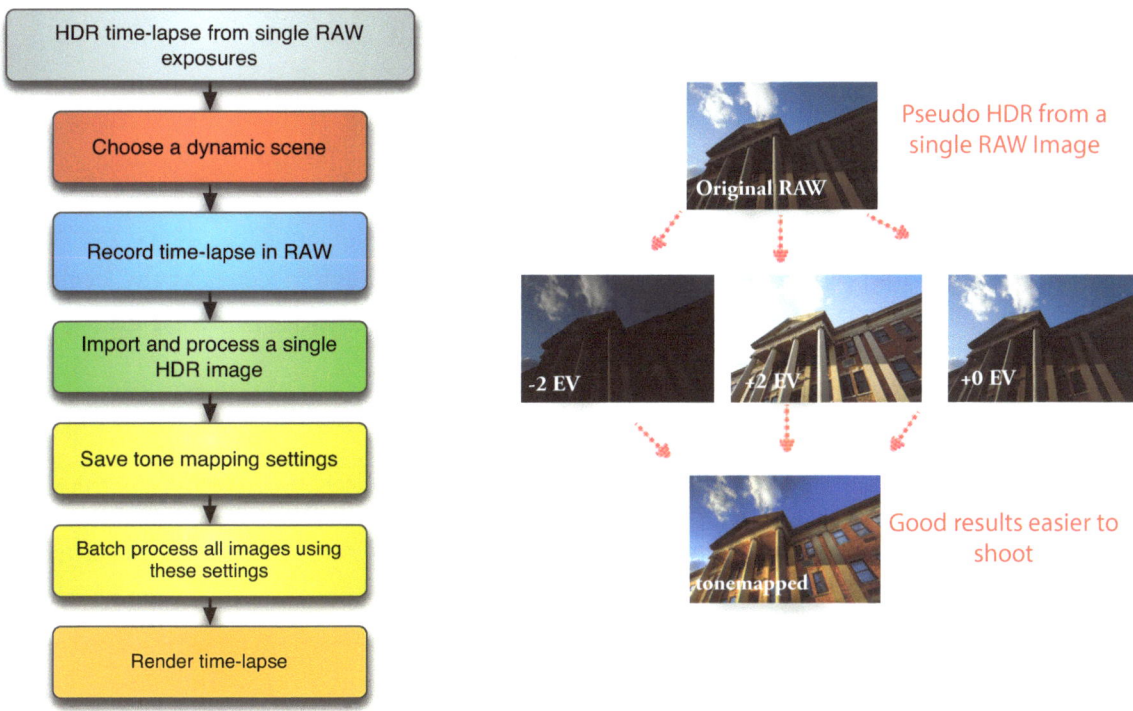

Since we are only concerned with regular old RAW images you'll follow the same setup as you normally would for any other time-lapse scene.

HDR really shines when you have lots of contrasting light and shadows and I particularly like how it pulls the detail out of materials like wood and stone. It offers great flexibility to capture amazing foreground detail while still showing the contrast and color in the sky. We'll take a look at multiple exposure HDR then jump into how to process both methods using Photomatix.

HDR TIME-LAPSE USING MULTIPLE EXPOSURES:

The full HDR effect is best done with multiple exposures. Since we are combining multiple photos taken over a short period of time, one right after the other, we have to be very sensitive about what movement is taking place in the scene. Since the world doesn't stop to allow us to snap three perfectly still photos sometimes parts of our images can appear too blurry or ghosted.

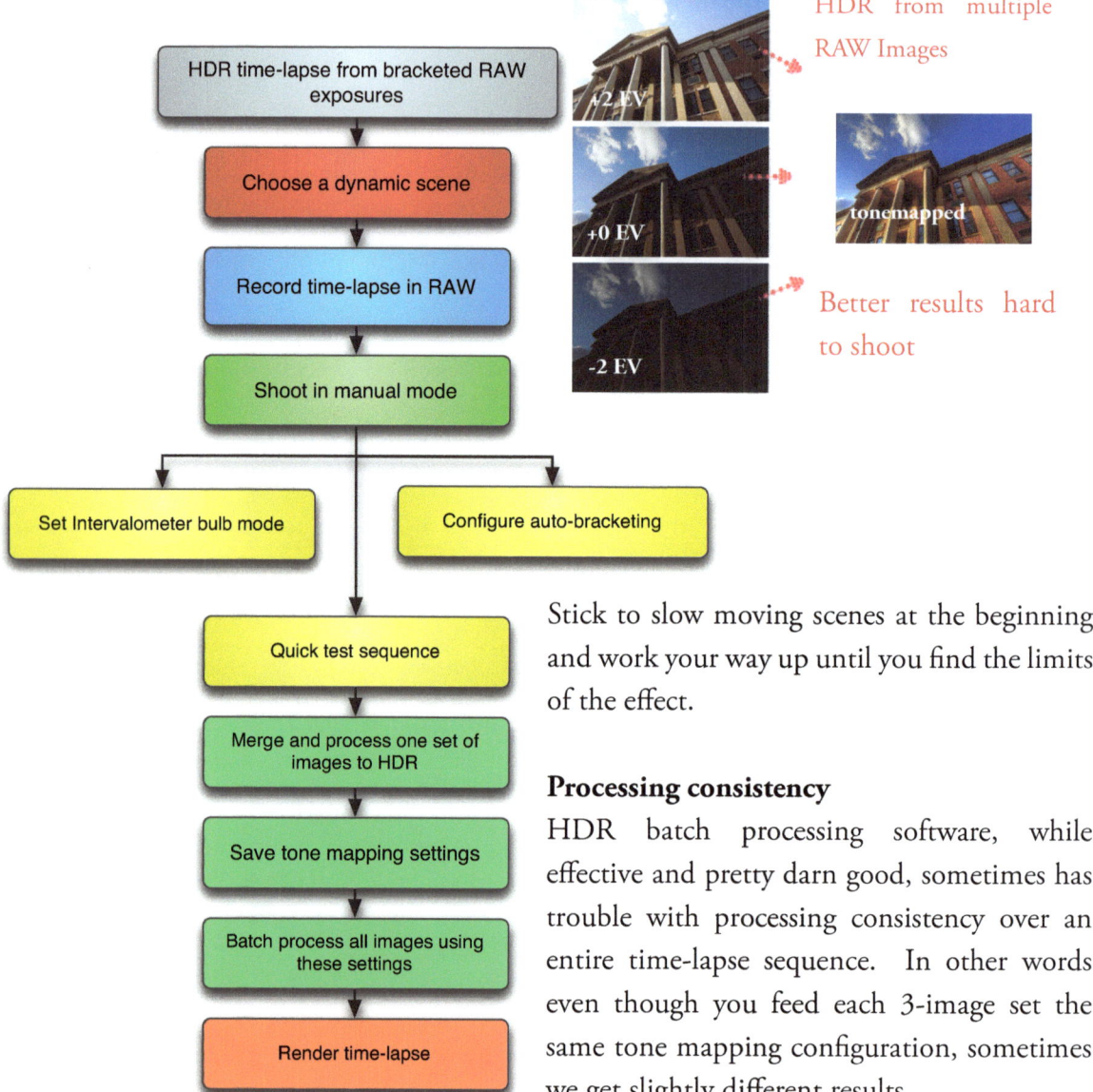

Stick to slow moving scenes at the beginning and work your way up until you find the limits of the effect.

Processing consistency
HDR batch processing software, while effective and pretty darn good, sometimes has trouble with processing consistency over an entire time-lapse sequence. In other words even though you feed each 3-image set the same tone mapping configuration, sometimes we get slightly different results.

We might also experience a similar problem with single batch processing. In short, be prepared to do some deflickering in post production to get the brightness we want.

Let's take a closer look at how to set up image bracketing while recording images at set intervals:

MULTIPLE EXPOSURE HDR CAMERA SETTINGS

Here are a few starting point exposure and set up recommendations for a multiple exposure HDR time-lapse.

1. Manual Mode: Configure manual exposure settings (White balance, ISO, aperture, focus). **2. RAW image format.**

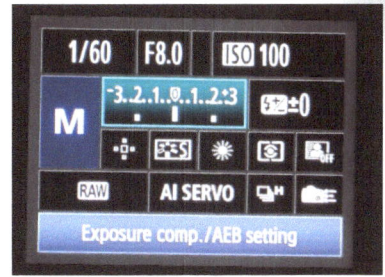

3. Set up Automatic Exposure Bracketing (AEB):
Configuring exposure bracketing will tell the camera to take three different photos with three different exposure values in quick succession. I recommend a 2 stop (+2EV, -2EV) exposure bracket to begin as this should capture a good range of light in most situations.

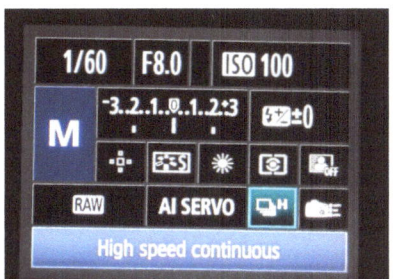

4. Select continuous shooting mode: You'll need the camera to take its three shots in rapid succession with one shutter trigger.

5. Programming the intervalometer:
Just like setting up our timer for a long exposure in bulb mode, we'll have a similar task when shooting multiple HDR exposures. Start by taking a quick test shot: Hold down the shutter trigger until all three photos finish. About how long did that take? 2 seconds, 3 seconds? This will be our bulb time.

Bulb setting:: This number simulates us pressing the shutter trigger and will need to allow sufficient time for all three photos to complete.

Interval Setting:: Our total interval time will be the time we programed for bulb mode plus the delay we want between brackets. For example if it takes the camera a little over 2 seconds to bracket all three shots and I am shooting a scene with a moving cloudscape, my interval might be 3 seconds for the shots + 2 seconds for the interval = 5 seconds total interval time.

Number of shots:: Start by taking a quick test time-lapse and program the timer to record 3 or 4 brackets. This will allow us to test if our bulb settings are correct and that the timing allows for all three photos.

Clear the test photos and program the actual desired number of shots. Don't forget for each frame of desired video we need to take three photos so make sure the memory card is able to handle the extra burden. That's it. Your camera will continue taking three or more photos for every time-lapse frame. Now begins the fun part: Batch HDR Processing.

PROCESSING THE IMAGES

There are many different ways to process HDR images and various strategies from basic to advanced. We'll walk through a quick batch process using a common HDR processor, Photomatix Pro, but no matter which application you use the workflow should be very similar:

Photomatix by HDRsoft (~$99 use code "learntimelapse" for a 15% discount) - hdrsoft.com
HDR Expose from Unified Color (~$149) - unifiedcolor.com
Photoshop from Adobe (~$199) photoshop.com

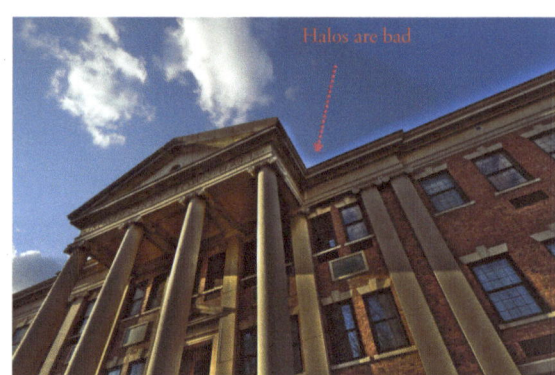

We'll walk through some basic tone mapping adjustments for your images, but it's perfectly OK to not necessarily know what each setting does and relying instead on just tweaking until you like the way it looks. Play with the settings until you find something that's interesting.

Know that there isn't really a right way or a wrong way to process your images, but there are a few things to look out for. Excessive halo effects are generally something to avoid. Keep an eye on the image as a whole to make sure what you are doing still makes sense and isn't going too flat. Too much detail sometimes takes away from the photo so keep in some shadows and highlights.

BATCH PROCESS A SINGLE IMAGE USING PHOTOMATIX

The HDR processing application will use your RAW image and essentially "expose" it multiple times to simulate the differences in brightness and tones then allow you to map them into a pseudo HDR image.

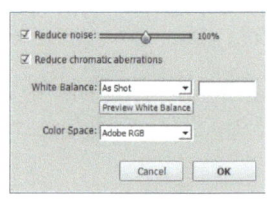

Step 1: Launch Photomatix and **open the single RAW file.**
Step 2: Create the initial merged image
Start with the initial default import processing settings (we'll look at other options when we merge 3 photos).

Photomatix will create the merged pseudo-HDR and allow you to configure tone mapping settings in one of two ways. The first labeled simply "tone mapping " takes our big 32 bit space of color and cherry picks colors placing them into a normal 16 or 8 bit space to print and use. The second, "exposure fusion", doesn't do full tone mapping effect, but instead stacks layers and changes blend modes for more of a normal photographic look. Don't worry too much about deciphering mode specifics but rather understand that you have a few different sets of options when it comes to creating the HDR effect.

You'll now be presented with a preliminary merged image that's ready for your tweaking using the HDR adjustments panel. While there are many different "looks", styles, and strategies for HDR processing (see the resource section), we'll simply walk through a few common adjustments to really bring out the detail in our images.

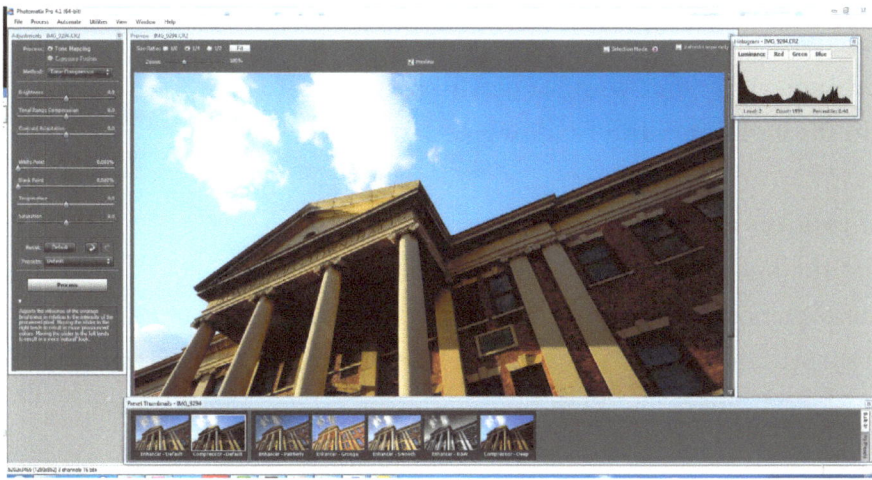

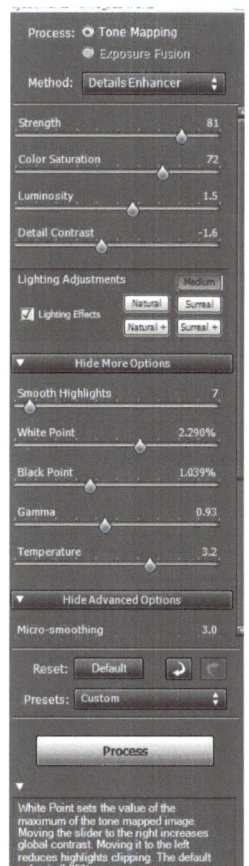

Step 3: Tone Mapping Adjustments

Most of our changes will take place inside the Tone Mapping Process. If at any time you need an explanation for what a setting does, use the tool tips shown below the process button and play with the sliders to get a feel for what each setting does. Here's a quick overview of what some of the options control:

Strength: Controls the strength of HDR effect (more color/detail/tones)

Color Saturation: Default is usually a good place to start, too much and you really exaggerate the HDR effect

Luminosity: Overall brightness but not uniformly, brightness of shadows

Detail contrast: Small adjustments to contrast creating that HDR detail effect

Lighting adjustments: Smooths areas of contrast (good for reducing halos in moderation). Changes the overall lighting look. You can also use different lighting algorithms by checking the lighting effects mode box.

Smooth highlights: Smooth out transitions from high to low contrast (watch your skies helps to remove the black undersides of clouds)

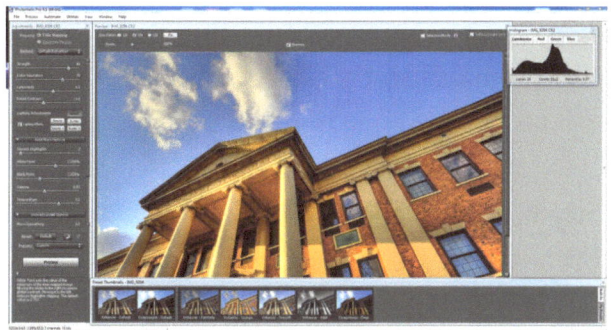

White Point: Adds brightness, spreads tones out across image

Black Point: Adds contrasts strengthens blacks

Gamma: Brightens middle tones

Temperature: white balance adjustment

Take a look at some of the advanced options but these are less commonly used:

Microsmoothing: control fine contrast details, reduce noise

Saturation in the highlights and shadows: add or drain colors

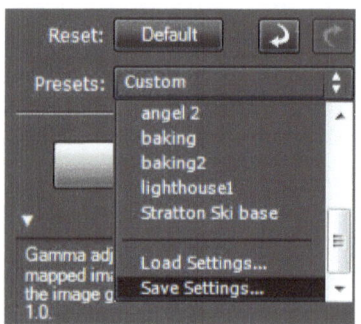

Step 4: Save your tone adjustment settings

Once you get the image the way you like it we will want to apply these changes to all our images in the sequence. Select "Presets: > Save As" and create a name to remember this configuration. Your settings are now saved into an instructions file that we can apply to the others. Now close out of this image and head back to the main Photomatix screen.

Batch Single Photos

Step 5: Setup the batch process

Choose "Batch Single Photos". Navigate to your time-lapse folder that contains only the RAW

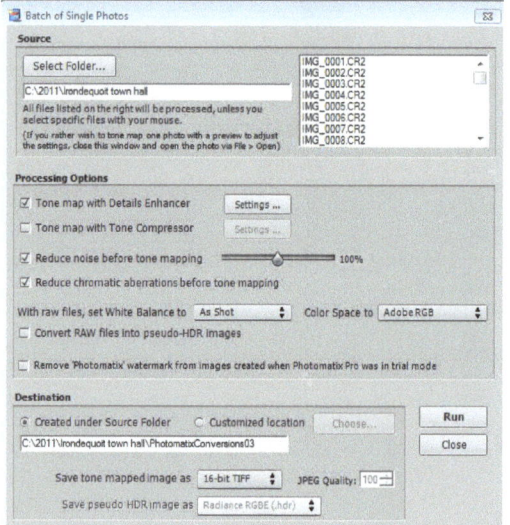

sequence you want to batch process. All files in the folder will be processed unless you select a specific subset.

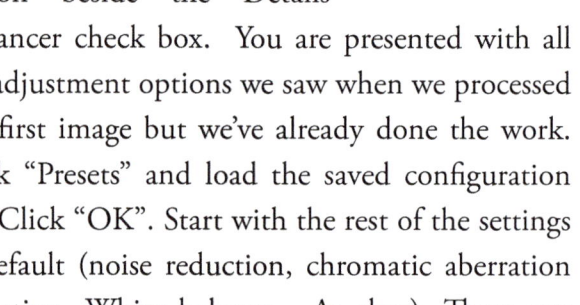

Now choose the "Settings" button beside the Details Enhancer check box. You are presented with all the adjustment options we saw when we processed our first image but we've already done the work. Click "Presets" and load the saved configuration file. Click "OK". Start with the rest of the settings at default (noise reduction, chromatic aberration reduction, White balance - As shot). These can come in handy if we experience certain problems.

Select a new source folder, usually within the same time-lapse folder and choose to export as a JPEG, 8-bit or 16-bit TIFF. 16-bit TIFF is the maximum quality settings for your images but will take a little more time and significantly more hard drive space.

Step 6: Click run and go to bed: This will take a long time and eat up your computer resources. I wouldn't try to anything else processor intensive (like rendering).

BATCH PROCESS MULTIPLE IMAGES:

Combining several different exposure into a single tone mapped HDR image will produce better results. You'll be able to capture more detail and experience less noise while doing so. We talked about some of the added challenges to capture the time-lapse but once you have your images batch processing is a cinch.

Most of the steps for multiple image HDR mirror the single image workflow with a few exceptions, here's where they differ:

Step 1: Drag your multiple exposure images into Photomatix

It's important that you select your three matching exposure images. The easiest way I've found to do this is to select the images in a browser like Bridge for example, and drag them into the Photomatix icon, that way I'm not trying to remember file names and numbers as I hunt through folders. Choose merge to HDR and confirm the three photos it will be using.

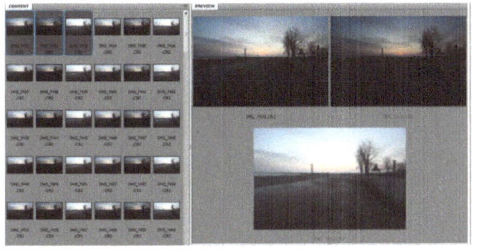 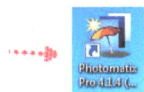 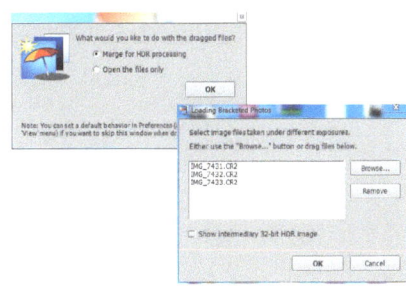

Step 2: Select preprocessing options

The default settings will work for most situations however you may need to explore alignment and noise reduction options if you find your results are lacking.

Photomatix will now merge the images into and 32-bit HDR space, reduce noise and chromatic aberrations.

Step 3: Make and save tone mapping adjustments

Just like we did for the single image HDR make some adjustments until the image looks they way you like it. Save those settings to a configuration file.

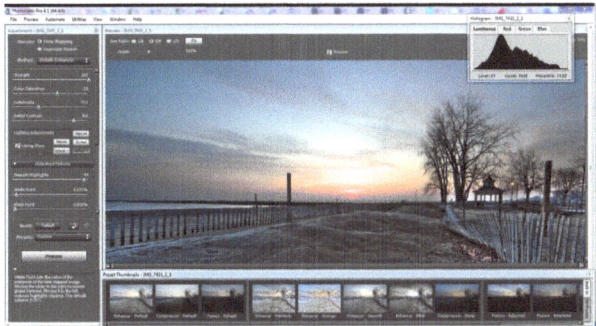 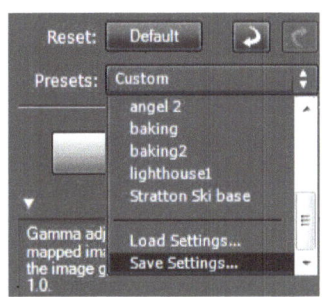

Step 4: Configure batch processing options for bracketed exposures

Select "Automate > Load Bracketed Photos".

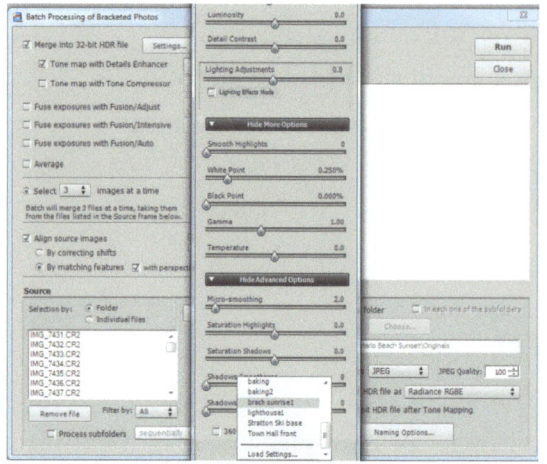

Check "Merge to 32-bit HDR file", "Tone map with Details Enhancer", and click the "Settings" button to load the saved configuration presets just like we did in single batch processing.

Make sure that the number of brackets is selected, in this case three images.

Under source select the folder that contains the bracketed images.

Double check your destination folder and processed image file types (TIFF for Lightroom/ LRtimelapse and Aftereffects rendering, JPEG for VirtualDUB or Timelapse Assembler) and quality settings.

Step 5: Run and go to bed.

This will take even longer than batch processing single images so I'd suggest overnight processing

CREATING THE HDR TIME-LAPSE MOVIE

We've only scratched the surface of HDR image processing but hopefully we can easily see how those settings can be applied automatically (although painstakingly from a computer processing perspective) across all images in our time-lapse sequence.

The next step is to take these tone mapped files and use them as our input images for a time-lapse video. We will likely see a little flicker due to the HDR processing algorithms but that should easily be corrected with deflickering software.

Experiment with the image processing settings and even with the HDR processing applications themselves. You'll find a good match of settings that will work for each individual sequence but it may take a few tests to get it right.

I have a lot of fun with HDR time-lapse and I encourage you to try it out.

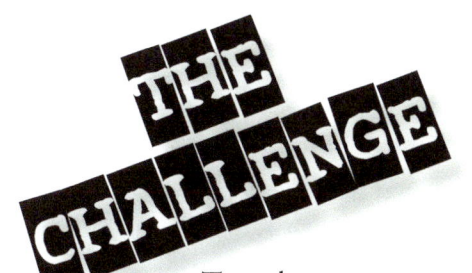

TIME-LAPSE MOTION CONTROL

Time-lapse cameras used to be stuck on stationary tripods...

"I'm a storyteller - that's the chief function of a director. And they're moving pictures, let's make 'em move!" --Howard Hawks

...but the last few years have shown incredible advances in the field of controlled camera movement, so much so that the average photographer can now afford movement devices that were once only available to big movie houses. We're talking precise panning (left and right), tilting (up and down), and dolly movements (smooth mounted movement along a track) at exact programed intervals over long periods of time. Here's a quick example of one form of time-lapse movement:

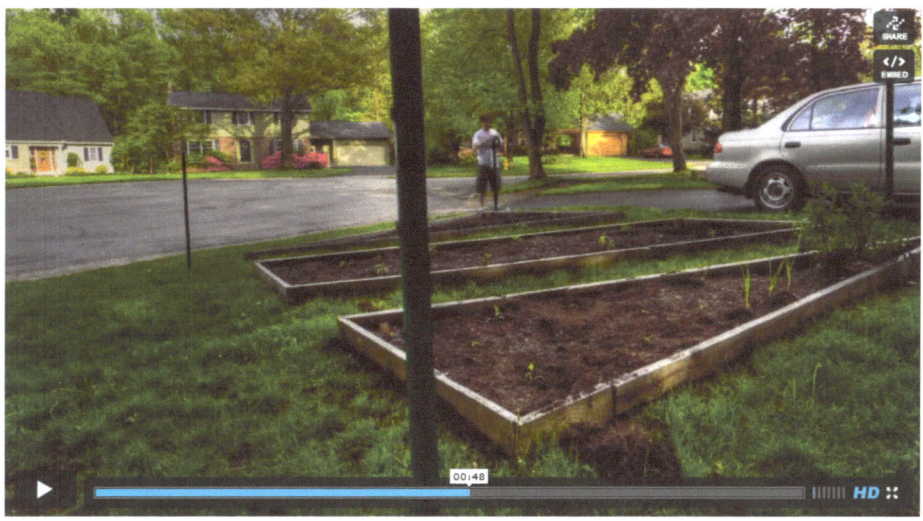

Time-lapse Challenge: This challenge involves learning what devices exist within the motion controlled space, how they can be used to add interest to our shots, and whether or not they should become part of your advanced time-lapse workflow.

Word of warning: some of these are expensive and once you start researching and the creative juices start flowing, well... let's just get started.

TIME-LAPSE DOLLY MOVEMENT

Dolly motion shots can add multiples of interest by highlighting components of a scene's unchanging foreground and the larger time-altered background. Some of the most popular time-lapse clips feature this kind of extreme moving contrast in almost every shot. By moving the camera slowly from left to right on a horizontal track or flipping the track system almost vertically to instead change the elevation of the camera, we can highlight stationary foreground objects in incredible ways.

Take this fun Christmas baking clip for example. I wanted to show the a cookie batter covered mixer in the foreground while my family and I toiled away making cookies in the background. A mixer in the corner of the shot might get boring after a few seconds, but moving the camera so the mixer enters and exits the field of view was much more interesting. Take a look:

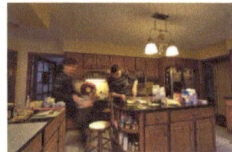 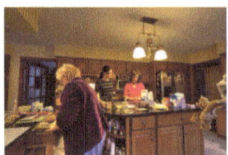 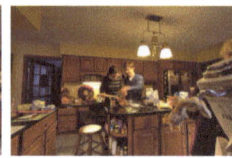 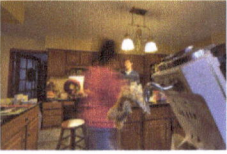 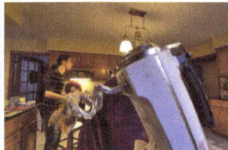

A time-lapse dolly system consists of a long track, usually 3 or 6 feet long, a small motor, battery pack and a programmable controller device that allows for movement of the entire camera between shots (move, camera takes a shot, move again...). Configuring the system for a shot can be as simple as setting a track movement speed and the total number of shots you want to take.

Dollies are all about linear motion and depending on how you set up the track and orient the camera you can achieve several different kinds of movement effects.

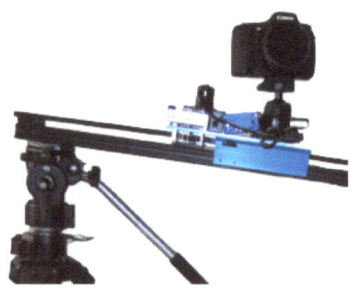

**LEFT/RIGHT
LATERAL MOVEMENT**

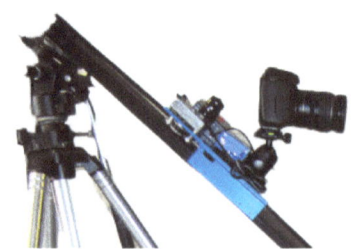

**UP/DOWN
VERTICAL MOVEMENT**

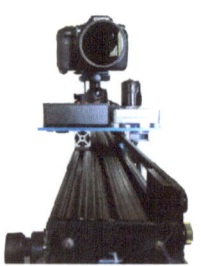

**IN/OUT
PUSH/PULL
MOVEMENT**

Build it yourself?

The movement seems pretty simple, and it is, but piecing everything together and programming a device to control it precisely is a challenge. Think you might want to build your own system? Don't start from scratch if you don't need to: a lot of great ideas and explanations are shared on the Open-Source Photographic Motion-Control Community at OpenMoco.org including controller hardware discussion, open-source firmware, motor recommendations and more.

Or start shooting now?

While I love to tinker, and I will certainly be doing some experimentation as I incorporate the next axis of movement, sometime you just want to get out start shooting right away. Here are some options for prebuilt dolly systems:

$895

Dynamic Perception Stage Zero Dolly-dynamicperception.com
This is the dolly system I have and recommend. I chose to source the aluminum rail locally and saved some money on shipping. Keep in mind you'll also need an extra tripod head to attach to the rail unless you want to keep attaching and reattaching during different shots.

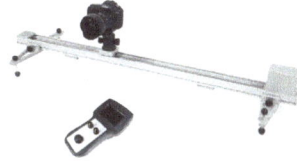

~$2,500

DitoGear OmniSlider - ditogear.com
More expensive but also clean and with advance controller features like joystick movement, auto playback of recorded motion, weatherproofing and more. Check out the website for a whole list of amazing enhancements.

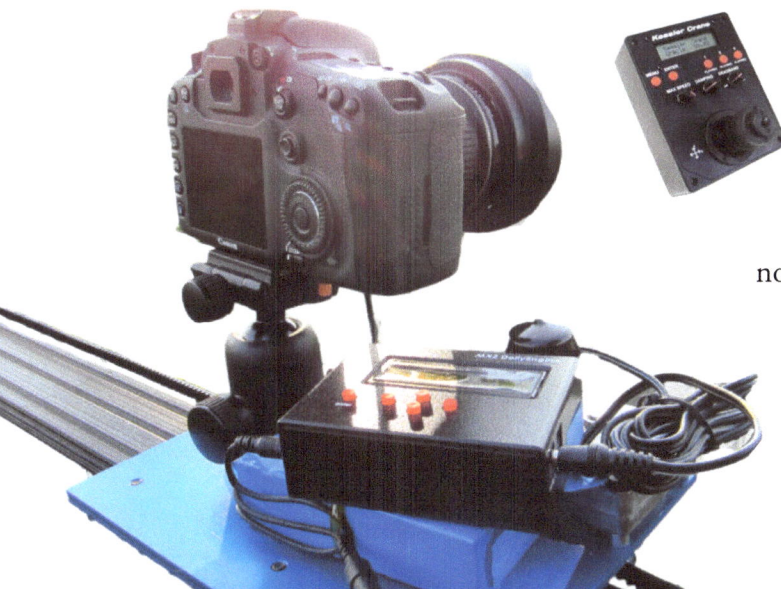

~$3,000

Kessler Oracle Controller and the CineSlider - Kesslercrane.com Kessler's line of innovative camera control equipment is nothing short of incredible.

TIME-LAPSE PAN/TILT MOVEMENT

The next two axes of movement can be accomplished by a single device aptly named a motorized panning and tilting head. There are a few different ways to go about incorporating one into your next time-lapse shot.

The first method employs the same controllers used in dolly motion but instead of connecting a standard linear motor setup we connect a hacked motorized telescope head using a special

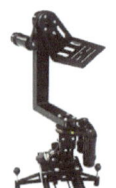

cable. The set up requires a little improvisation and if you are looking for more information and specifics head out to OpenMoco.org.
~$200-300
Motorized telescope heads: Orion Teletrack, Celestron Skywatcher, Merlin SkyScan, and a few others. Dynamic Perception will be releasing an inexpensive and completely modular pan/tilt solution for their MX2 time-lapse dolly controller soon. Way to go guys!

~$1,900
Kessler REVOLUTION Pan and Tilt Head System
Paired with the Oracle controller, I agree with the description when they list it as the most feature rich and best motorized head solution on the market, for under $5,000.

AND MORE...

Combine a 2-axis pan and tilt head onto a linear motion dolly and you have almost unlimited freedom of movement. Tracks, cranes, boats, stereoscopic 3D.... here are two of many cutting edge motion examples:

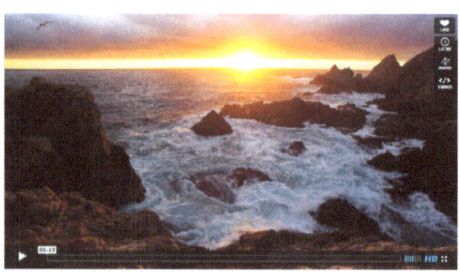
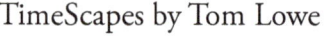

TimeScapes by Tom Lowe

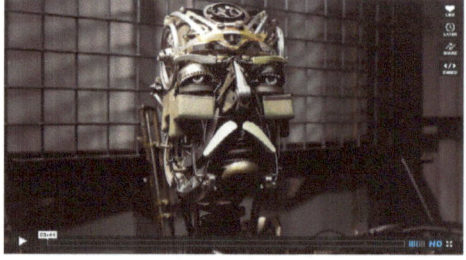

Deus Ex Homine by Peter H. Chang

Get's the mind working huh? While these clips really showcase what incredibly talented and experienced photographers with the latest gear can accomplish, don't think you *have* to have movement in your shots to produce a great time-lapse. There are many ways to control the viewers eye and telling a good story is by far the most important. Advanced gear don't let it get in the way of capturing and sharing what you enjoy.

WHERE TO GO FROM HERE

You now have a firm understanding of the basics of time-lapse shooting, flicker prevention, and rendering. You've gone through a few challenges to test your knowledge and you now have a good head start on a list of resources to continue learning. With all this information under your belt are you ready to head out and capture the changing world, or is there still a little skepticism inside that *you* can really create something great?

Eric Warren of Matadornetwork.com posed a related question:

Do you think time-lapse should be left to the pros?

> "Pros are the guys you call when you want to put a time-lapse in your car commercial. And while we tend to put pros up on a pedestal, they are often bogged down by their clients' needs. Most commercial advertising doesn't push the envelope of an art form.
>
> That job often falls to the independent artists, building their own equipment, and often not giving a rat's ass about whether their work is going to sell. Not that I want to be too demanding here, but I want to see something mind-blowing. Either something I've never seen before or something familiar, shown in a new way (one thing time-lapse excels at.) ....
>
> Consider this a call to all you independent filmmakers out there ready to push the limits of one of the most striking visual art forms."

I hope the information in this book has been helpful and I hope you find it useful. I also hope that it acts as a call to action to get you out there shooting, experimenting and sharing amazing time-lapse stories.

Take some of the stuff shared here and invest it in your next clip but also throw some of it away, do your own tests and rewrite sections how you please. Don't let anyone tell you that you are doing things the wrong way. If you are getting the results you want then that's all that matters. Never forget that you are the artist and it's your story.

If you need help or have further questions on anything, or just want to share some feedback or shoot the breeze, e-mail me at ryan@learntimelapse.com

It has been a pleasure sharing this information with you and I can't thank you enough for your feedback. I would love to hear some of your stories and see some of your work and again I hope this resource has been helpful.
Thank you.

TIME-LAPSE RESOURCES

I've been known to spend way too much time browsing some of these sites but if you are interested in learning more about time-lapse, DSLR photography and photo gear these resources might be a good place to start:

Time-lapse and related forums:
Timescapes Digital Time-lapse forum: http://forum.timescapes.org/phpBB3/index.php
OpenMoCo (photographic motion-control): openmoco.org
Magic Lantern firmware wiki: magiclantern.wikia.com

Other DSLR photography forums and resources:
The Photo Forum: thephotoforum.com/forum/
Cambridge in color: cambridgeincolour.com
Ken Rockwell's How to Take Better Photos: kenrockwell.com/tech.htm

Time-lapse Motion Control Equipment:
Dynamic Perception: dynamicperception.com
Kessler Filmmaker Tools: kesslercrane.com
Dito Gear: ditogear.com

Reviews specific to cameras:
Digital Photography Review: dpreview.com
Camera Labs: cameralabs.com

General gear reviews/new and used gear:
B&H Photo: bhphotovideo.com
Adorama: adorama.com
Amazon: amazon.com
KEH Camera: keh.com

Rent gear to try it out:
BorrowLenses.com
Lensprotogo.com
Lensgiant.com

DSLR and gear blogs/forums:
Planet5d: blog.planet5d.com
Cinema5D.com
Learningdslrvideo.com
nofilmschool.com

DIY gear:
The Frugal Filmmaker: filmflap.blogspot.com/
DIY Photography: diyphotography.net

Astronomical data and guides to our sky:
NOAA sunrise/sunset calculator: esrl.noaa.gov/gmd/grad/solcalc/
Dark Star Finder: jshine.net/astronomy/dark_sky/Clear Sky Chart: cleardarksky.com/csk/
Dark Sky Association: darksky.org/DSDestinations
City lights data: blue-marble.de/nightlights/2010
Stellarium Sky Map: Stellarium.org

For links and an updated listing visit: learntimelapse.com I am always looking for great new photography resources. Do you have a favorite you would love to share? send me an email at ryan@learntimelapse.com

TIME-LAPSE PHOTOGRAPHY

Quick reference summaries

TIME-LAPSE EXPOSURE SETTINGS CHECKLIST:

Here's a final review of the important exposure considerations for time-lapse photography:

Shoot in full manual mode:

Photographing in full manual mode prevents the camera from making independent exposure decision before each image is captured. Any drastic exposure changes in the middle of a time-lapse series might create a kind of flicker and should be prevented.

Configure the following exposure settings:

ISO: By deselecting automatic ISO determination and locking in a set number, we prevent the camera from creating brighter or darker images due to changes in sensor sensitivity.

Aperture: By setting a specific aperture we minimize time-lapse flicker by preventing the camera from jumping from one f-stop to another. We also prevent changes in depth of field throughout the sequence by keeping a constant range of focus.

Shutter Speed: By setting a specific shutter speed we minimize time-lapse flicker by preventing the camera from jumping from one exposure time to another.

Focus: Manual focus prevents the camera from focus hunting as each photo is taken and from seeking a different focus ranges throughout the compilation. Image stabilization off.

White Balance: Manual white balance prevents the camera from analyzing and adjusting each photo independently and avoids tint shifts in the final time-lapse compilation.

Create a little motion blur:

Since our time-lapse images are played back-to-back very rapidly, slight blurring in each individual photo helps to blend them together creating an added smoothness to the entire sequence. As a rule of thumb, try to keep your shutter speed under ~1/100th of a second. In order to get that low of a shutter in daylight conditions we will probably need to use an ND filter.

Watch your total exposure length:

Your exposure time MUST NOT exceed your interval length plus a little extra time for your camera to save the images to your card.

Check your file format:

Make sure you have enough room on your card all your required time-lapse images at the image size that you selected. Do you need to save space on your memory card for other shots today?

Consider a test photo and a quick mini-lapse:

Previewing an individual exposure and possibly scrolling through a few images in a test time-lapse might save a whole afternoon's worth of shooting. It's worth the extra time, trust me.

THE TIME-LAPSE EXPOSURE TRIANGLE:

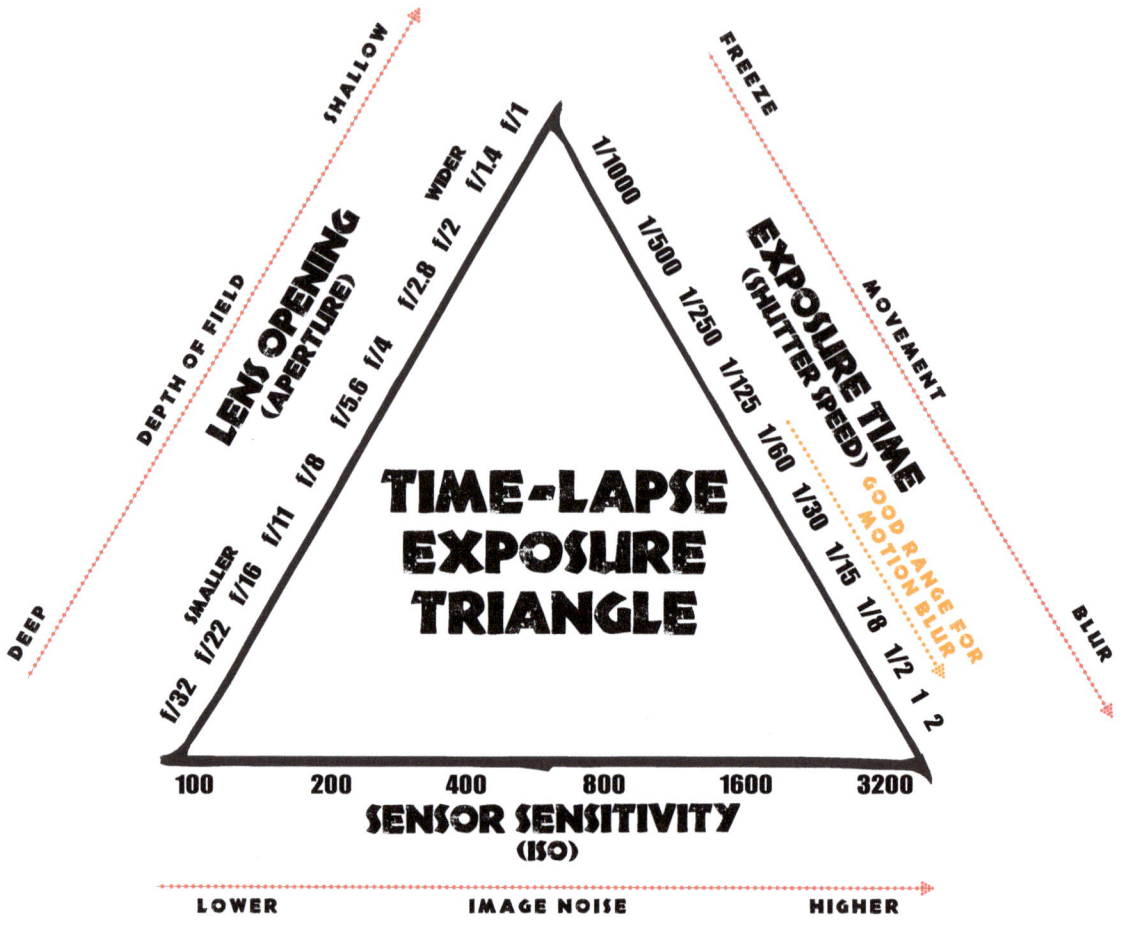

BALANCING IMAGE SETTINGS:

Shoot in the RAW image format:

If you can afford the large file size shooting in RAW will provide nondestructive creative control over your images in post production.

Shoot at high resolution:

Large images provide flexibility to crop, pan, tilt, zoom, or shrink when you edit your final video as well as the freedom to export to different destinations in at the highest quality.

Plan ahead for the HD aspect ratio crop:

When shooting to export to HD video don't forget to account for about a 15% (200 pixel) crop on the top or bottom.

FLICKER PREVENTION OVERVIEW

Here's a final review of the important considerations for time-lapse flicker prevention:

What is flicker?

Essentially instead of the camera's exposure settings and mechanical configurations remaining perfectly constant or purposefully changing in very slight and gradual ways, large unintended exposure jumps occur in some sequence frames which create images that look out of place when compiled together. **Flicker is caused by:** 1. Exposure settings 2. Mechanical inconsistencies

For scenes with constant light shoot in full manual mode:

Photographing in full manual mode prevents the camera from making independent exposure decision before each image is captured. Configure the manual settings discussed in the basic time-lapse shooting workflow.

For scenes with drastic changes in lighting we can take advantage of priority modes:

Automatic exposure control will allow more flexibility but we will experience much more flicker. We can usually correct this using de-flickering software in post production. Don't forget to cover your eyepiece.

Minimize the chances for Mechanical inconsistencies:

Inconsistencies in mechanical formations can occur between shots resulting in a slightly different exposures even though camera settings remain identical. There are two forms of mechanical flicker:

Aperture flicker

Minimize the chances for small frame-to-frame lens diaphragm inconsistencies by preventing movement:

- Use a manual lens
- Use the lens twist trick to fool your camera into thinking an automatic lens is manual
    1. Set your desired aperture setting in manual mode
    2. Press and hold the Depth of Field preview button to set the diaphragm (usually a small black button below your lens)
    3. Press the lens unlock button and slightly rotate the lens clockwise

Don't forget to fully reattach the lens before disconnecting from your tripod or packing it away.

Shutter flicker

Minimize the chance for small shutter curtain frame-to-frame inconsistencies by shooting at speeds slower than about 1/60th of a second.

SELECTING AND PROGRAMMING A TIME-LAPSE INTERVAL

With one number you have control over two things:

1. How fast the time-lapse change appears to be taking place
2. How smooth that action appears on screen

Common baseline intervals:

No two scenes are exactly alike. These common interval durations should give you a head start:

1 SECOND
- Moving traffic
- Fast moving clouds
- Drivelapses

1 – 3 SECONDS
- Sunsets
- Sunrises
- Slower moving clouds
- Crowds
- Moon and sun near horizon
- Things photographed with a telephoto

15 – 30 SECONDS OR LONGER
- Moving shadows
- Sun across sky (no clouds) (wide)
- Stars (15 – 60 seconds)
- Fast growing plants (ex vines) (90 – 120 seconds) Construction projects (5 min. – 15 min.)

Decide the length of your video:

Aim for at least a 8 - 12 second clip to allow for transitions and editing play if you are combining sequences or adding music.

Determine how many shots you need to take:

Video length (seconds) x frame rate (seconds) = Total number of images required
Example: 10 seconds of moon footage x 24 fps = 240 images needed

Calculate your shooting time:

Total number of images x Interval between each image = Total shooting time
240 moon photos x 3 second interval between each = 720 seconds or 12 minutes

PROGRAMMING YOUR INTERVALOMETER:

Delay (DE) : Just like a regular self timer. Program this delay time if you want to start your time-lapse recording at a later time.

Bulb (BU) : Controls your camera's bulb mode exposure time with the time you program here.

Interval (INT) : The amount of time that we program the camera to wait between each exposure. Your intervalometers will continue until your camera runs out of memory or you reach a programmed maximum number of exposures.

Number of shots (N) : How many exposures do we want. Most devices can be programmed from 1 to 399 or to infinity. For infinite exposures select " - - - " as the number of shots.

BASIC TIME-LAPSE WORKFLOW

Your time-lapse workflow will likely include these basic six steps from camera memory card to final rendering and post processing.

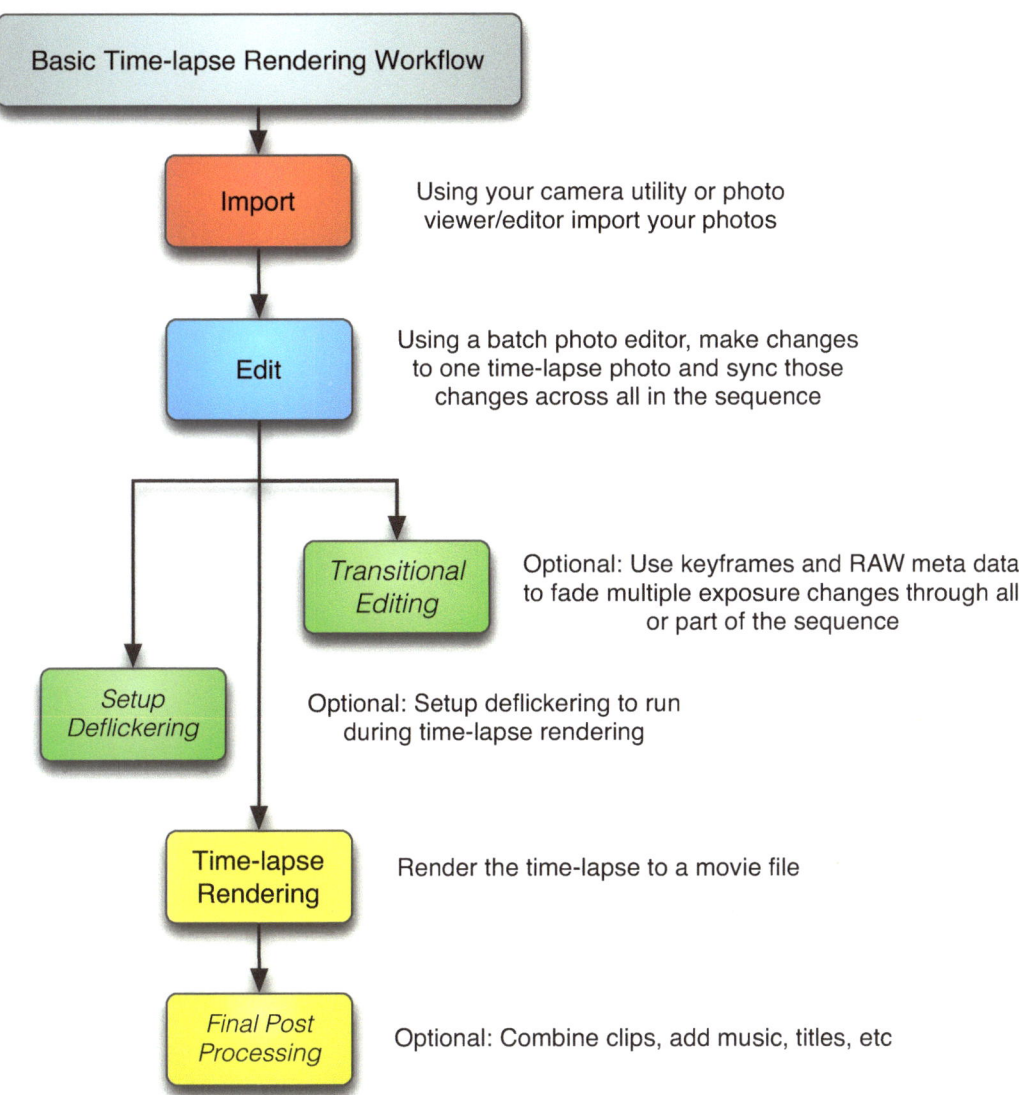

www.ingramcontent.com/pod-product-compliance
Lightning Source LLC
Chambersburg PA
CBHW050716180526
45159CB00003B/1041